AN ACCIDENTAL VILLAIN

AN ACCIDENTAL VILLAIN

A SOLDIER'S TALE OF WAR, DECEIT AND EXILE

LINDEN MacINTYRE

RANDOM HOUSE CANADA

Random House Canada, an imprint of Penguin Random House Canada Limited
320 Front Street West, Suite 1400
Toronto, Ontario, M5V 3B6, Canada
penguinrandomhouse.ca

Random House Canada and colophon are registered trademarks
of Penguin Random House LLC.

The authorized representative in the EU for product safety and compliance is Penguin Random House Ireland, Morrison Chambers, 32 Nassau Street, Dublin D02 YH68, Ireland. https://eu-contact.penguin.ie

Library and Archives Canada Cataloguing in Publication
Title: An accidental villain : a soldier's tale of war, deceit
and exile / Linden MacIntyre.
Names: MacIntyre, Linden, author
Description: Includes bibliographical references and index.
Identifiers: Canadiana (print) 20240449533 | Canadiana (ebook) 20240450833 |
ISBN 9780735282025 (hardcover) | ISBN 9780735282032 (EPUB)
Subjects: LCSH: Tudor, Hugh, 1871-1965. | LCSH: Royal Irish Constabulary
Reserve Force. | LCSH: Soldiers—Great Britain—Biography. | LCSH:
Ireland—History—War of Independence, 1919-1921. | LCSH: Ireland—
Politics and government—1910-1921. | LCGFT: Biographies.
Classification: LCC DA965.T83 M33 2025 | DDC 941.5082/1092—dc23

Cover design: Matthew Flute
Text design: Matthew Flute
Typesetting: Erin Cooper
Image credits: Sean Sexton / Contributor / Getty Images;
(back cover) Kimberly Boyles / Adobe Stock

Printed in Canada

2 4 6 8 9 7 5 3 1

Penguin
Random House
RANDOM HOUSE CANADA

CONTENTS

In memory

Derek Kennedy
1951–2022

Beyond this place of wrath and tears
 Looms but the Horror of the shade,
And yet the menace of the years
 Finds and shall find me unafraid.

WILLIAM ERNEST HENLEY, "INVICTUS"
(recitation popular in Dublin Castle, 1920–21)

PROLOGUE

THE TELEGRAM ON January 24, 1965, time-stamped 3:49 p.m., extended a formal invitation to an ailing, largely forgotten ninety-three-year-old British army general in Canada to attend the funeral of a famous ninety-year-old statesman in England. "Please cable if you can or cannot accept invitation to state funeral of Sir Winston Churchill St. Paul's Cathedral London Saturday 30th January 1965 Stop."

The invitation was delivered to a name and an address in a distant place, St. John's, Newfoundland, the recipient presumably unfamiliar and irrelevant to the organizers of an event of global interest and historical significance. Major General Sir Hugh Tudor had lived a quiet life in self-imposed exile in Newfoundland for nearly forty years and by 1965 was almost immobilized by the infirmities of old age.

He had not seen his old friend Winston Churchill in twenty-seven years, but the friendship obviously remained as fresh in 1965 as when it began seven decades earlier. Their correspondence had continued until, it would seem, both lost interest in the diminished empire they had served and a society that, over time, had disappointed them. Tudor's name was on the list because he was prominent among the people who were still loved and admired by the great Englishman Churchill as he approached the end of his life on earth.

Over the years Tudor had accepted several important invitations and requests from Churchill he might prudently have declined. This one he would have wanted to accept, but by January 24, 1965, his own mortality obliged him to turn it down. The general would follow his old friend to the grave eight months and one day later, on September 25, 1965.

The broad outline of their lives offers a superficial explanation of their friendship. They met as young men in a still robust British Empire, as ardent imperialists and English army officers; both had started military careers in India and had crossed paths often as they fought in or observed the various wars of their early years.

The essence of the friendship is harder to define. While Tudor shared a surname with British kings and queens, he had no genetic link to royalty or privilege. The army had offered him a departure from the conventional Tudor family experience in commerce and religion. For Churchill, the army promised the excitement of violent conflict. He had a seemingly voracious appetite for danger. War, he once insisted to his wife, was "a game played with a smile." His destiny, however, was determined by his DNA and British history. War would make him famous, but his role in the conflicts that would define his legacy would be, essentially, political.

It is possible that Churchill envied the clarity of his friend's career. He and Tudor met frequently during the First World War, when Churchill served briefly as a battalion commander on the Western Front while Tudor was rising through the ranks as an artilleryman, soon to be the youngest divisional commander in the British army. Their contacts at the front continued even after Churchill became a key minister in the wartime British cabinet.

By the end of the Great War, Tudor had been ten times mentioned in dispatches for gallantry in combat.[1] He was promoted in the field to the rank of major general. At forty-seven, he was still young. His reputation was solid. His rank guaranteed a comfortable living and, at the end, a pension that promised a sustainable retirement. He had a young family—four children whom he hoped to help through all their youthful challenges and nurture to maturity.

Instead, within two years, Tudor would be at war again, a brief war, but one that would consume his hopeful future. In the spring of 1920, he was summoned by his oldest friend to serve the British Empire in another conflict, this one close to home—in Ireland. Churchill was, by then, British secretary of state for war.

This would be a war that mocked the value of Tudor's prior military knowledge, a war that would, for future generations, provoke debate about who, if anybody, won it—or if, in fact, it ever ended. It would affect Tudor's life in ways he could not have imagined in the days of victory after November 1918 and then as a leader of the occupation forces in defeated Germany.

In Ireland, Major General Tudor would oversee a war for which he was personally and professionally unprepared—a war inflamed by hatred and propaganda too deeply sourced in history for a conventional response; battles fought in ditches, behind hedges; an enemy without uniforms or discipline or rules or scruples; an enemy who looked like him, who spoke his language. What he would experience in Ireland would bear little resemblance to the wars he had studied, the wars he'd fought. This would be a conflict that foreshadowed a future in which citizens demanding self-determination, freedom from colonial authority and institutions, would make armies of their own, deploying their own propaganda and any form of violence that might advance their cause.

His time in Ireland would mark the beginning of the end of the world as Hugh Tudor, his profession and his class, had known it. In Ireland, Tudor would be swept up by the primal energies that surface, even in the most seasoned military leader, when personal survival is at stake. And he would come to understand that the First World War was not, as his generation had hoped, "the war to end all wars." It was, instead, the beginning of a century of conflict, wars of liberation from the past and struggles to control the future of a world as it was being redefined by ideology.

Ireland was, in many ways, a hopeless war for both the British war minister and the British soldier on the ground. They both knew they had but one imperative—to win. Winston Churchill would find a way to define the outcome of the Irish war as a victory. But for Churchill's friend the soldier, his engagement with the Irish War of Independence would be the beginning of a long journey into personal oblivion.

Part I

A NEW FOUND LAND

Word over all, beautiful as the sky!
Beautiful that war, and all its deeds of carnage,
must in time be utterly lost . . .

WALT WHITMAN, "RECONCILIATION"
(a poem admired by Michael Collins, IRA leader and
commander-in-chief, Irish National Army, July to August 1922)

1.

Wednesday, November 25, 1925

THE RMS *NEWFOUNDLAND* was ten hours late as she slowly approached the narrow entrance to St. John's Harbour just before one o'clock in the afternoon. The North Atlantic was still heaving after a prolonged southeaster that had tied up shipping in and around the island through the night and for most of the previous day. The temperature hovered just above forty degrees Fahrenheit. Dark clouds raced across a broken sky, and a bitter autumn gale whipped the city streets clear of most pedestrians. Among the anxious passengers aboard the *Newfoundland* were two Irish doctors, an Irish priest, and a quiet English merchant who might have offered a distraction from the weather had the Irishmen been aware of who he was or inclined to start a conversation with a controversial Englishman.

Major General Sir Henry Hugh Tudor, now in transition to civilian life, had survived nearly thirty-five years of active service in the British army: colonial skirmishes and intrigues in India, Egypt and Palestine and in the Boer War, four years on the Western Front in the First World War, and, recently, a dirty war in Ireland. His name would have been familiar, thanks to the notoriety he had attained in Ireland as commander of policemen called the Black and Tans. Most of the English-speaking world was familiar with their reputation for brutality—part myth, part propaganda, but by 1925 rooted in enough reality to make anyone associated with the outfit a fugitive.

There was little else about him that would have sparked the curiosity of fellow passengers. Average height, dark eyes, a trim military
moustache. A female admirer had recently noted "a close-knit athletic
figure . . . the clear complexion of a boy; no one would imagine him
to be in his early fifties."[1] He was well dressed, reserved. He looked
the part of the provincial merchant he had decided to become.

While his name, in recent years, had been in the news, he'd rarely
been photographed. His job in Ireland as head of a police force with an
aggressive military mandate had made him permanently vulnerable.
He rarely ventured anywhere unarmed. In one of the few snapshots
from his time in Ireland, he is in civilian clothes, wearing a hat that
partially obscures his face and a long, baggy overcoat that conceals a
slim physique. He is pinning a medal on a policeman, and he seems
shorter than the man receiving the decoration—then again, perhaps
he stooped to conceal his fitness, age and height.

Being inconspicuous was a large part of a carefully managed survival strategy. People who were intent on capturing or killing him
wouldn't recognize him out of uniform. Efforts to track him around
Dublin had inevitably failed because he avoided predictable routes.
He abstained from socializing outside the walls of Dublin Castle.
Even in those presumably secure confines, headquarters for the British
administration in Ireland, the occupants ate with their revolvers
on the table.[2]

Some Castle colleagues had openly criticized Tudor's tolerance
for rough, sometimes criminal behaviour by his policemen. His tight
relationship with Winston Churchill, the British minister for war,
and what seemed to be a fawning admiration and unconcealed
encouragement by the prime minister, David Lloyd George, would
have limited the possibility of real collegiality among the bureaucrats and army officers with whom he lived and worked in Dublin.
But he had his own group of loyal friends, a half-dozen officers with

whom he had served in the Great War. They rewarded his unquestioning support by performing or at least tolerating often brutal duties without hesitation.

It was Tudor's first trip to North America. According to the passenger manifest, he was employed by Holmwood and Holmwood, a London trading company that also specialized in finance and insurance—two challenging professions for which the career soldier had neither experience nor expertise. There had been speculation in the British press in May 1925, repeated in a St. John's gossip column in June, that the British general was moving to Newfoundland to "engage in the fishery"[3]—another line of work for which absolutely nothing in his resumé could have prepared him. The son of an Anglican priest, he'd grown up in the shadow of cathedrals, untroubled by the unsteady fortunes of factories, fish plants or finance.

The November storm in the mid-Atlantic would have come as a shock after a pleasant voyage out of Liverpool under sunny skies a week earlier. Tudor's first impression of his new home might have come as yet another jolt. Travellers arriving in St. John's would sometimes comment on the twin spires of a grand cathedral that loomed over the low-rise city, or the dramatic citadel on the north side of the harbour entrance, Signal Hill, a memorable spectacle diminished by a squalid sprawl of shacks on the hillside and the shore below.

In the opinion of at least one visitor, it was preferable to arrive at night, when the only visible evidence of settlement was a warm glitter of city lights that "lend romance that is somewhat lacking by daylight."[4] Had his ship been on schedule, Tudor would have arrived in darkness. Now, in the early afternoon of a stormy day, the harsh daylight revealed ramshackle structures huddled along the waterfront behind rickety finger piers and tiers of wooden buildings sprawled against a steep hillside.

General Tudor left no record of his first impressions. That he would settle in St. John's, die there, and find eternal rest in a local cemetery might indicate that he grew to like the place.

Whether he knew it or not, Tudor shared a lot of history with the old North Atlantic city. He grew up in Devon, southwest England. Over several centuries, many Newfoundlanders had arrived as settlers from Devon, determined, like Tudor, to take up the fishing business. Near where he landed in St. John's, there was an old city neighbourhood called Devon Row.

It was a famous Devon man, Sir Humphrey Gilbert, who had first claimed Newfoundland for the English Crown. Another Devon nobleman, Sir Walter Raleigh, Sir Humphrey's half-brother, had attempted to colonize the island. Like Sir Hugh, both Sir Humphrey and Sir Walter had won their knighthoods for heavy-handed military operations in rebellious Ireland.[5]

St. John's was, in many ways, a microcosm of the world Tudor had left behind him. As a highly decorated British soldier with a knighthood, he would move easily among the anglophiles and Anglicans who dominated politics and commerce in Newfoundland. But he had a more visceral connection that drew him to this remote dominion, and it would serve him well through all the years he would spend here—his life-and-death experience with Newfoundlanders under fire in the final months of the Great War.

2.

HIS ADULT LIFE, like the lives of millions in his generation, and of almost everyone in Newfoundland, had been redefined by war. Henry Hugh Tudor had joined the British army at the age of seventeen. After two years at the Royal Military Academy in Woolwich, England, he had spent seven years refining military skills in India. In 1899, while back in Britain, an army friend who was recently married persuaded Lieutenant Tudor to replace him on a draft to South Africa to fight in the Boer War. The newlywed sweetened the deal by offering five hundred pounds in payment, which Tudor cheerfully accepted.[6]

The young lieutenant was only in the war a matter of weeks when he was nearly killed by shrapnel during an artillery barrage. The army tried to send him home after three months of surgery and healing. He balked. Four days after his release from hospital, Tudor walked up and over Table Mountain, a thousand-foot-high landmark near Cape Town, to prove his fitness for continued combat. He was promptly cleared for duty and remained in South Africa for the duration of the war.[7]

When war broke out in Europe, in August 1914, Tudor was travelling from Egypt, where he had been based for the previous five years, to begin a holiday in England. He was Major Tudor then, commander of a battery in the Royal Horse Artillery. Like most professional soldiers, he welcomed an important war. It would be good for his career and, in the minds of many, it wasn't going to last long—maybe until Christmas. As he wrote in the war diary that he kept for the four years he would spend on the Western Front, he "wanted no other job than to command [his battery] in war."[8]

But Tudor's battery was stuck in Egypt, and he was stuck in England. It was frustrating, but his "orders were definite and [he] just had to lump it." Which he did for more than three months while the enemy romped through Belgium and into France, threatening to end the war by Christmas by winning it decisively. Eventually, by mid-December, the enemy offensive had stalled and Tudor and his battery were on their way to the front. They spent Christmas Eve, 1914, digging four artillery emplacements just behind the lines on a muddy battlefield.

Then on Christmas Day, to Tudor's surprise, an unnerving silence descended on his sector of the Western Front, what was clearly a seasonal respite from killing—a bad idea, as he would record in his war diary. "It seems to me that regular armies can indulge in this sort of thing without impairing fighting efficiency; but that an army of ex-civilians must be stirred up by the propaganda of hate."[9]

Tudor need not have worried about the fighting efficiency of ex-civilians. Millions throughout the British Empire, stirred up by patriotism as well as propaganda, were itching for the fight. One of them was a thirteen-year-old boy named Tommy Ricketts, the son of a fisherman from Middle Arm, White Bay, a tiny village on the northeast coast of Newfoundland. His brother, George, who was four years older, had already volunteered.[10] If he could have pulled it off, Tommy Ricketts would probably have lined up right away with hundreds of young Newfoundlanders to join a regiment of "ex-civilians" that was destined to intersect with the life and the career of Major Tudor.

Newfoundland, as a British colony, had a long military history. A Newfoundland regiment helped fight off an American invasion of Quebec in 1775, and in the War of 1812, troops from Newfoundland were prominent in the defence of York (Toronto) and the British capture of Detroit. But the British government eventually withdrew its soldiers from the colony in 1870, and by 1914, the military presence in Newfoundland was almost nonexistent—four cadet brigades sponsored by the island's dominant religions, Anglican, Roman Catholic, Methodist and Presbyterian.

In a fit of patriotic fervour, the government of Newfoundland—no longer a colony, but now an independent dominion in the British Commonwealth—started enlisting five hundred men to become the core of a new regiment "for land service abroad."[11] The Newfoundland Regiment would win renown for its sacrifices and achievements on the battlefield. Before the war was over, it would become the Royal Newfoundland Regiment in honour of its battlefield heroics, the only British army unit to receive such recognition during the fighting.

But in August 1914, the reality of war was inconceivable to the office workers, fishermen and schoolboys who were suddenly determined to be soldiers. War offered immediate relief from civilian drudgery for many, the social status of an officer's commission for a few, and for almost everyone, a rescue from the tedium of peace.

The government delegated the creation of a regiment to a committee made up of fifty influential citizens. By October 2, five hundred newly minted soldiers were marching to the St. John's waterfront, on their way to Britain. The Newfoundland Bible Society had equipped every one of them with a copy of the New Testament. But their uniforms, like their military training, were conspicuously incomplete, part military, part civilian, trouser legs tucked into blue puttees.

The Canadian army had contributed five hundred military greatcoats. Winter wasn't far away. The coats were extra long, the bottoms left unhemmed so they could later be tailored to match the owner's height. But there hadn't been time for necessary alterations and so, in many cases, the heavy coats dragged on the ground. Only the officers had proper military headgear. The rank and file wore their best civilian caps and hats.[12]

Thousands of spectators lined the city streets as "the first five hundred" trudged from their camp on Quidi Vidi pond toward the waiting liner that would take them off for proper training at a military base in Britain. As one young officer later described the scene, "Marching was impossible, discipline vanished as the boys struggled to board the ship, tearing themselves away from the arms of their loved ones."

They were game for an adventure. If they were afraid of anything, it was that the war might end before they got to it. But as it turned out, they had no cause to worry that they might miss the action.

Before the conflict was finished, nearly twelve thousand men—10 percent of the male population of the island—would go to war.

Of the 500 volunteers who sailed away in October 1914, 429 became casualties. Only 71, almost all non-combatants, survived unscathed; 169 of the first 500 never saw St. John's again.[13]

By the summer of 1918, the officer who would lead the regiment through the final and decisive months of war had risen through the ranks to become a major general, commander of the 9th Scottish Division in the British army. By the time the Newfoundlanders came under Major General Tudor's command in September 1918, they had been hardened by experience. Heavy casualties in late 1917 and early 1918 had reduced their numbers to the point where they were forced out of the shooting war for months while they recovered and replaced lost fighters.

Tudor had been less than thrilled on learning that a battalion of Newfoundlanders would be joining one of his three infantry brigades, replacing a contingent of South Africans that he revered. The Newfoundlanders were, he observed in his diary, older than most of the Scotsmen serving under him. And half of this Newfoundland battalion, old or otherwise, had never been in battle. Fresh replacements for the dead or wounded of earlier encounters, they were about to be front and centre in an Allied offensive calculated to drive the Germans out of Belgium and, finally, to win the war.

The veteran fighters among the Newfoundlanders were also less than excited when they learned about the move. Since coming to the war, they had been in the British 29th Division, where they had survived Gallipoli in 1915 and had been almost wiped out at Beaumont-Hamel on July 1, 1916, on the first day of the Battle of the Somme. They had barely survived a more recent slaughter at the First Battle of Cambrai, in November and December of 1917.

Tommy Ricketts, now seventeen years old, was one of the battle-tested "old-timers." He'd been ready to join when he was thirteen. He was fifteen when he finally convinced a gullible recruiting officer that he was older and tougher than he looked. Though he was only five foot six, that was close enough to average height for Newfoundland men at the time. He could neither read nor write and, like his brother, signed his recruitment papers with an X.[14]

Shortly after his sixteenth birthday, he was at the Western Front, and soon after that, he was in the thick of fighting: Langemarck in August; Poelcappelle in October; and in November, Cambrai, two weeks of carnage in which eight out of ten Newfoundland soldiers were either killed or wounded in the fighting.

The Newfoundlanders might not have known, nor would they have been impressed to know, that General Tudor had designed the initial plan of attack for the Battle of Cambrai; or that, before the battle began, military analysts praised the innovative tactics he was recommending—a surprise attack, obscured by a heavy smoke screen and supported by an artillery barrage that would coincide with, rather than precede, a massive infantry assault. The battle followed Tudor's design except for one crucial detail—timing.

The attack appeared to have succeeded as planned on November 20, 1917, and almost immediately, Tudor was being congratulated by his superiors. The praise was premature.[15] The final battle plan had failed to include sufficient reserves of infantry support to stop a German counterattack. Over the two weeks of fighting, the Cambrai battle cost the British army 75,000 casualties. One hundred and fifteen Newfoundlanders died, including a renowned sniper, John Shiwak, who was an Innu hunter from Labrador, and George Ricketts, Tommy's older brother.[16]

Tommy himself was seriously wounded. A bullet in the leg would take him out of action for the next ten months. By September 1918, he was back in the front lines in time for some of the most decisive fighting of the war. He was only seventeen, but he was destined for a date with history, a battle that would make him Newfoundland's most famous soldier and fame that would in time become an insufferable burden.

3.

EVEN AS A young man Hugh Tudor was obviously destined for the military career that Winston Churchill, had he been less ambitious, less political, less weighted down by history, would have wanted for himself. Tudor was dedicated to the civilizing mission of the British Empire, as was Churchill, and he proved in the Boer War that he was brave and resilient.

Churchill had joined the South African campaign as a "fighting journalist," writing action-packed war stories for the London newspapers. While technically on leave from the army, usually he was able to place himself front and centre in his sensational accounts of combat. After a shootout in December 1899, he was briefly captured and held prisoner by the Boers.

He escaped captivity to great acclaim back home, an experience that launched a long, adventurous political career. But when he discovered, just days later, that his friend Tudor had been seriously wounded that same month and was recuperating in a hospital in Cape Town, Churchill took the trouble to send a get-well telegram.

Their paths would cross again in the chaotic drama of the First World War. In 1915, Churchill was forced to take a break from parliament because of political controversy over his role in a failed attempt to seize the offensive in the war by attacking Turkey through the Dardanelles Strait and Gallipoli peninsula. He was demoted within cabinet, and, when completely excluded from decision-making, he kept his seat in parliament but quit the government of Prime Minister Herbert Asquith, put on a uniform and went to war as a relatively junior army officer. He took charge of an infantry battalion in the 9th Scottish Division, where his old friend, Hughie Tudor, now a brigadier general, significantly outranked him.[17]

In Tudor's Great War diaries, there are more than thirty references to encounters with Churchill on the Western Front between 1916 and 1918. They hadn't seen each other since the Boer War, but in his account of February 7, 1916, the day they reunited on the Western Front, Tudor noted that Churchill was "the same as ever."

Churchill, in a letter to his wife, Clementine, on February 8, wrote how pleased he was that they were back together, in uniform: "I had tea with General Tudor yesterday. He commands all the artillery of the Division and is quite young—my age about. He and I were friends in Bangalore as lieutenants—and much good polo did we play together."[18]

In personality, they were polar opposites. Tudor was reserved; Churchill was flamboyant. His arrival at the Western Front on Monday, January 3, 1916, would not have gone unnoticed by either British soldiers in the 9th Division or the nearby enemy. A junior officer in his battalion would recall the spectacle:

> Just before noon an imposing cavalcade arrived. Churchill on a black charger, Archie Sinclair [his second-in-command] on a black charger, two grooms on black chargers followed by a limber filled with Churchill's luggage—much more than the 35 pounds allowed weight. In the rear half we saw a curious contraption: a long bath and boiler for heating the bath water.[19]

The enemy acknowledged the new high-value target in the neighbourhood by maintaining a heavy artillery bombardment on the battalion for as long as Churchill was there.

Tudor, the professional soldier, avoided unnecessary risks. Churchill seemed to thrive on danger, leading hair-raising nighttime reconnaissance patrols into no man's land, displaying what appeared to be a careless indifference to crashing shells and snipers' bullets and the possibility of sudden death. After a heavy enemy bombardment while Tudor and Churchill were observing action from a front-line trench on February 8, he described the experience in a letter to Clementine: "I found my nerves in excellent order and I don't think my pulse quickened at any time. But after it was over, I felt strangely tired."[20]

One of his battalion officers, Lieutenant Edmund Hakewill-Smith, would write that Churchill was like "a baby elephant out in No-man's land at night . . . He never fell when a shell went off; he never ducked when a bullet went past with a loud crack. He used to say, after watching me duck: 'It's no damn use ducking; the bullet has gone a long way past you by now.'"[21]

Even after a tragic incident on the night of February 26, when one of Tudor's guns miscalculated distance and landed an artillery round on one of Churchill's night patrols, Churchill didn't seem especially concerned, though the shell killed two British soldiers and seriously wounded four others. Over lunch the next day, Tudor expressed regrets to Churchill, but Churchill seemed to shrug off the episode. Bad things happen during wars. War was "a game," as he told his wife in a letter home, recounting a pep talk he had recently delivered to his junior officers: "Laugh a little and teach your men to laugh—great good humour under fire—war is a game played with a smile. If you can't smile, grin. If you can't grin, keep out of the way till you can."[22]

Tudor's frequent meetings with his friend while Churchill was at the front were mostly social, but the war was impossible to ignore when drinks and dinners were interrupted by enemy artillery exploding just outside their bunker. Churchill clearly trusted Tudor and he would often seek the perspective and advice of the more experienced

soldier. Tudor's diary entry for February 11, 1916, records "a very pleasant dinner" during which they drank their favourite champagne, Veuve
Clicquot, which was readily available in Bailleul, a French town just
two miles from the Belgian border.

That evening Churchill laid out plans for a new fighting machine
that was already on the drawing boards and would soon revolutionize
the technology of war—what he then called "land cruisers," soon to
be better known colloquially as "tanks." Tudor wrote, "Churchill
visioned them lined up some dark night behind our front trenches
and, just before dawn, advanced them to smash through the enemy
wire and trenches. I was greatly impressed."[23]

For his part, Tudor bent his friend's ear with his own idea for
improving the effectiveness of infantry assaults by cloaking no man's
land in smoke. Conventional assaults, in which men went "over the
top" of their trenches, were generally preceded by heavy artillery
bombardment by mostly high-explosive shells. The shelling would
destroy barbed wire and intimidate the enemy, but the attacking soldiers remained easy targets for enemy machine guns. But what if the
shelling also produced a pall of smoke that concealed the advance
and, at least partially, blinded defenders?

At the beginning of May 1916, Churchill abandoned his brief
adventure in the trenches and returned to the political battlefield in
England. Four days before he left the front, in a letter to his wife, he
reported: "The Germans have just fired 30 shells at our farm hitting it
four times, but no one has been hurt. This I trust is a parting salute."

Tudor's May 7 diary entry was wistful: "I saw Churchill off in the
afternoon. I shall miss him very much . . . but he is right to go back
to a more important duty than a battalion commander."

His friend would eventually join a new wartime cabinet, a coalition led by a Liberal, David Lloyd George, as minister for munitions.
It was a job that would enable fulfillment of the two initiatives he and

Tudor had discussed in the field, tanks and smoke. Both would play a major role in the first successful round of the ultimately disastrous Battle of Cambrai in November 1917.

In March 1918, Tudor was given temporary command of the 9th Scottish Division when the divisional commander went on leave. Almost immediately, the German army launched a desperate offensive to regain control of a war that, for months, they had been losing.

On March 19, Churchill showed up at Tudor's headquarters in Nurlu, at the Somme, during a brief period of calm before the anticipated battle. The general and the cabinet minister strolled among the front-line trenches on March 20, clearly visible to enemy observers. No one shot at them. The silence was ominous.

At 4:40 the next morning they were awakened by a series of explosions followed by what Churchill would describe as "the most tremendous cannonade" that he would ever hear. It was the beginning of what the Germans would call Operation Michael, a major offensive to split and overwhelm the French and British armies. Churchill wanted to stay to watch the action. Tudor was in favour. But Churchill's travelling companions thought it was a bad idea for a senior British cabinet minister to risk his life and the lives of those around him by lingering in what would soon be a ferocious battle.

In the early days of the attack, the Germans threatened to wipe out two British armies. Tudor's 9th Division helped enable a tactical British withdrawal when the Third and Fifth Armies were forced to fall back to new defensive positions. The prime minister, Lloyd George, later credited Tudor and his division with "a gallant and successful fight" that helped prevent the annihilation of the British Fifth Army.[24] Field Marshal Douglas Haig, commander-in-chief of the British forces, conveyed high praise through a subordinate: "Tell Tudor that but for him and the 9th Division the situation of Flanders would have been very much worse."[25] On March 28, 1918, Tudor was informed that for the rest of the war he would remain commander of the 9th Scottish Division, soon to include a group of battle-hardened Newfoundlanders.

Tudor's tenacity—in Churchill's words, his division had been "an iron peg hammered into frozen ground"—would be remembered two years later when Lloyd George and Churchill were recruiting talent for another war, a conflict close to home, a rebellion that would mark "the fighting general," Henry Hugh Tudor, for a lifetime.

Part II

IRELAND: FROM MUTINY TO MURDER

... the hands of the sisters Death and Night, incessantly
softly wash again, and ever again, this soil'd world ...

WALT WHITMAN, "RECONCILIATION"

4.

IT IS UNCLEAR exactly when General Tudor first became a part of the Irish war. Though he had kept a diary during the Boer War and diligently recorded his experience on the Western Front, he left no record of his time in Ireland, even though the twenty-three months he spent there redefined his life, his career and, arguably, his personality.

Tudor and Churchill were frequently in touch on the Western Front during critical moments in an evolving Irish crisis in April 1916. It is not unreasonable to speculate that the two old friends, both die-hard imperialists, would have exchanged tactical ideas about Ireland during long discussions about politics and war. Irish independence had been a cause of violent conflict for centuries and had dominated British politics for decades. Easter week that year became a historic flashpoint.

Churchill was still a member of parliament while in uniform and had returned to London on April 19 for a debate on conscription that would inevitably focus on Ireland's contribution to the Great War. While in London he had dinner on April 24 with Edward Carson, a hard-line Protestant leader of Irish unionists in the British parliament and vehemently opposed to any form of Irish independence. It isn't hard to imagine what they spoke about. April 24 was Easter Monday, the first day of the rebellion that would define Anglo-Irish politics for all time.

On April 26, two days into the Easter week uprising in Dublin, Tudor commented in his diary that "the papers are full of the Irish

rebellion. We all hope that [Sir Roger] Casement will be hanged."
(And he surely was, in August, after a controversial trial for treason.)[1]

Churchill saw Tudor shortly after he returned from London to the
front lines the next day, April 27. The timing of the Irish crisis would
be difficult for two high-ranking British soldiers, one of them an
ambitious politician, to ignore.

As they socialized in the final days of Churchill's service at the front,
brutal British military justice was polarizing Ireland, where fourteen
accused rebels were shot by army firing squads in Dublin between the
third and twelfth of May. It would soon be obvious to both Churchill
and his friend that Ireland's long campaign for self-determination
wasn't going to lose momentum, as many British politicians had hoped
it would during the distraction of the First World War.

After Easter week, 1916, Irish nationalists made ever more provocative demands for a republic, once and for all divorced from Britain,
her Empire and her Crown.

Before the Great War, the demand for Irish independence might
have been satisfied by some form of Home Rule, perhaps the status of
a self-governing dominion, like Canada or Newfoundland. But by 1920,
Irish politics were dominated by radical nationalists. The most aggressive independence party, Sinn Féin, even had a military wing: the Irish
Volunteers, more widely known as the Irish Republican Army (IRA).

The Lloyd George coalition government was unimpressed by the
popular support for Sinn Féin politicians. Unlike earlier Irish nationalists, they refused to sit in the British House of Commons. Their
power, to the pragmatic Lloyd George, was therefore largely symbolic. The violent tactics of the IRA were becoming a problem, however. The government was determined to keep Ireland in a United
Kingdom no matter the cost, and it had formulated an aggressive new
strategy for defeating the republicans.

A key part of the strategy was a militarized Irish police force, with manpower recruited among English veterans of the Great War, and new leadership, also to be found in the senior ranks of the British army. The objective was to achieve the practical advantages of military force without the messy political implications of declaring martial law so close to home. The answer was to launch a hybrid campaign in which military rules would be enforced by the police, the Royal Irish Constabulary (RIC)—rearmed and repurposed under new military leadership. It was a plan that met immediate resistance among senior British military ranks.

The general officer commanding (GOC) in Ireland, General Nevil Macready, refused to consider taking on command responsibility for a civilian police force with an unconventional paramilitary mandate. The chief of the imperial general staff (CIGS), Field Marshal Sir Henry Wilson, was hostile from the outset and would become a persistent critic of the militarized police force and its leadership. The first army officer General Macready approached to take the job, euphemistically titled "police adviser" to the Anglo-Irish government, flatly turned it down.[2]

After a few days of dithering by the military brass, Winston Churchill, now the British minister for war, stepped in—he knew just the man for the position, an old friend, Major General Hugh Tudor. The speed with which General Tudor accepted the assignment might suggest that he already knew exactly what the new job would entail. The position was approved by cabinet on May 11, 1920. Winston Churchill made the call and by May 15 the job was filled. Tudor arrived in Ireland on May 16.[3]

Did General Tudor ever wonder whether he could meet the tough challenges ahead? There's no record that he had any reservations about the job in Ireland, but he must have had at least a few. He had no experience in police work. He also had no experience with working in a political spotlight that exposed him to close public scrutiny and criticism. But he knew he did have the unqualified support of the powerful

minister for war and, even more important, the backing of the prime
minister, David Lloyd George, who was familiar with the general's
achievements on the Western Front and, like Churchill, was a fan.

The admiration in the Churchill-Tudor friendship was mutual from
the outset. Churchill was from an aristocracy that was not quite royal,
but prominent in British history. He had a magnetic personality, bound-
less energy and brains. Tudor was a dedicated military man. He was
also an all-round athlete, a skilled horseman, an avid polo player and a
dedicated golfer. He had been a British army boxing champion, winner
in his lightweight class twice in the 1890s. Near middle age, Tudor still
exuded an aggressive masculinity, a quality much admired and maybe
envied by both Churchill and Lloyd George.

The sights and sounds of Dublin in 1920 could have made an
Englishman like Tudor feel at home. Ireland's peril for an imperial
bureaucrat or soldier might have been obscured by her physical famil-
iarity, the Irish charm and the deference of friendly, witty people.
Tudor was clearly warned before he took up his post not to be deceived
by first impressions.

He had never been to Ireland and was indifferent to the long Irish
fight for self-determination. As he later told a friend, he didn't care "a
whoop in Hell" about it. He was more familiar with the intrigues of
Asia, Africa and continental Europe. He was fluent in, along with the
proper English of an officer and gentleman, French and Arabic and
was competent in Urdu. Tudor's interest in Irish history and politics
extended only to recent episodes of what he viewed as Irish treachery:
the Easter Rising, at a time when Britain and her allies had their backs
against the wall fighting the Germans in France; Roger Casement's
effort to recruit Irish rebels among British prisoners of war in Germany;
Irish resistance to conscription when Britain desperately needed fresh
blood for the war in Europe.

Were he of a more volatile disposition, Tudor might have shared the hostility revealed by his military counterpart in Ireland, General Sir Nevil Macready. "I loathe the country . . . and its people," Macready had written in 1919, "with a depth deeper than the sea and more violent than that which I feel against the Boche."[4] But Tudor, when he arrived in Ireland, was not a sentimental man. He believed that shallow sentiments like loathing, anger and a desire for vengeance, proper motivation for a conscript, should be suppressed by military leaders in case they triggered unprofessional behaviour.

While he knew little about Ireland, he did know, from his experience on the Western Front, a few hard-nosed army officers, British patriots with Irish links who could help him crush the expanding insurrection Churchill had described.

He soon recruited Lieutenant Colonel Gerald Smyth, a soldier from Ulster, who had the kind of brutal pluck the British campaign in Ireland badly needed. Smyth would quickly pivot to a challenging police assignment as one of Tudor's senior officers.[5]

Another officer whose resumé and personality Tudor believed were ideal for the assignment was Brigadier General Cyril Prescott-Decie. He had Irish connections through his wife and a visceral hatred of Irish rebels. More important, he had caught the eye of Winston Churchill when Tudor introduced them on the Western Front in 1916.[6] Prescott-Decie didn't try to hide his anti-Irish bias. He described his enemy succinctly—the typical IRA man was either a "burly ruffian" or "a moral and physical degenerate."[7]

A third member of the Tudor team, William Y. Darling, was, in Tudor's estimation, "a man of great personality and exceptional efficiency at any job he undertakes."[8] Darling had been Tudor's camp commandant on the Western Front. During one of Churchill's visits to the front lines, in October 1918, he'd met Captain Darling and was impressed. In the spring of 1920, Churchill urged Tudor to take

Darling with him when he went to Ireland. Tudor wrote, "So, Darling accompanied me and became the life and soul of our little party in Dublin Castle and a great help to me."

Colonel Charles Wickham was another Great War veteran and, like Tudor, a long-standing member of the exclusive Army and Navy Club in London.[9] He would take on one of the most challenging policing jobs in Ireland, RIC commissioner in Belfast. Wickham was joined by two other artillery officers from the Western Front, Brigadier General Guy Barron,[10] who would, like Smyth, serve as a divisional commissioner in Munster, and Ormonde de l'Épée Winter,[11] who became General Tudor's deputy police chief and director of intelligence.

Dublin Castle, a sprawling fortress in the middle of the city, was the pinnacle of British authority in Ireland. While the Castle had occasionally served as a palace for visiting British royalty, by 1920 it was mostly an administrative hub. By the end of that long, hostile summer, the Castle would be overcrowded as British government officials, including Tudor and two members of his team—Captain Darling and Colonel Winter—abandoned less secure accommodations in the city for safety behind its ancient granite walls.

It was in many ways a prison for the people living there. Mess dinners were the high point of most days. Social life was limited to card games, usually bridge and poker, and musical performances by the more talented inmates. *The Beggar's Opera* was a reliable source of songs most people knew by heart; an assistant undersecretary, Alfred (Andy) Cope, would be remembered for stirring renditions of "Invictus," a poem that was particularly poignant for its familiar closing line: "I am the master of my fate, I am the captain of my soul."[12]

Central Dublin, in 1920, was a tightly packed community of tenements and slums, small shops and pubs crowding narrow streets, a maze of lanes and alleyways running off the streets in all directions, the River Liffey bisecting the population of about 230,000. As a result, it was a relatively safe haven for fugitive rebel gunmen and leaders of the Irish independence movement. The guerrilla leader Ernie O'Malley, who had been a medical student in Dublin in 1916 and lived there incognito in late 1920 when he was on the run, wrote of "a definite friendliness and ease about Dublin."[13]

Cellars and countless hidden spaces below the ancient slums offered hideouts for gunmen and storage for weapons and munitions, and safe workshops for making bombs and bullets and repairing rifles and revolvers. A section of Camden Street, O'Malley recalled, was known as the Dardanelles, a reference to the First World War battle site, "on account of the narrowing of the houses and the number of ambushes that took place there."[14]

General Tudor had wasted little time tackling his assignment. Within days, he had the beginnings of his team gathering around him in Dublin, and by early June, he had an aggressive plan in place that he had obviously explained to his subordinates. General Prescott-Decie, in a letter to an assistant undersecretary in Dublin Castle dated June 1, gave a vivid assessment of their intended strategy. The letter is significant for two reasons: it was written just fourteen days after General Tudor's arrival in Dublin, and it suggests that terror tactics by the enemy would now shape a deliberate but undeclared government response.[15] "I have been told the new policy and plan," Prescott-Decie wrote, "and I am satisfied, though I doubt its ultimate success in the main particular of stamping out of terrorism by secret murder."

The oddly punctuated sentence could be read two ways: the policy and plan simply involved tough new measures to stamp out "secret murder" by the terrorists, or the "new policy and plan" for pacifying Ireland involved "secret murder" *by the RIC*. Significantly, historians have interpreted the words as written to mean exactly what they seemed to say. Dublin Castle was embracing a bold new policy of intimidation and assassination.[16]

Prescott-Decie wasn't sure that it would work, but he had been assured by his superiors that the RIC would be getting all the support they needed—more weapons, vehicles and manpower—"and when the support we are promised arrives, we shall know how to employ it in carrying out the policy outlined to me."

Days later, on June 6, 1920, just three weeks into his new job, General Tudor was in London. Over a private dinner with the prime minister and one of Lloyd George's most influential confidants, the newspaper baron Sir George Riddell, he offered a candid assessment of how he saw the challenges before him.[17] According to Sir George, who wrote about it in his diary, it was a "graphic" briefing, after which the prime minister was "very emphatic about the necessity for strong measures."

Lloyd George had agreed that "when caught *flagrante delicto* you must shoot the rebels down. That is the only way." The next day, June 7, the prime minister reported to the cabinet on his chat with General Tudor the night before and made it clear that the government and the country should be prepared for aggressive new initiatives in Ireland.[18]

Twelve days later, on June 19, the strong measures explicitly approved by the prime minister were being spelled out in even more graphic detail to a squad of RIC policemen in a barracks day room in Listowel, County Kerry.

5.

JUNE 19 WAS a lovely spring day in Listowel, a quiet market town of about three thousand. The trip to Listowel was just one of many visits the new police adviser was planning in a campaign to boost morale among the constables and officers of the Royal Irish Constabulary. Tudor wanted them to know that the RIC was about to become Ireland's unofficial army, with the regular British army as backup. The police force would soon be bigger, more aggressive, better armed and better led than at any time in the living memory of any Irish man or woman, friend or foe. The RIC was rebuilding for a major role in shaping Ireland's future.

But even more important than new firepower, individual policemen needed to rebuild their self-confidence and cultivate a more aggressive outlook. All over Ireland, the RIC had been under siege for more than a year. Policemen had become targets of an organized campaign of intimidation, social isolation and murder by Irish militants. In January 1919, two officers had been killed by rebels in County Tipperary. It signalled the beginning of a war in which Irish police would be portrayed among their own people as the bad guys.

The "peelers," as they were known, had never been entirely popular.[19] They were symbols of an alien authority, and they enforced that authority's law, sometimes gently, often zealously. But they were also local people, mostly wearing uniforms for economic reasons. The RIC provided steady work with a pension at the end of a career. Any Irishman could understand the motivation to join up.

But this violent persecution by their fellow Irish men and women, even children, was new. It wasn't just from the radicals, but the radicals—the political Sinn Féin and their military wing, the Irish Volunteers, now generally known as the Irish Republican Army— were driving it, insisting on harassment of policemen as evidence of Irishness. *Make the peelers suffer. Make them quit their jobs to prove they're really Irishmen.*

From January to May 1920, when General Tudor arrived in Dublin, forty RIC officers had been killed on the job, compared to fifteen for all of 1919.[20] It was hard on the nerves. It was hard on the family. Veteran policemen were quitting in record numbers, and they were hard to replace, for the same reason that made it hard for them to stay on the job. The paycheque wasn't worth the danger and the personal aggravation.

Tudor wanted members of the RIC to know that a new day was dawning. He was starting his rejuvenation tour in Listowel because he realized that Listowel could become a special problem. Poor morale had metastasized there into an anxiety that had the makings, if unchecked, of mutiny.

Since the beginning of the year, the RIC had been actively recruiting replacements for departing Irish peelers in England, hiring unemployed British army veterans of the Great War. The constables in Listowel had expressed profound resentment of this strategy, arguing that the last thing the Irish constabulary needed was unemployed English soldiers. Tudor had decided from day one that, in fact, Ireland needed more of them—that it was the best way to guarantee that from now on, policemen no longer had to feel that they were sitting ducks for rebel gunmen. He wanted the men in Listowel to be among the first to know that.

Earlier that week, the RIC policemen in Listowel had been ordered to evacuate their barracks and to hand over principal policing duties in the area to British army personnel and the new police recruits.[21] They were about to be reassigned to other places as, in strategic towns, the Irish constabulary was expanded, rearmed and fortified, reinforced by soldiers and new peelers who mostly came from England.

Some smaller, more remote and more vulnerable stations had been closed and their officers reassigned. The frequent response to both these reassignments and the growing perils of police work had, in recent months, been resignation or retirement. In Listowel the officers decided to respond to what they considered to be unreasonable orders the more authentically Irish way. They decided to rebel.[22]

They passed along the word to their superiors that they were not leaving their barracks and they were not abandoning responsibility for policing Irish men and women, mostly law-abiding people, many of whom they knew personally, to a crowd of English soldiers who were nothing more, in their estimation, than thugs dressed up as Irish constables. No, they were staying put. When they were reminded by their district officers that the orders came from Dublin Castle, the seat of British government in Ireland, and that they had sworn allegiance to the King, they held their ground.

The arrival of senior police and military personnel in Listowel that morning was meant to send a reassuring message to the constables and to all the loyal citizens of County Kerry. *Be patient. We are all in this together. Don't do anything to make matters worse.* But the officers watching the high-powered gathering of police and military brass outside their barracks didn't see it that way. To them, it was another act of British imperial intimidation.

Tudor was one of the first of the senior officers to arrive, under armed escort. He was soon joined by the Kerry County police inspector, arriving from Tralee with another armed escort. He and the officers in his party were decked out as if for a parade, with helmets, swords and rifles.

And then an army truck pulled up behind the police cars, and a regular British army unit from a military encampment just outside of town clambered down, weapons clattering. The locals had been aware of the soldiers since their arrival several weeks earlier, but they had made nothing of their presence. Now, it seemed, these soldiers were about to occupy the barracks by force if necessary.

The last arrival came all the way from Cork, the second-largest city in southern Ireland and the capital of Munster province, the heartland of the Irish republican insurrection. Lieutenant Colonel Gerald Smyth was the new RIC district commissioner for the rebellious province, which included County Kerry and the town of Listowel.

In the words of one of the Listowel constables, Jeremiah Mee, Colonel Smyth was "in full dress uniform and wearing at least a dozen war medals across his chest . . . escorted by British soldiers fully armed with rifles and swords." A sleeve on Colonel Smyth's army tunic was flipped up and pinned, revealing that his left arm was missing below the elbow, one of many combat injuries he'd survived. It was obvious from their greetings that Tudor and the new arrival were old friends. In fact, Smyth had served in the 9th Scottish Division when Tudor was divisional commander.

Now there were four Crossley tenders—menacing military trucks— parked along the road in front of the barracks. Milling among the regular soldiers and familiar cops in familiar uniforms were the "English" newcomers. They were conspicuous for their mismatched uniforms— military khaki and the near-black tunics of policemen—and known since their arrival as Black and Tans.

Knowing they had been recruited to restore manpower but, more important, while it wasn't said aloud, to stiffen backbones among the Irish constables, these Black and Tans tended to exude an attitude of superiority. There was, of course, the incitement of an English accent, aggravating even for people who were politically indifferent. And there was also the unmistakeable swagger of an occupying military force.

6.

HISTORY WOULD RECORD the Irish situation in 1920 as a war: the Irish War of Independence, the Anglo-Irish War, the Tan War. By 1920, war was the key to understanding what was going on in Ireland, but official British policy was to treat the violence as a crime wave. The job of the police would be to restore law and order in the midst of an armed disturbance, whatever it was called. How Tudor and his team would stifle this brazen criminal threat to British interests in Ireland was basically up to them.

Ireland had a long history of failure in the quest for independence, but the struggle playing out in 1920 was buoyed by a new revolutionary spirit that was shaping nationalist ambitions in disintegrating empires around the world. Britain's imperial grasp was no less vulnerable to the global volatility, and nowhere in the colonies and provinces of the British Empire was the movement for self-determination more active and more advanced than in Ireland. Britain's leaders regarded it as imperative for what was left of their sphere of global influence that the Irish appetite for independence be suppressed. There could be political accommodation short of nationhood, but first, the Irish insurrection had to be decisively demolished.

That objective was, for General Tudor's time in Ireland, the mission of the Royal Irish Constabulary. The British policy was classic stick-and-carrot. They would carry on a patient but continuous flirtation with the enemy in the backrooms and back channels of Dublin, but the sharp end of the stick would be the RIC and the rowdy, ruthless Black and Tans.

The new recruits were from all over the United Kingdom, with a few from elsewhere in the Empire, but from a strictly Irish point of view, they were all Englishmen. Soon they would be joined by a new paramilitary outfit, the Auxiliary Division, also raised in England but dressed in more conventional military uniforms. The "Auxis" would be more carefully selected, all former commissioned British military officers with battlefield experience, many highly decorated in the recent war. But they were destined to be merged in Irish memory with the ruthless Black and Tans.

———

Constable Jeremiah Mee was more than a casual observer of the scene in Listowel that Saturday morning. He was, in fact, one of the reasons for the high-powered response to what, until that day, had been a muted resentment toward the expanding British military presence in the south and west of Ireland.

Tudor would have argued that the expanding presence of regular army as well as veteran soldiers repackaged as policemen was unavoidable. The rebel strategy to shun, insult and persecute policemen and their families, threaten them with death and, with increasing frequency, gun them down, was working. Before the year was out, the 1920 death toll for policemen in Ireland would total 168.[23] By that summer, officers were abandoning police work at the rate of more than one hundred a week. In the months after Tudor's arrival, between July and the end of September, the RIC lost more than thirteen hundred men through resignations and retirement.[24]

Because almost all of the new recruits were veterans of a savage war, most of them from England, their recruitment was accelerating a change in the personality and culture of the RIC and in the direction of the Irish War. This was where the constables in Listowel decided, collectively, that their leaders had gone too far.

Tudor understood that the smouldering revolt in Listowel was serious. Britain didn't need this insubordination. Open mutiny, even on a small scale, could not only spread but could also give comfort to the enemy. In Tudor's regular army career, though, he'd been known for empathy with fighting men. His objective in Listowel that day was to be encouraging. The last thing these men needed was more intimidation.

This situation called for reassuring spectacle and perhaps a lecture on tradition and the importance of military discipline, of doing what you're told. But it was not to be heavy-handed. If they had been soldiers disobeying orders, they could have been shot. But they were policemen, subject to a different form of discipline. Tudor meant to be firm, but essentially collegial.

Inside the barracks, Jeremiah Mee and his fellow mutineers were braced for punishment. By refusing to leave, they knew that they were seriously out of line, risking unemployment, perhaps prosecution. They were certain they would soon face the fury of the senior officers who were lingering outside. As Constable Mee wrote years later, "To say that I myself was anxious would be to put it very mildly. This display of force was no doubt intended to terrorise and overawe our little garrison within, and I will admit that I never felt less cheerful in my life."

It remains unclear how Jeremiah Mee became the front man in what turned into a direct challenge to the power of a new and more aggressive team of leaders who were trying to revitalize a demoralized and increasingly ineffective police force. Mee was an unlikely rebel. He had been born and raised, one of nine children, on a subsistence farm in Galway. He had been in Listowel for just a little over six months. He had an unremarkable face, memorable mainly for a carefully sculpted handlebar moustache. On a force where many of the Irish policeman stood six feet tall, Jeremiah Mee barely passed the minimum five foot nine.[25] He did, however, have a stubborn streak and had recently annoyed his RIC superiors by trying to organize a union for policemen.

Their orders to vacate had arrived on the evening of June 16, a Wednesday. They were told that at noon the next day, soldiers would take possession of the barracks. One constable and three sergeants would remain in Listowel to act as guides for the outsiders, but everyone else would be reassigned.

Possibly for the first time in his life, Mee felt the sting of nationalist outrage. "After a lot of discussion, I personally addressed the men in the day-room. I pointed out that a war had been declared on the Irish people and that . . . we had to consider our own position," Constable Mee would recall.

> I pointed out that in a war one of two things must happen. We had either to win or lose. I assumed that we would win the war with the assistance of the British military.
>
> When we had defeated our own people, the British military would return to their own country and we would remain with our own people whom we had, with the assistance of the British Government, crushed and defeated. That would be the best side of our case. If we lost the war, the position would be still worse.

Mee's simple logic was irrefutable. The Irish police were being used to undermine a political movement that the majority of Irish citizens supported. There could be no happy ending to this story. Win or lose, Mee and his fellow constables were doomed to be pariahs in their own country for all time to come. The more he spoke, the more aggressive were his feelings and his language.

> I suggested that, instead of going on transfer, we would hold the barracks and refuse to hand over to the British military. We had bombs, rifles and revolvers, and any amount of ammunition; and there was no reason why we could not hold the barracks at least for a few days.

But first he and his comrades decided to see how much they could achieve by talking sense to their Irish superiors. Leave the English out of it. Mee wrote to the Kerry County RIC inspector, Poer O'Shea, explaining that there were two substantial reasons for their defiance. First: "There was no crime in Listowel district and we felt that, as policemen, we were quite capable of doing any police work in the district without the co-operation of the military."

The second reason was more subjective and more provocative: they refused "to co-operate or work in any capacity with . . . men of low moral character who frequented bad houses, kept the company of prostitutes and generally were unsuitable and undesirable characters."

The county inspector refused to submit their "filthy document" to his superiors in Dublin Castle until they had removed the references to the "low moral character" of the newcomers, who were all, until quite recently, gallant British soldiers. The Listowel policemen refused to retract a word. Now, in the harsh light of day, staring down the barrel of British military power, Constable Mee might have been having second thoughts about their hard line.

Colonel Gerald Smyth was the kind of Irishmen that Englishmen could understand, admire and even like. He was of an admirable social class, but with little of the rigidity that seemed to infect the British upper crust. Smyth's kind were the sons and daughters of the law-abiding people who owned, managed or worked on the great estates and in the linen mills of northern Ireland and in the factories and shipyards of Belfast.[26]

They were part of the economic lifeblood of the United Kingdom and, when properly led, became great soldiers and frequently went on to be great leaders themselves. These were people who truly wanted the law and order General Tudor had undertaken to restore with the help of reliable Irishmen like Colonel Smyth. They considered the trouble-makers in the republican political movement, Sinn Féin, to be nothing more than terrorists. Through intimidation they had compromised the Irish public as they had intimidated the Irish police.

Tudor and the British leadership believed that the widespread popular support for the mob that they referred to as the "Shinners" was no more complicated than a visceral response to fear. "The whole country . . . would thank God for strong measures," General Tudor declared shortly after his arrival. And by mid-June, when he went to Listowel, he was satisfied that strong measures were already under way. Given a few more months of resolute support from politicians like Churchill, and the help of half a dozen of his other friends, all military professionals like Smyth, he was confident that he could "crush the present campaign of outrage" without any difficulty before the year was out.

Colonel Smyth, though he insisted he was Irish, had actually been born in India, in the Punjab, the son of a British high commissioner. He had been educated in England and in northern Ireland. He was fluent in Spanish and a gifted student of mathematics—he could have had a career as a translator or a teacher.[27]

But, like Tudor, he was barely out of adolescence when he'd answered the call of opportunity and duty and joined the army. Like Tudor, he was commissioned as a second-lieutenant at the age of twenty. He wasn't yet thirty-five when he returned to Ireland in late May 1920. Much decorated for his bravery, Smyth was also admired for what one of his British superiors described as his "Irish humour and pluck" when morale and discipline among the rank and file required a special boost from leadership. Tudor was counting on those qualities to restore morale and discipline among the constables in Listowel on June 19, 1920.

7.

THOUGH CONSTABLE MEE stayed up late on the night of June 18, preparing and practising the little speech he planned to deliver to the high command the next morning, he was possibly more afraid that he would bungle the delivery than he was of potential consequences of his insubordination. He was almost tongue-tied as the senior officers paraded into the barracks day room and lined up facing him and his fellow mutineers.

To his surprise, Colonel Smyth's tone, when he stepped forward to speak to them, was friendly. It might have been an opportunity for the policemen to step back from the brink of confrontation, but Mee didn't see it that way. As Smyth began to speak, the constable interrupted. Politely, he objected to the presence of so many military officers. This was supposed to be a conference about policing for policemen. Smyth hesitated, but before he could react, "the military officers smiled at each other and quietly walked out of the room."

Smyth resumed his speech, and from the outset it was clear that he was about to radically redefine police work. "Sinn Féin has had all the sport up to this; we are going to have the sport now," he declared.

Late that night, Mee would write down what he remembered of Smyth's speech. His recollection would read like a verbatim transcription, which would inevitably raise questions about its accuracy. But he would insist that he had faithfully recorded what he'd heard and that he'd circulated his reconstruction to fourteen constables for their approval. Each of the fourteen eventually signed it.

In Jeremiah Mee's version of the speech, Colonel Smyth, with General Tudor at his side, was encouraging policemen to throw away their rule books, to follow their most violent instincts in dealing with their enemies. They were to adopt the tactics of the terrorists on clandestine night patrols and ambushes:

Take cover behind fences, near the roads, and, when civilians are seen approaching, shout "hands up."

Should the order be not immediately obeyed, shoot, and shoot with effect. If the persons approaching carry their hands in their pockets or are in any way suspicious looking, shoot them down.

You may make mistakes occasionally and innocent persons
may be shot, but this cannot be helped and you are bound to get
the right persons sometimes. The more you shoot, the better I will
like you, and I assure you that no policeman will get into trouble
for shooting any man.

Whatever Colonel Smyth's precise words were, there was little disagreement about the essence of what he had to say: Smyth was instructing them to kill anyone they even suspected of militant opposition to
British rule—members of the IRA and even the more aggressive politicians in Sinn Féin and their supporters. He was giving the police a
green light to shoot people only suspected of subversion—shoot to
kill, in fact—and he promised the political and legal support of their
commanders when they inadvertently shot innocent people, as they
inevitably would.

The official version of Smyth's statement in Listowel, later quoted
in the House of Commons by the Irish attorney general, was less
inflammatory but hardly less aggressive in tone:

> I wish to make the present situation clear to all ranks. A policeman
> is perfectly justified in shooting any person seen with arms [guns]
> who does not immediately throw up his hands when ordered.
>
> A policeman is perfectly justified in shooting any man whom
> he has good reason to believe is carrying arms . . .
>
> Every proper precaution will be taken at police inquests that
> no information will be given to Sinn Féin as to the identity of
> any individual or the movements of the police.[28]

Jeremiah Mee was in no doubt about what Smyth was telling
them to do.

In desperation, I stepped forward and said, "By your
accent, I take it you are an Englishman. You forget you are
addressing Irishmen."

I said, "I am an Irishman and very proud of it." Taking
off my uniform cap, I laid it on the table in front of Colonel
Smyth and said, "This too is English; you may have it as a
present from me."

Having done this, I completely lost my temper and, taking
off my belt and sword, clapped them down on the table, saying,
"These too are English and you may have them. To Hell with
you, you are a murderer."

The meeting went downhill rapidly from there. Smyth ordered
Mee arrested. His fellow constables intervened, some suggesting that
Colonel Smyth deserved to be shot. The senior police officers retired
to another room to consider what should happen next. General Tudor
opted for a gesture of conciliation, decided to be the "good cop."

According to Mee's later account, Tudor's friendly manner was
reassuring. He shook hands all around. He seemed to understand what
they were up against. The stress, the sense of never being off duty. He
could relate, just on a human level. He wasn't there to punish. He was
there to reassure. He promised them unqualified support. He promised them a raise in pay.

General Tudor had good reason to feel confident and be generous.
It is unlikely that while Colonel Smyth was laying out the details of
a brutal strategy, the general was hearing anything he hadn't heard
before. Smyth's was a plain-spoken description of the mission as
Tudor understood it and as he himself had explained it to the British
prime minister, who, just two weeks earlier, had explicitly approved it.
If General Tudor was surprised by anything that morning in Listowel,
it would not have been the content of Smyth's pep talk. Smyth was

only describing the unpleasant job he understood that they had both signed on for—stamping out terrorism by killing terrorists.

The prime minister had suggested shooting people "caught *flagrante delicto.*" Smyth, as a fighting man, would have known that on a dark night in an unfamiliar place, *flagrante* is rarely flagrant—that almost always there is a moment of doubt that, for a soldier or policeman, defines a narrow space between life and death, a moment when any hesitation could be fatal. Smyth's message to the troops, in essence: *When in doubt, shoot first. If there are questions later, your leaders will provide the answers.* How could any soldier or policeman not be inspired by such unqualified support?

8.

BY EARLY 1920, the Irish conflict had become a war fought on rebel turf on rebel terms. The action happened where and when the IRA wanted it to happen; the rebels always had the upper hand and almost always had the advantage of surprise.

The IRA campaign of intimidation and assassination had been a calculated escalation to deplete RIC morale and discipline. It was obviously working, but in one respect, it had produced an unintended outcome months before Tudor and his team had even arrived. The policemen who hadn't run away or quit were showing signs that they were capable of fighting dirty too. In a violent moment, they could be as terrifying as the "terrorists."

Black and Tans had quickly earned a reputation for ham-fisted law enforcement. Perhaps emboldened by the Black and Tans, many Irish-born policemen were, unlike the constables in Listowel, starting to appreciate the aggressive spirit of the new recruits. Discipline be damned.

The responses to Sinn Féin intimidation in the early months of 1920, by both the old guard and the Tans, had been invariably chaotic, with a lot of booze involved. After what the RIC called "outrages," houses of suspected Sinn Féin sympathizers were burned down, barns and animals were destroyed, pubs and businesses were vandalized and looted.

As General Tudor saw the situation, rage was understandable. But if the objective was restoring law and order and winning Irish friends, spontaneous retaliation wasn't helpful. Acting out in mindless anger, often when drunk, was an admission of despair. Such frustration was a natural response to impotence, but what if the energy that sprang from being outraged could be harnessed? What if righteous passion could be turned to an advantage by directing the rage toward a controlled retaliation? Vengeance could be rebranded, reclassified and called "reprisal"—a more palatable word, implying deliberation and control.

By the end of the summer of 1920, reprisal, a word that also suggested punishment for criminal behaviour, would be a regular topic in cabinet discussions about police and military tactics. It was controversial, but the impulse was ancient—a concept sanctioned in the Bible: an eye for an eye, a tooth for a tooth. A template for the new "crime fighting" strategy might well have been established by a high-profile murder in Cork city more than two months before the Tudor team took charge.

At about ten thirty on the night of March 19, the IRA gunned down a Cork policeman, Joseph Murtagh, forty-six, a widower with three children. Murtagh had a reputation for treating rebel suspects harshly when he caught them. He had attended a policeman's funeral earlier that day.[29]

Just over three hours after Murtagh was shot, a group of armed men arrived at the home of Cork's lord mayor, Tomás MacCurtain, a popular politician and an easy-going businessman with friends across the spectrum of Irish politics. He was also, everyone knew, a brigade commander in the IRA.

MacCurtain had visited the local Sinn Féin club near midnight and broken up a friendly card game—warning the card players that an RIC officer had just been shot and that they could expect a police raid at any moment.[30] In recent months, policemen had been more likely to lash out in anger when one of their own was injured or, as was more frequently the case, gunned down by Irish Volunteers. The Sinn Féin men promptly put the cards away and several walked the mayor back to his house and watched him until he was inside and presumably safe.

Armed strangers at MacCurtain's door demanded to see him, and before they got a response, forced their way inside. By now everyone in the household, including MacCurtain's wife and children, was awake and terrified. The mayor's sister-in-law, Susanna Walsh, who was living with the family, later described what happened.[31]

She said the mayor was in bed when "two big men with blackened faces and big rain coats on them got to his [bedroom] door." She continued, "I heard the first man say, 'Come out. Curtain!' And my brother-in-law said, 'Give me time to dress. I am not yet ready.'" The intruders "spoke like members of the RIC. They had a most peculiar accent."

Walsh then heard three pistol shots. "I rushed upstairs," she said. "I thought I would die with all of them. And as I went upstairs, I heard heavy moaning . . . and I looked, and my brother-in-law lay just outside his door with blood oozing from the region of his heart."

MacCurtain died there in the early morning of his thirty-sixth birthday. The police didn't bother to investigate the murder. The RIC district inspector in Cork, Oswald Swanzy, declared that he believed the mayor had probably been murdered by IRA extremists.

Swanzy's theory was repeated by the prime minister, Lloyd George, and the Irish viceroy, Sir John French. The viceroy was still simmering after an assassination attempt on him by the IRA four months earlier. MacCurtain, they all claimed, was too reasonable for hard-line elements in the IRA, so they'd killed him as a warning to other moderates.

It was a lie. MacCurtain's murder was clearly retaliation for the recent murders of policemen, and probably of one policeman in particular— the man gunned down just hours before the mayor was attacked. An IRA investigation of the incident predictably concluded that the shooters were policemen, probably Black and Tans. The killers had been careless and someone saw them entering a nearby police station shortly after the murder.

A Cork coroner's jury reached the same conclusion and cast a wide net in assigning criminal responsibility. The killers were "unknown members of the RIC," but the ultimate responsibility was assigned to Lloyd George, John French and assorted other government officials. The man named last on the jury's list, RIC District Inspector Oswald Swanzy, would pay the greatest penalty.

Swanzy had disappeared from Cork shortly after the mayor's death. The Cork IRA were on the hunt for him, but by July, they had a more recent and potentially more serious provocation to respond to—Colonel Gerald Smyth's pep talk to the constables in Listowel on June 19. Smyth had quickly become the embodiment of a dangerous new British strategy in Ireland. He represented a threat that had to be eliminated as soon as possible.

General Tudor hadn't gone to Ireland with a violent game plan in mind. But conversations on the ground, and with senior members of the British cabinet, persuaded him that brutal tactics by the enemy justified brutal countermeasures by the government. Then came the savage murder of a friend.

9.

POLITICAL FALLOUT CAN be immediate and violent. Or it can be soft and silent like snow, tiny flakes accumulating imperceptibly until a landscape disappears. After Listowel, General Tudor returned to Dublin Castle and the challenge of implementing the new strategy for policing all of Ireland. Colonel Smyth went back to Cork. One of the Kerry RIC commanders advised the Listowel constables who had been rattled by Smyth's blunt instructions to calm down. Smyth was "a fool," he said, and not to be taken seriously.

Jeremiah Mee, however, couldn't help but take Smyth seriously. For the next two weeks, he stewed quietly, waiting for the fallout. But nothing obvious was happening. He wasn't suspended, arrested or disciplined, and neither were the other mutinous constables.

Then came the news about a mutiny in India in late June. Soldiers in an Irish regiment, the Connaught Rangers, were protesting British military policy back home. The protest grew into a brief and futile confrontation. A court martial sent seventy-seven mutineers to prison. Their leader, a private named James Daly, was sentenced to be shot.

Luckily, the Listowel mutineers weren't soldiers, just policemen. But now they were expected to do the work of soldiers. They were being given soldiers' weapons and, if Colonel Smyth was to be believed, a soldiers' mission, for which they were neither trained nor morally inclined.

Most of the Listowel policemen would quit before the summer ended. One inspector would be punished, shoved into early retirement with a reduced pension. Four would remain policemen in Listowel and become prolific information sources for Sinn Féin. One of the constables would reassess his life, enter a religious order and, later on, become a Roman Catholic bishop in West Africa.[32] Jeremiah Mee would take a different path entirely.

———

General Tudor and his man in Cork, Colonel Smyth, soon seemed to have put the incident in Listowel behind them. The Castle was preoccupied with a larger issue than tantrums by individual policemen—how to put the Shinners in their place once and for all. Phase one was outgunning them. Phase two would be out-talking them, negotiating some permanent basis for a long-term peaceful relationship on British terms.

Inevitably, there were debates at Dublin Castle about the effectiveness of declaring full-scale martial law for as long as it might take to win phase one and set the stage for the second and more important phase, peaceful co-existence. Given there were forty thousand British soldiers in Ireland, why not just cut to the chase by turning law enforcement over to the military? But declaring martial law, though tempting to some hard-liners in the British government, would be playing into the hands of Sinn Féin and the IRA, not only increasing their already rich reserve of grievances but also adding to their self-importance by dignifying their criminal campaign with the status of a war.

Martial law in Ireland would look bad in places like the United States, where displaced Irishmen were well-heeled and influential and where Britain wanted to appear to be on top of a manageable internal problem, its civil laws and civil rights intact. A military response to past crises, including the Easter Rising of 1916, had disturbed American politicians to the point where, as Lloyd George would eventually speculate, "had there been no Irish grievance, it is by no means improbable that America would have come much earlier into the [First World] War."[33]

Martial law, as the minority of moderates in Dublin Castle understood, was never a long-term solution for any situation, whether political or criminal in nature. Even when martial law produced a good result, the optics were invariably bad. However, disguising martial

law as something less offensive to democratic sensibilities made a lot
of sense. A "war on crime," perhaps. The deployment of repurposed
soldiers, granted special powers and proper weapons, could allow the
politicians time and space to implement solutions that would be com-
patible with British security and economic interests without the political liabilities of exerting military justice—an oxymoron, in the
opinion of many lawyers.

Tudor's tour of RIC barracks in late June left him confident—
even after Listowel—that the police force was ready to take on an
aggressive new role in the campaign against the rebels. On June 27,
eight days after the "mutiny," he confidently informed Churchill,
in a letter with the salutation "my dear Winston," that "we are
gradually persuading the RIC that they are being backed up and
will continue to be backed up . . . The situation is worse than it was
a year ago but it is better now than it was two months ago; that is
to say that we are more in a position to take effective action against
Sinn Féin."[34]

He hoped that "the public . . . at home realize the cowardly and
abominable nature of the Sinn Féin murder campaign against the
police." Further, he wrote, "but for the conduct of the RIC, one
would almost be driven to think that the Irish were a nation of cow-
ards. It really is the RIC who are preserving the honour of Ireland as
a fighting race."[35]

Ironically, even as Tudor wrote such reassurances to Churchill, the
general was frantically recruiting seven thousand reinforcements who
were mostly Englishmen to prepare the RIC for the coming showdown with determined Irish fighting men.[36]

The early response to the call for British soldiers to become policemen was underwhelming. But by the end of the summer of 1920, British
war veterans were flocking to Ireland for general service in the RIC and
in a new paramilitary section of the police, the Auxiliary Division

(ADRIC). Tudor had delivered on a promise he had made in Listowel—a raise in pay for policemen. RIC wages were doubled by late that year.

Members of the new Auxiliary Division had an even better deal. They were freelance police on short-term contracts, mercenaries paid more than the average constable and given a broader mandate and the proper motivation to get things done without too much interference from above. Tudor and his team were confident that they could turn the conflict around in a year or less. They were to be led by another former Tudor comrade from the Western Front, Brigadier General F. P. (Frank) Crozier.

They were all professionals, experienced in what was turning into a war, no matter what the politicians called it. They understood the importance of leadership and discipline in maintaining order and morale when under fire. Soldiers are prepared for confrontations with other soldiers, to deal with enemies in other uniforms. But a soldier can become confused and unpredictable when the enemy is a cluster of bloody-minded citizens dressed in their own clothes. There was nothing in the soldier's training that equipped him for the hidden perils in civilian violence. From a soldier's point of view today, the situation hasn't changed much in a hundred years.

Constable Jeremiah Mee saw that there would be no retreat from what was now a policy and a trend—merging soldiers and policemen into one potentially destructive enterprise, pacifying Ireland by making war on Irishmen.[37] He was a trained and experienced policeman. But above all else, he was an Irishman. The soldiers being hired to be the new policemen in his country were mostly foreigners to him. If he had to pick a side in a war that now seemed unstoppable, he would have no hesitation in deciding where he stood.

Seventeen days after the barracks showdown, Mee and three of his fellow mutineers opted for desertion. They packed up their personal possessions, their police revolvers and ammunition, and they left the barracks without farewell or explanation to catch a train from Listowel to Limerick. Four days later, on July 10, their account of Colonel Smyth's inflammatory speech appeared prominently in a widely read Dublin publication, the *Freeman's Journal*.

The next day, Jeremiah Mee sat down in Dublin for a serious conversation with some of the senior leaders in the Irish revolution. Officially, they were cabinet ministers in an upstart republican parliament, the Dáil Éireann. But behind the political facade, they were top-tier strategists in Sinn Féin's military campaign. Michael Collins had been adjutant general for the Irish Volunteers and was now director of intelligence for the IRA. Erskine Childers was Sinn Féin's English-born head of propaganda. A third member of Sinn Féin's provisional government was Countess Constance Markievicz (originally Gore-Booth), also English born, a high-profile socialist and suffragist married to a Polish artist. She had fought on the barricades in the Easter Rising of 1916. Her social status and her gender had saved her from a firing squad. Jeremiah Mee had now entered a secret world of conspiracy and revolution at its highest echelon.

Collins seemed convinced that Smyth's words were mostly bluster. He told Mee that he didn't believe the British were "dastardly enough" to follow such a policy. Childers disagreed. He had served in the British army in the Boer War. He'd worked as a parliamentary assistant among the top politicians and bureaucrats in Westminster and knew the English upper classes from personal experience. They were, in his opinion, capable of anything when it came to protecting their dwindling imperial authority.

As Mee was meeting with the rebellion's senior leaders, Colonel Smyth was on his way to London to offer his personal reassurances to the chief secretary for Ireland, Hamar Greenwood, that his words as reported in the Dublin press had been deliberately misconstrued. The next day, Monday, July 12, he sat down with senior Irish administration officials and managed to persuade them that the *Freeman's Journal* story was at best yellow journalism, at worst Sinn Féin propaganda. Some disgruntled constables had misunderstood him and blown his words out of all proportion.

Two days later, in the House of Commons, a member of parliament, T. P. O'Connor, a strong supporter of the Irish cause who represented Liverpool, asked for an adjournment to debate the incident in Listowel and the outrageous comments of the Cork divisional commissioner. Were Smyth's careless words a reflection of official government policy?[38]

Sir Hamar Greenwood, the cabinet minister responsible for Ireland, brushed O'Connor off, insisting that the reporting on the speech had distorted Colonel Smyth's words. But the Listowel story now had legs and was provoking outraged chatter in the mainstream British press and, to the alarm of Dublin Castle, in the United States.

By the end of their meeting, Colonel Smyth had managed to reassure the politicians. And perhaps his plain talk was exactly what the situation needed. Even the exaggerated interpretation of the words he spoke was no more bloody-minded than the spirit Lloyd George was hearing in his cabinet, a spirit with which, deep in his pragmatic heart, the prime minister could not disagree—a point of view most firmly held by Tudor's friend, the secretary of state for war, Winston Churchill.

For Jeremiah Mee, soon to become a player on the other side, working closely with Countess Markievicz and Sinn Féin, the version of the incident in Listowel as he reported it, while perhaps not scrupulously accurate, was true in essence. As he recalled it decades later, the British government had to play down the controversy because Colonel Smyth had inadvertently revealed a fundamental strategy that was already being implemented by the new police adviser in Ireland. And he asked a crucial, if rhetorical, question: "General Tudor, with other high-ranking officers, was present when Colonel Smyth delivered his infamous ultimatum to the R.I.C. at Listowel. Why was General Tudor not summoned to London to give evidence of Smyth's speech?"

Mee already had an answer. "The reason is that the British Cabinet were already committed to a policy of outrage and murder in Ireland. Investigation or inquiry was the last thing that the British Cabinet then desired."

Tudor, of course, could easily have verified Smyth's version of the speech or, at least, corrected the interpretation published in the newspapers. But surely he didn't have to. Wasn't Smyth articulating, if not official policy, the implicit understanding now? If a dirty fight was what was happening, the men in Tudor's RIC were up for it.

The explanations all made sense to the hard-line members of the British government. On the night of July 14, Colonel Smyth was on a boat, sailing back to Ireland. The constables' mutiny was officially considered to have been insignificant, already blowing over. But for Smyth, the reckoning had only just begun.

10.

SEÁN CULHANE WAS seventeen years old when he joined the Irish Volunteers in Cork in 1917. He took "a particular interest" early on in making primitive "tin-can bombs," crude explosives filled with metal filings. When, during tests, some of his bombs fizzled, he decided to become a spy. By the time he was nineteen, he had become an intelligence officer for the Cork city IRA. His commander was Tomás MacCurtain.[39]

Culhane was well positioned for a spy, working as an apprentice draper in a clothing store that was a popular destination for military officers and policemen. He was boyish and chatty, with a talent for asking innocuous questions that would sometimes draw useful information from his customers.

And Cork was a hot spot for unrest in Munster province. The mayor's murder in March had profoundly shocked republicans, none more than young Seán Culhane. The verdict of the coroner's inquiry into the mayor's murder was unequivocal and, to Culhane and most of Cork, unsurprising.

> Ald. Thomas McCurtain [Tomás MacCurtain], Lord Mayor of Cork, died from shock and haemorrhage caused by bullet wounds and that he was wilfully murdered under circumstances of the most callous brutality and that the murder was organised and carried out by the R.I.C. officially directed by the British Government.[40]

Colonel Smyth's arrival in the city had already been noted by Culhane and the rest of the brigade as an escalation in the growing British military presence in the city and the region. On July 10, when the *Freeman's Journal* reported on Smyth's speech to the Listowel constables, the details were much discussed by the local IRA leadership at brigade level and viewed as an official endorsement of a policy of retaliation—reprisals like the murder of MacCurtain, gunned down in his home, in the presence of his family. Was this the kind of war the republicans could expect as official policy under the new Tudor regime? The Cork Brigade had many scores to settle with the British, and now there was this provocative signal from a tough-talking new police commander who wanted to play hardball. So, if it was hardball Smyth was after, hardball he would get.

The brigade was already committed to avenging MacCurtain's murder by eliminating the man considered most directly responsible,

RIC Inspector Oswald Swanzy, who had vanished from the area shortly afterwards. They were still hunting him, but the speech by the new RIC commissioner in Cork would briefly push revenge for the mayor's death off the IRA's agenda. As Culhane recalled, the Cork Brigade put Inspector Swanzy's fate on hold after the press report of the incident in Listowel so they could "effectively deal with" Colonel Smyth.

The County Club in central Cork was, in the words of a local IRA foot soldier, "the resort of landed families and high military officers" and a place where high-profile British visitors thought they could relax in safety.[41] Security was tight, club employees carefully screened for politics. Most people working there were unionists committed to the political status quo: the union of Ireland with the United Kingdom and the British Crown. But one republican slipped through the tight club screening process.[42]

Ned Fitzgerald, a personable young waiter in the club's lounge, kept Seán Culhane informed of the comings and the goings of interesting guests. Colonel Smyth, he reported, would be living at the club until the middle of July and had become a regular visitor to the club's smoking lounge. Brigade leadership quickly came to a decision: Smyth would die at the County Club on the night of July 13.

But before the appointed execution day, Fitzgerald reported that Smyth, carrying a suitcase, had abruptly left the club a day or two before. No one knew where he had gone or for how long. He had, in fact, been summoned to London to explain the story everyone was talking about—the *Freeman* newspaper's account of his speech to the constables in Listowel.

On the morning of July 15, at a conference in Dublin Castle, senior officials reviewed the Listowel controversy and its aftermath. After Smyth's explanation in London, was there anything more that should be done to calm things down? Smyth's friend General Tudor had been present in Listowel and surely knew that the reports of Smyth's instructions to the constables were accurate. But still he argued that the *Freeman* should be prosecuted for "publishing false information." John Anderson, the senior British bureaucrat in Dublin, backed him up, insisting the newspaper should be sued on principle, if nothing else.

The Castle's lawyers disagreed. They thought a prosecution would be futile. So did the assistant undersecretary, Mark Sturgis, who wrote about the conference in his diary. "The Irish lawyers are dead against it . . . I am dead against it on grounds that newspapers love being prosecuted."[43] For the moment, the idea of a lawsuit was on hold.

Smyth was back in Cork by July 17, a Saturday, a fact Ned Fitzgerald dutifully reported to the IRA brigade. Culhane consulted the acting brigade commander, Seán Hegarty, who had replaced the murdered Tomás MacCurtain, and he, once again, approved the hit. That evening, half a dozen IRA men armed with revolvers gathered at the Sinn Féin hall, where they were soon joined by three others. After a brief consultation, they set off for the club. It was shortly before ten.

Ned Fitzgerald met Culhane on the street out front and confirmed that Smyth was relaxing in a smoking room. Since no one but Fitzgerald knew for sure what he looked like—except that one arm had been amputated at the elbow—Fitzgerald led the way through the club with six Volunteers, guns drawn, following so closely it might have looked like the waiter was being forced at gunpoint to lead the intruders to their quarry. It was after ten o' clock on a slow summer Saturday, so there were hardly any guests. They found Colonel Smyth at a corner table in the lounge, chatting with a Cork County RIC inspector, F. W. Craig.

According to an official RIC statement, the killers

burst in through the door and one of them shouted where is he, the leader shouted hands up then opened fire riddling his [Smyth's] face, forehead and neck with bullets.

After being shot he [Smyth] sprang from his seat, but it was evidently a death effort for he was fatally wounded, he rushed to the hallway but after a few yards he dropped dead.

Years later, when Culhane recalled the incident, he remembered minor differences in the details. But the outcome was the same. "We opened fire simultaneously, without any preliminaries, and most of our shots hit the target. Smyth made an effort with his one arm to make for his gun but collapsed in the attempt—he must have died at once."

Culhane then recognized Inspector Craig, who was scrambling for safety. A week earlier the RIC inspector had bought a pair of socks from the young man who was now about to shoot him. "I opened fire . . . although I aimed at his heart, I only succeeded in shooting him in the leg. My comrades did not know Craig, hence did not understand until later why I turned my gun on him. Had they known, Craig's fate would also have been sealed."

By Sunday night, agitated policemen and soldiers were thronging Cork's main streets. Two off-duty officers found themselves in a brawl with two local men, one a forty-year-old former soldier named James Burke, with no known political affiliation. Soldiers caught him on the street sometime afterwards and killed him with their bayonets.[44] Later, soldiers opened fire with a machine gun and a stray bullet killed an eighteen-year-old IRA member named Jackie O'Brien.[45]

By Monday, Cork was quiet. Seán Culhane was back at work behind the counter selling fabrics, socks and other clothing to unsuspecting customers.

———

There was never an official inquiry into the killing of Colonel Smyth; it would have been impossible to find a jury in Cork to conduct an inquest into the incident when so few would admit that they considered it a crime. Even the senior Roman Catholic clergyman in Ireland, Michael Logue—who deplored the murder—understood the motives. He said there was little point in efforts to prevent assassinations when the British government routinely provided "the excuse for these men to commit such outrages."[46]

The murder of Gerald Smyth was an unofficial act of retribution by a local IRA brigade, a response to the words attributed to him after his visit to the RIC in Listowel, June 19. A few IRA gunmen who were already famous or notorious in the public imagination would get the blame, or credit, for his death. None of them were on the team that did it. It would be a long time before anyone involved was identified—long after legal notions of accountability had any relevance. By then the concept of reprisal would be the centrepiece in military strategy on both sides of the Irish war.

Colonel Smyth's military funeral in Banbridge, County Down, on the afternoon of July 21, 1920, has been described as the largest funeral ever held in that little town about thirty miles from Belfast.[47] This was Ulster province, where conservative politics infused a Protestant tradition of resistance to the influence of the three other, largely Catholic, provinces of Ireland—Munster, Leinster and Connaught.

General Tudor was one of thousands who turned out. Smyth's coffin was draped with a Union Jack. On top of the flag there was a wreath from Smyth's mother, Helen Ferguson Smyth. His service cap and belt were conspicuous beside the wreath.

Lurgan Road in Banbridge was thronged with mourners and admirers as the gun carriage bearing the coffin moved slowly toward a nearby cemetery. A marching band and a hundred police officers followed the coffin, along with an honour guard of one hundred members of the 1st Bedfordshire and Hertfordshire Regiment; among the many commemorative wreaths, there was one from Inspector Craig, still recovering from his bullet wound in Cork.

There was already a palpable throb of anti-republican, anti-Catholic rage in Banbridge and it erupted even as the final notes of the Last Post faded, with the echo of the ceremonial volley at Smyth's graveside still hanging in the air. The assassination had horrified Smyth's fellow Ulstermen. But, exacerbating an already explosive situation, on the day of the funeral the "marching season" for Ulster Orangemen was just coming to an end. "The Glorious Twelfth" of July had marked the start of the annual celebration of a 1690 battle in northern Ireland when a Protestant claimant to the British crown (William of Orange) defeated the last Catholic to occupy the British throne, King James II. It's a day of religious tension every year and sectarian tempers were already hot when word of the killing in Cork on July 17 struck like a bolt of lightning.

After the funeral, Colonel Smyth's mother was among local mill-owners who declared they would no longer employ overtly nationalist Catholics. Catholic workers in linen factories throughout Ulster were, on pain of losing their jobs, made to swear not to support Sinn Féin.[48] During three days of what has been called a "pogrom," a loyalist mob estimated to number more than 2,000 trashed and looted pubs, businesses and homes owned by Catholics.

To the loyalists, it didn't matter who had pulled the trigger in that Cork smoking lounge. The villains were Sinn Féin, and Sinn Féin was predominantly Catholic. There could be no Sinn Féin without Catholic support, and that support threatened the future of the Irish connection with Britain, which, for centuries, had guaranteed protection for Protestant interests and Protestant social and economic hegemony in Ulster.

There had been inflammatory speeches on these themes on July 12, Orangemen's Day, one in particular by Edward Carson, leader of the Irish Unionist party and a powerful opponent of any form of Irish independence that would break the country's ties with the United Kingdom. He was part of the British political elite, a recent member of the British cabinet, but his speech was practically seditious. "If you [the British government] are unable to protect us from the machinations of Sinn Féin and you won't take our help," he warned, "well then, we tell you we will take the matter into our own hands. And these are not mere words."[49]

Ulstermen didn't need much further provocation, but when republican railway workers in Cork refused to transport Colonel Smyth's body by train to Banbridge, it was a final insult to the memory of a son of Ulster and a British hero.[50]

The only evidence of what might have been in General Tudor's heart as he sat through his friend's funeral that day lies in how he approached his job as a policeman in the days and months that followed the events in Listowel and Cork. The Smyth assassination would have hit close to home. Not only was Smyth a friend from the Western Front, part of an exclusive brotherhood, but it was Tudor who had persuaded him to join the RIC campaign. Decades later, he would remember bitterly how his friend Gerald Smyth had been "foully murdered by the Shinners with no chance to defend himself."[51]

In late July, British troops raided Jeremiah Mee's family home and, failing to find him there, burned it to the ground.[52] On July 30, a dynamite blast destroyed a house in Limerick. The owner, Michael Hartney, was wrongly believed to have been involved in the murder of Colonel Smyth. He escaped injury, but the explosion killed his neighbour, John O'Sullivan, an apolitical watchman and father to six children.[53]

The principal triggerman, that teenaged sales clerk in Cork, was shielded from suspicion by his friendly charm. More than thirty years later, a middle-aged Seán Culhane would calmly tell the story of Smyth's death to Irish archivists who were recording the personal experiences of seventeen hundred men and women who had served in the Irish War of Independence. Part of his story would be a grisly description of yet another deadly mission he undertook just a few weeks later, when he finally tracked down and killed Oswald Swanzy—publicly accused, along with Prime Minister Lloyd George, of complicity in the murder of Tomás MacCurtain.

Culhane had found Swanzy 250 miles from Cork, in northern Ireland, living with his sister under an assumed name. On a quiet Sunday morning, August 22, 1920, Culhane waited outside a church in Lisburn, County Antrim, until the end of Sabbath service. As Inspector Swanzy strolled away from the church, on his way home for a private Sunday lunch with his sister, Culhane walked up behind him and shot him in the head. The weapon that Culhane used to kill Swanzy was a revolver previously owned by his IRA commander in Cork city, the late Lord Mayor Tomás MacCurtain.[54]

11.

THERE WAS A message waiting at the Castle for General Tudor when he returned to Dublin from Smyth's funeral in Banbridge—a summons from Prime Minister Lloyd George. Tudor and most of the senior people in the Castle administration were ordered to London as soon as possible for a conference about what was clearly a deteriorating security situation in Ireland. Mark Sturgis, the prodigious diarist who was an assistant undersecretary at the Castle at the time, noted in his diary: "The PM is waking up."[55]

Suddenly, events were waking many people up. When General Tudor first heard that his friend was dead, it would have been almost impossible to believe the news. It was easier to believe, as Gerald Smyth had often demonstrated during the war, that he was indestructible. His assassination could only have happened in a place where he felt it safe to let his guard down. A smoking room in a quiet club, supposedly a sanctuary. But sanctuary anywhere in Ireland for a British officer was an illusion. There was no safe place, no friendly Irish face that could be trusted. Tudor's own survival now depended on old army comrades of proven loyalty, and the Webley revolver that was never out of reach.

Smyth had been in a special category of friends. They'd shared experiences on the Western Front, in Ploegsteert, the village just inside the Belgian border that they'd called Plug-Street, in the decisive months of 1918. One of Tudor's most vivid memories: on October 2, near Ledeghem, in Belgium, how Smyth had practically apologized to Tudor when he received the news that he would be leaving the 9th Scottish Division to command his own brigade. As Tudor noted in his war diary, Smyth was "very sick about having to leave the 9th Division." The sense of loss was mutual. Tudor wrote: "He is an exceedingly brave and efficient battalion commander and we shall all miss him badly."

Gerald Smyth was one of the first officers who came to mind when General Tudor accepted Churchill's call to serve in another war, and he had responded as Tudor knew he would—enthusiastically. And now, through malice or misunderstanding, Smyth had paid for his enthusiasm with his life.

Tudor would have had to shake off the memories and regret and move on, but he would not allow himself to forget. The funeral in Banbridge was a great strain. Even just getting there from Dublin had been an effort, and then there were the overwhelming crowds, the grief. But Tudor would also have found some solace in the moving ceremony, the loyal Ulster spirit, a reminder that there was more to Ireland than separatists and treachery.

In Dublin Castle after July 1920, there was a noticeable change in General Tudor's attitude toward his enemies, the Shinners. John Anderson, the senior bureaucrat in Dublin and a consistent voice for moderation, noted later that Tudor came to Ireland without strong views about the Irish but that he became "embittered" when the Irish started killing people he cared about.[56]

By the time Tudor was seated among the political and bureaucratic heavyweights in the cabinet room at 10 Downing Street on July 23, his mind was clear, focused on ten specific points he had to make. For someone with less personal self-confidence—the kind that comes with rank and battlefield experience—it would have been an almost overwhelming challenge. The room itself was daunting, nerve centre of the empire, with Sir Robert Walpole, fat and satisfied, berobed, bewigged, staring out from a gilded picture frame just above the fireplace. Tudor would have been well aware of the scenes Sir Robert witnessed in this place, of the crises dealt with, the wars won and lost here, life-and-death outcomes on battlefields determined by discussion, argument, decisions. Here.

Tudor knew he would be called upon to speak as the senior civilian law-enforcement officer in Ireland. He would be logical, practical, unemotional, but he would not hold back. His audience would include some of the most influential politicians in the country. At the long rectangular table—cluttered with documents and files and blotters, important men busily scribbling their thoughts, notes on what they were hearing, what they planned to say, composing arguments to make to shape decisions—sat seven key officials from Dublin Castle, representing, as would soon be obvious to the politicians, opinions that were irreconcilable.

Among the politicians, there were the hard-liners and the pragmatists, Lloyd George being perhaps the most pragmatic of them all. On the Castle side of the table, those attitudes were represented too, as well as a third faction—the moderates. Their position would be well represented that day by the legal adviser to the Irish administration, William E. Wylie.

Wylie was an Irishman, a lifelong unionist dedicated to the Anglo-Irish partnership. He had been in Dublin during the Easter Rising in 1916, and he had been part of the legal follow-up—the speedy trials of rebel leaders and the speedier decisions, legally correct and swiftly executed. But something had changed in Wylie's thinking since then. More recently, he had begun to advocate for conciliation, for opening a space for conversation with the more reasonable Shinners.

To Tudor, a hard-liner, the notion of "reasonable Shinners" was an oxymoron. Wylie, and some of his associates, were giving too much credence to "the other side." Wylie stated their ideas clearly that day. As reported in the conference minutes, he said there were, in his opinion, "two remedies for the present state of affairs. The first was to proclaim at once martial law of the most stringent kind . . . The second remedy was a settlement with Sinn Fein."[57]

Wylie, in that moment, was confessing to a dramatic personal conversion—heresy, as far as Tudor was concerned. The minutes continue: "[Wylie] himself had started life as a Unionist, but now, after seeing the marvellous organization which Sinn Fein has built up, he was of the opinion that the Irish were capable of governing themselves."

Wylie had done his homework. Sinn Féin had been sending conciliatory signals, a reality implicit in everything he said. And, explicitly, he had spent three weeks speaking to Irish policemen. He told the meeting that it was his opinion that within two months "the Irish police force as a police force would cease to exist." They had been polarized, either resigning from the RIC because of terrorism, or staying on and taking the law into their own hands. For Wylie, "both conditions of mind were disastrous." The situation in the courts was worse. "With regard to the civil courts, the entire administration of the civil government has ceased."

Negotiation with Sinn Féin might seem like condoning murder, but that take would be a mistake. As far as Wylie was concerned, "these murderers were not real criminals. Fanatics they might be, and probably were, but they were themselves convinced that through murder was the only path to freedom." Coming only six days after the assassination of a senior police official whose friend was sitting just down the table from him, Wylie's words were brave, even fortified as they were by new insights and strong conviction.

General Tudor spoke next and he was tactful. He agreed with Wylie—as matters stood, within a few months the RIC would cease to function as a police force. "But as a military body," according to the minutes of the meeting, "he thought they might have great effect. He had just recruited 500 ex-officers and a number of ex-soldiers, which formed a fine body of men, and he felt that given the proper support, it would be possible to crush the present campaign of outrage."[58]

Tudor then spelled out the basis of the anti-terrorism campaign he had in mind. His constabulary, fortified by Black and Tans and Auxiliary recruits, could dominate the countryside, but it would take stringent laws to put an end to the rebellion. Trials by military officers; all criminals tried by military courts martial; ID cards for citizens in all towns in Ireland, as had been required by the army of occupation in Germany; power to restrict where people lived by controlling change of domicile; passports required for entry to Ireland; communal punishment—fines and seizure of livestock—in places where there were murders; flogging for "outrages against women"; a purge of "traitors" from post offices . . .

It was a hard-line wish list, a measure of how seriously Tudor viewed the challenge they were facing. Essentially, he called for a suspension of democracy without a formal declaration of martial law. The strategy resonated with many of the most influential people in the room. Lloyd George asked Tudor if he thought that, given the legal powers he had suggested, he "could control the situation." According to the minutes, "General Tudor said he thought he could, provided enough men were obtainable. The whole country was intimidated and would thank God for strong measures."

Both of the Irish undersecretaries from Dublin Castle, John Anderson and James MacMahon, clearly saw the danger in General Tudor's formula for peace and lectured him at the meeting on the peril of his remedies. "The measures which General Tudor advocated were those of martial law and were not the ordinary methods of administering civil government . . . Under martial law there must be one military administrator who would have the whole power in his hands, and the civil authorities would be subordinate."[59]

A military dictatorship wasn't exactly what General Tudor was suggesting, given that he had no intention of handing the job he was describing over to the military high command. What he had in mind would amount to, at least temporarily, a police state.

Tudor was already confident that he had enthusiastic backing from the top—from Lloyd George, who seemed to clearly understand that a charade was playing out in front of him. The way ahead was already being written into hard-line legislation, the Restoration of Order in Ireland Act, a peacetime law with wartime penalties, including death. But the prime minister was coy. He turned to the lawyer Wylie, asking if, perhaps, a little dose of General Tudor's strong medicine might check the Irish fever long enough to enable a more democratic cure for the republican disease.

Wylie was emphatic. Tudor's medicine "would only create a feeling of intense hostility in Ireland, and the Irish would regard it as another piece of English tyranny."

Winston Churchill raised an even more inflammatory notion, inquiring "what Mr. Wylie thought would happen if the Protestants in the six counties were given weapons and definitely charged with the duty of maintaining law and order and of policing the country?"

Mr. Wylie "thought that such a policy would be disastrous . . . Sinn Féin would arm a more numerous and an equally efficient force." It was a certain formula for civil war.[60]

The one Catholic in the room that day, Sir James MacMahon, bluntly warned that "any attempt at repression would fail" and would "deprive the government of any friends among the Nationalists whom they might have left." And the government certainly had friends among the nationalists, he assured them. When he had visited the eighty-year-old Irish prelate Cardinal Michael Logue a few days earlier, he said that he had found him "weeping over the murder of Colonel Smyth."[61]

Except for his query about the possibility of arming loyal Ulsterman to keep the peace in Ireland when all else failed, the minister for war, Winston Churchill, had been uncharacteristically low-key throughout the conference. But it was obvious that when General Tudor spoke, he spoke for both of them. And the subtlety of the prime minister's question to Wylie—whether perhaps some of the "inconveniences" suggested by Tudor might be helpful—would, in retrospect, provide a clue about where Irish policy was headed.

Churchill was far more forthcoming in his thinking at another meeting of the cabinet later that same day. He noted with some approval that General Tudor had dissented from the "formidable" unanimity of the other speakers from the Castle, the moderates— Wylie, Alfred (Andy) Cope and the undersecretaries, MacMahon and Anderson. Churchill's opinion was that "prolonged strain was breaking down the officials in Ireland." Half measures wouldn't work.

"It was necessary to raise the temperature of the conflict to a real issue and shock, and trial of strength."

Churchill's close friend and political ally, the hawkish Lord Birkenhead (F. E. Smith), thought "the government should put in force at once General Tudor's suggestions."[62]

Sir John French, the King's representative in Ireland, was at the meeting but kept his opinions to himself that day. He would, however, later express his point of view directly to Lloyd George. The one speaker with whom he agreed entirely, he said, was the police adviser, General Tudor. "I am of the opinion," he wrote the prime minister, "that the only way to save Ireland is to adopt all his suggestions."[63]

Not long after the momentous meetings on July 23, it would become apparent that the government was already prepared to propose a form of martial law that offered military justice with civil law enforcement—in essence, the Tudor/Churchill formula. It would take only a few days to ram the Restoration of Order in Ireland bill through parliament before it was proclaimed as law on August 9.

Under it, military officers would preside in military courts to try all offences; they would have the power to impose the ultimate penalty for crime, death; they could administer summary justice; military enquiries would also replace coroners' investigations; they could force witnesses to appear in court and impose communal punishment through financial penalties and, later, by destroying private property. The difference between declaring martial law and this arrangement? Enforcement would be led by the police, with military backup, if required.

It was a major setback for the morale of the senior officials at Dublin Castle who disagreed with Tudor. The path to peace was obvious to the lawyer William Wylie. Allow semi-independent parliaments for both Ulster and the rest of Ireland. Reach out to the wise men of Sinn Féin, of whom there were a few worth talking to. July 1920 was, as he had plaintively advised the meeting on July 23, "a golden moment for settling the Irish question."

Now wasted. Wylie knew it wasn't going to happen. Not yet, not while the hawks controlled the thinking of the man in charge, Prime Minister Lloyd George.

In early August, six weeks after the "mutiny," the stillness of a Sunday evening in Listowel was shattered by gunfire, an opening salvo to announce the latest chapter in a long serial drama—the "restoration of order" in Ireland. Several military vehicles raced through the streets, the occupants firing rifles and pistols wildly in the air, shouting as if in celebration. They were policemen. Witnesses later testified that many of them appeared to be drunk.

Drunk or sober, they were announcing to the town that they had arrived to bring law and order to the place and that they had come to stay. It was like a scene from the mythical American Wild West—a new sheriff and his posse charging through the streets, proclaiming to an anxious population that from now on law and order would be delivered through the barrel of a gun.[64]

Part III

RETALIATION

"It is not they who can inflict the most,
but they who can suffer most, will conquer."

TERENCE MACSWINEY, 1879–1920,
POLITICIAN, IRA COMMANDER, CORK

12.

MAJOR OSBERT SMYTH might as well have written "vengeance" on his application for a transfer. Most people would have understood his motivation. He was based in Cairo. He had missed his brother's funeral in Ireland. Now he needed to go home, he had a duty to fulfill. Call it honour.

Everyone in the army, at least anyone who mattered, knew the story of how Colonel Gerald Smyth, a legend, was murdered by a gang of Irish rebels in the smoking room of a private club in Cork on July 17. Permission for his younger brother to transfer from Egypt back to England was an easy call.

Major Smyth sailed out of Alexandria on July 30, "hell-bent on revenge."[1] Eleven days later he was staring at the looming coast of England, approaching Folkestone. Getting the green light to go to Ireland was the next challenge. It would require some string-pulling by a close friend of his late brother, Major General Hugh Tudor. Once again, all the right people understood his need. The timing was propitious, now that retaliation was the covert "anti-terror" policy of the British government.

Like Tudor and his brother, Osbert Smyth had served on the Western Front. Like his brother, he had suffered multiple wounds and won multiple military decorations. Gerald had lost half of his left arm. Osbert had also been badly wounded in his left arm and, while doctors saved the limb, it would never again be fully functional. All three—Tudor and the two Smyths—were artillery officers who had graduated from the Royal Military Academy at Woolwich.

With such connections, it wasn't long before Major Smyth was living in a military barracks in the Dublin Castle complex, joining most of the senior personnel in the Irish administration, including Tudor. When he'd first arrived in Ireland, Tudor had occupied the surgeon's residence at the Royal Military Infirmary, near Phoenix Park, a high-risk two-mile drive away from central Dublin. By the time that Smyth arrived in mid-August, Tudor had moved into less comfortable but more secure private quarters in the castle.

General Tudor introduced him to his director of intelligence, the deputy police chief Ormonde Winter, another ex-artillery officer from the Western Front. Winter, working closely with the army, was trying to rebuild an intelligence network that had been practically destroyed in the IRA campaign to neutralize the Royal Irish Constabulary and the Dublin Metropolitan Police (DMP). The distant Irish country-side had gone dark and silent for the bureaucrats in Dublin Castle. The capital, Dublin, was by then close to a blind spot.

Winter hadn't been in Dublin long when he defined a fundamen-tal problem and came up with an obvious solution. The most ruthless of their IRA enemies were strangers to the police; many came from distant parts of Ireland. It was difficult to deal with an enemy if you didn't know what he looked like.

Winter created an "identification squad," recruiting about a dozen officers from small towns and rural areas, people likely to recognize the faces of wanted rebels, and he put them under the command of a soon-to-be notorious policeman, Eugene Igoe from County Mayo. Soon they were called the Igoe Gang, or, by some, the Cairo Gang, and their responsibilities only really started when they recognized a wanted man—at least according to the urban legends that they encouraged. Identification was usually followed by pursuit, arrest and, occasionally, assassination.

General Tudor knew Ormonde Winter well—their military service went all the way back to India, where they'd first met. Like Tudor, Winter had no police experience and hardly any background in intelligence. But Tudor knew that Winter could be ruthless and had the guts for fighting dirty when he felt he had to. As a young army officer, Winter had chased down and killed a fifteen-year-old English boy after a minor altercation. He'd used an oar to beat the boy to death. Winter was charged with manslaughter but was acquitted. The boy was said to have antagonized Winter by throwing stones at him.[2]

Ormonde Winter was a performer. He was flamboyant. A whiz in a poker game. A linguist. He was a master of magic tricks, one of which was to create illusions of his own importance. A senior Castle colleague described him as "a little white snake . . . probably entirely non-moral. . . and a most amazing original."[3] He came across to almost everyone who met him, or heard of him, as "a dapper, if somewhat stagy, raconteur: eccentric and adventurous."[4]

But Tudor knew Winter from the trenches and knew that he was both shrewd and fearless under fire. He was described by one officer who had served with him as the bravest man that he had ever known.[5] Winter was the first man General Tudor wanted Major Osbert Smyth to meet.

Both Tudor and Winter understood the urgent need to improve the collection and analysis of intelligence if the republican rebellion was to be suppressed. Tudor's predecessor as head of the RIC, a Belfast Orangeman named T. J. Smith, had been working to rebuild the DMP since he'd taken the job in late 1919. He had brought a team of Belfast colleagues with him to restore morale and muscle.

Smith had been in Dublin only a month or so when he discovered what he was up against. One of his new police enforcers from Belfast was an RIC inspector, Forbes Redmond. Smith assigned Redmond to rebuild the DMP intelligence operation, which had been decimated in the IRA campaign to neutralize the police.

Redmond arrived on January 1, 1920. The IRA soon had a photograph of the new man. Three weeks later, gunmen from an IRA
assassination team called the Squad shot him down outside his hotel
on Harcourt Street in central Dublin.

The man who pulled the trigger, Paddy Daly, described the hit
succinctly: "When Redmond was about two yards from me, I fired
and he fell, mortally wounded, shot through the head."[6] Several of
Redmond's new police recruits soon gave up on Dublin and headed
back to Belfast. Three months after Tudor's appointment as police
adviser, Smith was gone and Tudor was, as he renamed the position
he now occupied, police chief.

The British secret service had been struggling for months to infiltrate
Sinn Féin and the IRA. The biggest prize of all would be to capture
the elusive Michael Collins, head of IRA intelligence. But Collins
had an uncanny ability to sense when they were getting close and slip
away uncaught; it soon become obvious that his spies had penetrated
even Dublin Castle.

In January 1920, Jack Jameson, a secret agent who had infiltrated
the senior ranks of the IRA, was making headway when he was
exposed, possibly by a tip from a source within the Castle. His real
name was John Byrne and he was controlled by London's Special
Branch, reporting to the British spymaster, Basil Thomson. The
Squad tracked him for weeks, confirmed that he was a British spy and
then tricked him into believing they were leading him to Collins.

Paddy Daly, who had assassinated Redmond, was now assigned to
deal with Jameson. "We brought the spy down the side road leading
to the back entrance to the Albert College," he explained years later.
"I told him that we were satisfied he was a spy, that he was going to
die, and that if he wanted to say any prayers he could do so. The spy
jumped to attention immediately and said, 'You are right. God bless

the King. I would love to die for him.' He saluted, and there was not a quiver on him."[7]

Alan Bell, another agent reporting to the London Special Branch as part of the new security initiative, was working in the Castle as an intelligence adviser but living in a city neighbourhood. He was an experienced sixty-two-year-old, confident of his spy-craft. By March 1920, the Squad had a physical description of Bell and knew that at nine thirty every morning he took a tram to work. On March 26, four men boarded his tram in central Dublin, sat beside him and asked his name. When he confirmed that he was Alan Bell, they dragged him from the tram onto a platform and shot him dead.

Once again, Squad member Paddy Daly was on the scene: "When Alan Bell was shot, I did not know why he was listed as a man to be eliminated. We knew in some cases, but in others we did not know. We were soldiers carrying out orders and we did not ask any questions."[8]

These failures and losses in early 1920 were among the reasons that, by May, the British government was looking for new leadership for the RIC. When Tudor was brought in, he and his deputy, Ormonde Winter, would work closely with (and eventually run) a combined military-civil intelligence offshoot of the London Metropolitan Police, the Dublin District Special Branch (DDSB). Many of its agents had worked in military intelligence. Many had either worked for or been trained by Britain's secret service operation, MI5. The DDSB's mandate was, in military jargon, "part intelligence and part executive"— part basic espionage and part assassination.[9]

By the time of Osbert Smyth's arrival, Winter had established an official Raid Bureau within the DDSB. Over the next year, the bureau conducted 6,311 searches of homes and businesses in Dublin alone.[10] They sometimes led to significant arrests and the discovery of crucial information on the inner workings of the IRA. With suspicious frequency, the raids also turned into homicides when suspect fugitives resisted, tried to run away or were too hesitant in opening a door.

The raids became a crucial part of the government anti-insurgency campaign, part of a larger strategy that would become notorious for wild, seemingly spontaneous rampages by soldiers and policemen, invariably—if not always accurately—described as Black and Tans. Osbert Smyth was soon an enthusiastic participant on DDSB raids, always alert for leads that might help identify his brother's killers.

13.

WHILE WINTER AND the military worked at penetrating the inner circle of the IRA, General Tudor was preoccupied with the creative challenge of making a mercenary army look like a civilian police force while upgrading the firepower of the police to a wartime standard. The police were getting better guns, tanks and trucks, and armoured vehicles, as well as better wages. Ernie O'Malley, a senior IRA commander, noted:

> Police barracks now had machine guns and rifle grenades; the
> approaches were protected with barbed wire and often mined . . .
> Police and military shot prisoners: "Shot dead whilst trying to
> escape," was their explanation.
>
> Raids became more destructive and rings, watches and valuables
> disappeared. Officers wore masks on their faces and Tans used
> blackened cork when they came at night to shoot men who were
> on their blacklist; bloodhounds sniffed while the family cowered.[11]

O'Malley admitted that the terror cut both ways—"police and tans were shot down on the street by the IRA; houses which police or military were about to turn into posts were burned."

The official insistence that the speech in Listowel by Colonel Smyth had been distorted for propaganda purposes would soon ring hollow. Smyth, if anything, was understating what had become British policy. The police were getting increasingly explicit instructions from the top: *When provoked, don't pull your punches; when in doubt, shoot first, shoot to kill. We've got your back.*

Major Osbert Smyth had one specific reason for showing up in Ireland at this time, and from Winter's point of view it was a worthy one. It neatly dovetailed with the strategy he and General Tudor were implementing. The fact that no one was quite sure who exactly had killed his brother was but a minor complication. In the complex picture that was Ireland's independence struggle, it was sufficient to know that Colonel Smyth had been murdered by Irish Volunteers, which was just another label for the IRA, which was just the muscular extension of Sinn Féin.

The way Osbert Smyth and his new comrades on the Dublin District force saw their mission, anyone connected with Sinn Féin was fair game. All IRA men could fairly be considered gunmen, potential killers, and so they would all become potential targets. His brother had been shot in Cork, but his killers could have been from anywhere in Ireland, and whether or not they had any personal connection with the capital, Dublin was both an ideal place to hide and a likely place to look for them.

In fact, two of the most wanted men in Ireland were, that August, lurking somewhere in the city. Dan Breen and Seán Treacy were members of the team that had fired the shots that historians consider the beginning of the Anglo-Irish War, on January 21, 1919, near Soloheadbeg, Tipperary. They had ambushed and killed two RIC officers who were guarding a delivery of gelignite to a rock quarry near Tipperary town. Treacy and Breen had earlier concluded that it would take a shooting war to get the serious attention of British politicians. Bloodshed would guarantee results. Breen, who apparently knew one of the dead officers, later lamented that they had been primed to confront a team of *six* policemen. He felt that it was a pity there were only two to kill.[12]

This was the mentality that, for Tudor and the hawks in Dublin, justified an implacable determination to eliminate a ruthless enemy. Breen and Treacy were poster boys for the Irish revolution. In the popular imagination, they were involved in every "outrage" by the IRA, including, falsely, the assassination of Colonel Gerald Smyth— and prime targets for the hunters on the Dublin District force.

Acts of vengeance generate new bitterness, building momentum until the bitterness is self-sustaining. The IRA had smashed or trashed hundreds of police barracks since the beginning of the year, killed dozens of policemen, bullied hundreds into resignations or retirement, made life hellish for their families, and were tracking down and executing anyone suspected of collaborating with the Crown. Now, police and military units were launching their own campaigns of retribution. The message to the IRA was clear: *You hit us and we'll strike back, twice as hard.*

At first, the reprisals still seemed to be spontaneous responses by frustrated, frightened, angry officers, understandable reactions to the maiming or the murder of a comrade. Over time, revenge became strategic.

An incident in Fermoy, County Cork, on September 7, 1919, had offered a preview of what would soon be commonplace in Ireland. The IRA, always short of weapons, saw a Sunday morning military church parade as an opportunity to relieve some British soldiers of their rifles. It was supposed to be a bloodless operation. A soldier's rifle was replaceable. Why would he resist an Irish patriot's attempt to steal it? But several soldiers did, and one was killed during the commotion. When a local jury refused to treat the killing as a murder, "two hundred soldiers invaded the town . . . and wrecked the shops of the tradesmen who had been on the jury."[13]

In time, word of an IRA ambush or assassination in a village would send frightened families fleeing, scattering through the countryside, hiding in the haystacks, sleeping in the fields, knowing that "the Tans" would inevitably descend upon their homes, shooting, shouting, burning, looting. The avengers might have been soldiers or Irish members of the RIC or Auxiliaries, but in the public nightmares, they were the Tans, and that name became synonymous with terror.

Shocking murders by policemen and soldiers made the point that no one was exempt from punishment, including death, not even clergy, not even elected politicians; entire communities could suffer economic violence, small shops and factories destroyed, the homes of suspected rebels and rebel sympathizers looted, vandalized, burned down even when there was little or no evidence of culpability. If Tipperary was the scene of a rebel "outrage," Tipperary would be punished.

Along with "outrage," the word "reprisal" entered the political vocabulary. Inevitably there was pragmatic calculation at the highest levels of the government of the potential value in retaliation, including the strategic value of assassination. And it followed that there was a cost-benefit element to orchestrating counter-outrage.

By late summer 1920, the political discussions had evolved to analyzing such gritty details as whether "gunning" was more productive and/or less offensive to British public sensibilities than "burning." The British cabinet consensus favoured gunning, but the burning—the destruction of homes and farms and businesses—carried on. Town halls. Libraries. On the front line in Dublin and beyond, abstract policy made in Downing Street would become life-and-death instruction for the RIC.

Nearly a century later, in 2019, the historian Eunan O'Halpin was unsparing in his judgment: "The British government, which had made such justified propaganda against Hunnish barbarism when German forces destroyed the great library of Leuven [Belgium] in 1914, sat unperturbed while its forces burned a succession of municipal libraries along with local creameries, town halls, shops and private dwellings across Ireland in 1920 and 1921."[14]

Inside the secure walls of Dublin Castle, General Tudor must have struggled to understand the politics that were driving the peculiar war he had taken on. He had experience with the hill tribes of the northwestern frontier provinces in India—unpredictable and unconventional in every way. But the tribal warriors made no secret of their plans to kill. You could see them coming on their horses, or on foot, screaming down the hillsides or up from hidden gullies. The Boers invented much of what Tudor knew about the ambushes and tactical surprises of guerrilla war. But they also resorted to conventional military tactics and they usually wore uniforms. All the major players in the Great War were experts on the writings of Carl von Clausewitz and worked from the same strategic playbook. For most of his four years on the Western Front, Tudor felt relatively safe, protected by tradition and unspoken rules of discipline.

Dublin placed him in a different kind of war. An undeclared war. The real enemy in this war was idealism, a force that mobilized an irrational determination to achieve a speculative outcome. As von Clausewitz had warned, a war can't end "as long as the *will* of the enemy is not subdued."[15]

In Ireland, Tudor was learning that to subdue the will of the enemy would require suppression of a large and growing segment of a stubborn "civilian" population. By mid-summer 1920, it was probably becoming clear to him that if this war in Ireland didn't kill him, it would consume him. Like Jeremiah Mee, the policeman who had defied him in Listowel, he could find no personal satisfaction in any aspect of the Irish war, anticipate no outcome that could secure his future.

Throughout his career to this point, Hugh Tudor had always managed to sustain a life beyond the military. In the two years he spent in Dublin, even his closest family connections disintegrated. His friend and secretary at the Castle, Captain William Y. Darling, would write that "life in the service of the government of Ireland in these days was for many of us nasty, brutish and short . . . social life was impossible."[16] And Tudor is rarely mentioned in any social context in the diaries and the memoirs of his colleagues in Dublin. There wasn't much that offered even a brief escape from the pressures of his work.

Tudor occasionally made time for golf—but always in the company of armed and watchful bodyguards. He was an avid horseman, a champion rider and polo player in his younger days. Some of his Castle colleagues regularly exercised their thoroughbreds in the security of Phoenix Park, two miles away from their headquarters, near the residence of the viceroy and the main depot of the RIC. They made time, despite the ever-present danger of the conflict, for cautious visits to public racetracks and betting rooms, but it seems they never thought of asking Tudor to go along.

Even if he longed for companionship, everyone knew it could be suicidal to go anywhere in public with the man who ran the Black and Tans. It wasn't prudent to be noticeably close to Tudor, a lightning rod in an electrical storm.

A younger Tudor would have been appalled by the reputation of the Black and Tans. They carried out their duties with a zeal inflamed by racism, and it seemed to be contagious. As the historian Peter Hart has noted, "The Tans' ethnic hostility was shared by the English soldiery who usually began to lump all Irishmen together as dirty and treacherous soon after their arrival. The resulting distaste and hatred are deeply etched in nearly every regimental journal, letter or memoir from this period of service."[17]

One keen-eyed Irish observer memorably summed up the more glaring peculiarities of the English Tans: "They spoke in strange accents, called the Irish 'natives,' associated with low company, stole from each other, sneered at the customs of the country, drank to excess and put sugar on their porridge."[18]

In his new role, Tudor was learning to exploit the foibles and the fearsome reputation of "the Tans." If they frightened or offended people, fair enough. If the Tans were blamed for the worst excesses of the Irish peelers or the British soldiers, he and they had thick skins and could handle any fallout. As one who placed loyalty among the highest of military virtues, Tudor honoured his undertaking to encourage and support the Black and Tans and all his constables, even in their wildest moments.

A younger Tudor might have taken young Osbert Smyth aside on his arrival at Dublin Castle and advised him to go back to Egypt. As a senior military officer, he would have been obliged to warn the younger man about the danger of personal and emotional motivation in a job that was supposed to be, for people of his rank, rational and disciplined, professional. But when they spoke in August 1920, General Tudor might have seen in Major Smyth's determined outrage following the murder of a beloved brother a reflection of his own.

14.

IN LATE AUGUST 1920, policemen and soldiers were now ubiquitous in Ireland. Ordinary law-abiding citizens found it difficult to tell the difference between cops and soldiers, even when they worked together.

And they found the situation ever more frightening as the body count kept rising through a blood-soaked autumn. Tudor's leadership was soon to be the subject of quiet speculation in Dublin Castle. There were military gains, but the political exposure was becoming unpredictable. The Irish war was slipping into chaos. The violence was becoming manic, uncontrolled.

Fourteen British soldiers died violently in August, six of them by accident, some by suicide. In October, in County Wexford, fourteen Irish Volunteers were making bombs by candlelight in a dark abandoned hut. As one of them trimmed wires on a detonator, his penknife slipped. There was a spark, the detonator flashed and there was a bang like a gunshot. A survivor described a sudden "blue light" in the room, and then the hut was gone. Two Volunteers died instantly, two more shortly after, and a fifth died the next day. The blast scattered nine into the weeds of a surrounding field; all of those survived.[19]

Their rebellion was always perilous, but the IRA seemed to have the upper hand. They picked the time and place for confrontation. There was less risk in murder by surprise, especially when the victims were alone and unarmed. Small police patrols on unfamiliar narrow country roads, often on bicycles, made easy targets as they wound between the hedges and the gullies. Since the IRA gunmen were mostly in control of the action, from time to time they even felt they could afford a gesture of civility.

As recently as June, the IRA had managed to kidnap a senior British army officer in County Cork, held him for a month, then allowed him to escape. General Cuthbert Lucas had been on a fishing trip near Fermoy with friends who were fellow officers. His rebel captors, hard men from the #2 Cork IRA Brigade, eventually released the two other officers after one was injured in an escape attempt. They kept Lucas as a hostage but in time, apparently, the enemies grew fond of one another. "Lucas was a very decent man and could even see our point of view," one IRA man later wrote. "He said to me once that if he were an Irishman, he would be in the I.R.A."[20]

They brought General Lucas his mail. They drank and talked together about war and politics and life. They let him go for walks alone, after one of which he didn't come back. Once free, the general declined to incriminate or even name the kidnappers. The incident exposed a capacity for chivalry on both sides of the conflict, a quality that would vanish as the ruthlessness intensified.

For a few months in 1920, "catch and release" became a common practice when IRA commanders found themselves with enemy prisoners they didn't want to have to feed. In three weeks, between July 2 and July 23, the IRA claimed to have captured, disarmed and freed, unharmed, 156 policemen and members of the military.[21]

But the tide was turning. Ormonde Winter's "identification unit" roamed the streets of Dublin day and night watching for familiar faces. For a known IRA man, answering a knock on his door in rural and small-town Ireland in the dead of night was already often fatal. And now, the peril was afoot in Dublin. Unlike the random brutality earlier in 1920, this new remorselessness appeared to be deliberate, a change that seemed to coincide with the arrival of the Tudor team in May and June, and to escalate after the murder in July of Colonel Gerald Smyth.

By late summer, kidnappings on both sides had become preludes to inevitable murder. Life-and-death decisions could be spontaneous, a whim or a mistake or a random encounter with someone with a grievance and a gun. In Dublin on July 30, the IRA's assassination squad shot an Irish businessman named Francis Burke apparently on impulse when they noticed he was working in his office unprotected. Opportunity became a key factor in the calculus of murder. Burke was on a list of enemies, as Paddy Daly recalled, but there had been "no definite plans to shoot him."

Patrick Lynch, forty-nine, was a harness maker in County Limerick with no apparent political connections. But his name, common among IRA men, obviously rang a bell with a military raiding party when they invaded his home on August 14. Liam Lynch, a senior Cork Brigade commander, was on a hit list for every soldier and policeman.[22] The soldiers marched Patrick Lynch in his bare feet to a village green and shot him six times in the head and body. Later they claimed he'd been trying to escape.

"Murder gang" had been a standard government description of the IRA. But in Thurles, County Tipperary, by late 1920, people were whispering about a "murder gang" that was operating from the local barracks of the RIC.

Even after two policemen were killed at Soloheadbeg, Tipperary, in January 1919, murder was still shocking when the IRA in Thurles assassinated a district inspector, a hard-nosed Catholic policeman named Michael Hunt, in June that year. There was a stunned silence for a while, then an ominous expansion of the police and military presence in the area.

When the IRA learned that a constable in Thurles, Tipperary, an Irishman named Luke Finnegan, was creating a master list of local rebel activists for the intelligence files of the police and military, the local leadership decided that he had to be eliminated for their own protection. He had been stationed in Thurles for nearly two years and knew everyone in town.

The unarmed Finnegan was nearly home, just after 10 p.m. on January 22, 1920, when gunmen shot him in the abdomen. Finnegan staggered into his house, crying out to his horrified wife, "Oh Mary, I am shot." He died later that night in a Dublin hospital.[23] Hours later, policemen rampaged through Thurles, trashing fourteen houses belonging to known rebel sympathizers.

On February 24, local Sinn Féin supporters awoke to discover that, during the night, someone had painted the letters RIP on their doors.[24] The rebels were undaunted by the threat, and ten days later, on March 5, IRA men gunned down a policeman named John Heanue while he was buying groceries in a local pub. Heanue had been stationed in Dovea, five miles from Thurles.

In the weeks that followed, the intensity of police and military raids increased dramatically. On March 27, at one thirty in the morning, masked policemen showed up at a house in Thurles where four known IRA men were living. One of them, Jimmy McCarthy, twenty-seven, died instantly after being shot in the chest while opening the door.

The next night, masked RIC officers killed Thomas O'Dwyer, twenty-one, in the home he shared in Thurles with his sister, a niece and an invalid uncle. Like McCarthy's, his death was believed to be revenge for the killing of Constable Heanue. Though neither McCarthy nor O'Dwyer had been involved directly, O'Dwyer had been seen talking to one of the men who had taken part in killing the constable. (More than a year later, on the night of July 7, 1921, the RIC sergeant who had led the raid on O'Dwyer's home, Anthony Foody, was killed by two masked men who left a note on his body— "Revenge for Dwyer.")

The same night they murdered O'Dwyer, RIC officers bombed the home of Richard Small, whose son, Michael, was a senior IRA commander and had been one of the gunmen who killed Constable Luke Finnegan in January. Michael wasn't home, but the RIC, led by Detective Inspector Michael Wilson (who'd replaced the murdered inspector, Michael Hunt), caught up with him on July 4 and gunned him down when he was crossing an open field on his way to Mass. Then, on August 16, Inspector Wilson was assassinated in revenge by the same IRA man who had killed his predecessor, Hunt, fourteen months earlier.

When soldiers and policemen from the area heard what had happened to Wilson, they burned the town hall and three creameries in the area. The destruction of creameries had by then become a standard collective punishment by the police in agricultural communities.[25]

Revenge killing by the police was by late summer, 1920, quietly but generally applauded in Dublin Castle and in London. But some, especially at senior levels of the British army, had misgivings, believing the strategy was not only terribly unsporting but also inefficient. Common sense and history decreed the most effective way to victory—martial law for all of Ireland. Give everyone a taste of military governance and see how quickly the rebels disintegrated. As they had done consistently throughout their trouble-making history.

The strongest voice among the critics was that of Sir Henry Wilson, chief of the imperial general staff. His preferred formula: make a list of enemies, make it public, then kill them legally. He wasn't troubled by the morality of an official murder policy, but he believed it was a mistake to let General Tudor run it haphazardly and without apparent political or military oversight.

The practical reality was that Lloyd George was committed to what he saw as a solution with credible deniability. To him, "political oversight" was a feeling in his own politically calibrated gut. Murder was an essential element in his strategy for keeping Ireland in the kingdom, and so far, it was working.

In September, Sir Henry confronted Tudor's friend and political mentor Winston Churchill, claiming he'd been told that Tudor's people talk "in the calmest way of murdering the S.F's [Sinn Féin members]." This was a bad idea, he said, because it was basically uncontrollable. Churchill didn't deny it but assured Sir Henry that the strategy was being monitored at the highest levels and that Tudor "could rely on L.G. [Lloyd George] to support him."[26]

———

A peculiar calm settled briefly over Tipperary that month, thanks to the intercession of no less a luminary than the Blessed Virgin Mary. It had been reported in August that she had visited a humble Irish cottage near Templemore and communicated with a sixteen-year-old farm labourer named Jimmy Walsh.[27]

Walsh would later claim to a skeptical IRA commander that the Mother of God enthusiastically supported the IRA campaign to drive the British out of Ireland. When word of the apparition got out, Templemore was besieged by pilgrims from all over Ireland, Europe and even the United States. Eventually, confounded by the crowds, the IRA, police and military leaders respectfully stepped back from their hostilities. They even managed to collaborate on practicalities like crowd control.

Both sides seemed to regard the entire spectacle as a scam, a skepticism shared by some of the most influential leaders in the Catholic Church. But it soon turned into an opening for peace talks—one of the senior churchmen who turned up in Templemore was a bishop from Australia, an Irishman named Patrick Clune, originally from County Clare, who was soon to become an important voice in efforts to begin negotiations for a truce.

While he was in Templemore, the bishop met with the local IRA brigade commander, Jim Leahy. Clune told Leahy he disapproved of the Sinn Féin policy of persecuting RIC policemen, tormenting them into quitting. Leahy said it was a policy that wasn't going to change. Clune invited the IRA to direct unemployed policemen to Australia, where he'd find safer jobs for them. Leahy was noncommittal but he reported on their conversations to Michael Collins in Dublin, suggesting that Collins should talk to Clune when he was in the city.[28]

Collins and the bishop met, and within weeks, Clune was working cautiously behind the scenes, exploring possibilities for a ceasefire with members of the "peace party" in Dublin Castle and with Prime Minister Lloyd George in London.

Then September came to an end and the war in Tipperary resumed with what Jim Leahy would describe as "a police campaign of unprecedented violence." Throughout October, policemen "masked and disguised" went door-to-door in Sinn Féin neighbourhoods, shooting men suspected of being in the IRA. On the night of October 25, they killed two suspects, one of whom was sick in bed. Three others they shot that night managed to survive.

Later in October, a sympathetic RIC policeman from Thurles approached Leahy to share a document he'd copied from police files—a list of twelve Tipperary men selected by the RIC for assassination. Leahy's name was the first one on the list.

15.

IN EARLY SEPTEMBER, Winston Churchill was on vacation in southwestern France, in a place called Mimizan on the Atlantic coast. He spent much of his two-week holiday painting and relaxing, but Ireland was never far from the centre of his hyperactive mind.

Hamar Greenwood, as chief secretary for Ireland, was politically responsible for Irish policy and administration. But as a Canadian-born anglophile (from Whitby, Ontario), Greenwood lacked the zeal of the prime minister, Lloyd George, a Welsh Gaelic speaker who saw Ireland through a sentimental Celtic mist. Churchill, too, had Ireland in his boyhood memory.

Churchill's grandfather had been the Irish viceroy. His father had worked in the viceroy's office as an adviser. Winston had happy childhood memories of loyal, friendly Irish maids and gardeners and nannies—more reason for him to loathe the Irish radicals who were turning Ireland into a war zone on Britain's doorstep.

He understood the fundamental Irish problem: there were two Irelands and their differences were irreconcilable. One Ireland wanted independence from the United Kingdom. The other Ireland wanted independence from the rest of Ireland. The Sinn Féin goal was, and remains a century later, a united Ireland. But the British government saw partition as a convenient, if perilous, political escape hatch, and eventually the Ulster loyalists shared that pragmatic view.

There would soon be new legislation in place—the Government of Ireland Act—that would provide for two moderately independent Irish parliaments, one for the northern counties, one for those of the south. But the new law was still in limbo. As always seemed to be the case throughout Irish history, compromise was fraught with peril and consequently slow, even as the need for a viable settlement grew more urgent by the day. There were preliminary hints of a willingness by moderate Sinn Féin leaders to consider peace talks. Lloyd George was always open to the conversation. But there were lines that neither side would cross.

Anyone following events in Ireland in September 1920 could see the glimmering of sparks that, at any moment, could burst into flames. One of the more ominous Irish problems was glimmering just four miles away from Downing Street—in Brixton Prison.

The lord mayor of Cork, Terence MacSwiney, who had replaced the assassinated Tomás MacCurtain as both mayor and Cork IRA Brigade commander, had been scooped up in a raid on Cork's city hall on August 12. There was a hunger strike under way that day by Sinn Féin prisoners in Cork jail. MacSwiney promptly joined it. The British moved him to Brixton Prison in London, where he continued what was beginning to look like a suicidal protest. He was physically frail to begin with and seemed to be on the threshold of tuberculosis.[29]

Jailing MacSwiney in London was a political miscalculation. His case became more visible there than it might have been in Cork. In addition to being politically radical, he was spiritually pious. Now his emaciated image, with his rosary in his hands and his chaplain at his bedside, was getting media attention around the world.

Churchill could have let the Irish cabinet minister, Greenwood, fret over Ireland while he was enjoying France. But Churchill's old friend Tudor was in the Irish hot seat, and his already difficult assignment was being complicated by static from the military. The last thing either he or Churchill needed was a starving martyr conspicuous at centre stage in London.

Tudor and General Macready, the head of the British military in Ireland, had been collegial and warm when they were both new to their assignments. But ambiguity about the boundaries of their authority—especially in General Macready's mind—was causing tension at the Castle. In the bureaucratic pecking order, Macready had the higher rank and his responsibilities were explicit. He was the GOC, the general officer commanding military operations. He also had spent two years as commissioner of the London Metropolitan Police, and he couldn't seem to keep his fingers out of General Tudor's business. The two generals saw eye-to-eye on rare occasions—the fate of Terence MacSwiney created a brief moment of hard-line unanimity—but harmony was inevitably lost in fundamental differences over how to win the war.

Like his admirer Sir Henry Wilson, Macready was a persistent advocate for martial law for all of Ireland. He was confident that only heavy-handed military management would settle Ireland's conflict, and straightforward martial law would also give him unprecedented power. Under martial law everyone in uniform, including Tudor, would be a soldier.

But Tudor's personal relationship with Churchill gave him an undefined authority that overshadowed almost everyone around him, including General Macready. It was not in Tudor's nature to swagger. (Perhaps, in his own best interests, he should have swaggered more in asserting his considerable political influence while he had it.)

Cracks in the relationship between the police and the military leaders were soon becoming obvious. Macready complained to anyone who would listen that policemen were behaving like vigilantes. Policemen were getting away with murder. Regular soldiers were confused. Was such police behaviour deviance or policy? As GOC in Ireland, Macready was supposed to be running the war. Instead, he was playing second fiddle to a police chief whose men, many of them former army officers, appeared to be out of control. It was unconventional and it was messy.

By the end of August, he was complaining loudly to Sir Henry Wilson about the Black and Tans and their "wild reprisals." Wilson, himself vocally hostile to the notion of policemen doing soldiers' work, happily relayed the complaints to Churchill, with the personal observation that the situation, as described by General Macready, was "a scandal."

Churchill, understandably, resented the complaints. As Wilson noted in his diary, Churchill became "very angry" and defended Tudor and his men. "He said these Black and Tans were honourable and gallant officers, etc. etc., & and talked much nonsense."[30]

Angry or not, while still in France, Churchill contacted General Tudor to suggest that Tudor and Wilson have a heart-to-heart talk. It was time to bring Sir Henry on side with what was an irreversible aspect of official policy. And so, on September 13, while in London for meetings at the War Office, Tudor dropped in on Wilson and tried to clear the air. Sir Henry, who unlike Tudor was a prolific diarist, wrote later that day: "Tudor came to see me & had a long talk about the RIC & his Black and Tans and [Auxiliary] cadets. He says . . . that when the police carry out reprisals the authorities look the other way."

General Tudor told Wilson that he had, a few days earlier, been in Galway during a reprisal by the RIC. His version of the episode, as Sir Henry would remember it, was sketchy but it obviously illustrated what Tudor meant by the authorities, himself included, looking the other way.

> For instance, when he was in Galway last Wednesday [Sept. 8], he had just gone to bed when he heard a few shots and a policeman was murdered. On that, the other policemen saw red, went straight to the houses of 3 notorious Sinn Feiners, pulled them out of bed, put them up against a wall and shot them.
>
> He quoted other cases where these reprisals had a most salutary effect but he agreed with me that this procedure would never solve the Irish question and that the only chance was for the Cabinet to rouse England and then exterminate or transport the rebels.[31]

The Galway story was more dramatic and more revealing than either Tudor or Sir Henry seemed to understand. A Black and Tan named Edward Krumm, who had been a member of the RIC for only a month, had shot and killed an IRA man on the railway station platform shortly before midnight. It is unclear what started the shootout, but Krumm was promptly killed by a second IRA gunman.

An American tourist, Agnes King from Ironton, Ohio, a former schoolteacher, was on the platform, and witnessed the confrontation and the killings.

There was a man on the platform to whom I paid little attention, and could not give a description of him in a satisfactory way. He wore what I think was a loose cap. He did not appear to me to be a regular soldier, nor did he seem to me to be the customary Black-and-Tan . . .

[She witnessed a sudden struggle after] the man in this peculiar uniform whipped out a revolver. He was standing with another man in ordinary attire. And he slashed the revolver around and began shooting. One shot hit a boy in the leg . . .

And then a harsh shot rang out and this soldier fell to the ground.[32]

A Galway police rookie, John Joseph Cadden, was sleeping in the Galway RIC barracks at about 1 a.m. when another officer woke him up to report that a fellow constable had just been killed at the railway station. There were fifty policemen in the barracks at the time and none of them were Black and Tans, but soon they were all up and armed and heading for the streets.[33] They shot up the neighbourhood, staged a mock execution of two young men they'd roused from their beds, set houses on fire, terrorized the occupants, then tried to murder a young man who'd fled a burning house.

A rumour spread that the man who'd killed Krumm was named Seán Turke. In one of the houses they were torching, they found a lodger named Séamus Quirke, whom, presumably, they mistook for Seán Turke. Quirke was dragged out of bed and "taken barefoot, his rosary beads in his hands, about 300 yards . . . shot ten times and left for dead." Agnes King was in a group that viewed his corpse the next morning. She noted nine bullet holes in his body below the waist. He was, she remembered, "virtually disemboweled."

General Tudor, it would seem, slept through most of the disturbance but investigated early the next day. The young RIC policeman,

Cadden, reported a visit to the RIC barracks from "a British general" in the morning. Cadden was just nineteen and new to the RIC, and he clearly didn't fully understand the importance of the British general, unquestionably the commander of the RIC, General Tudor.[34]

When he was later asked how he knew the officer had been a general, Cadden replied that it was "because he was so well guarded. He had two motor lorries of soldiers there to guard him. He had two other officers with him. The [RIC] county inspector was there and two district inspectors, and the men in the barracks were there."

The words the general spoke to the men in Galway that morning would sound familiar to anyone who had been present in the Listowel RIC barracks on June 19. As Cadden remembered it, the man was forceful and direct:

> "This country is ruled by gunmen, and they must be put down."
> He talked about giving home rule to Ireland, and he said home
> rule could not be given until all of these gunmen were put down,
> and he called on the R. I. C. to put them down.
>
> He asked them what they required in the barracks, and that
> whatever they wanted he would give them, and that they were
> also going to get a raise in pay. And they said they needed
> machine guns, and he said that they would get them, and also
> tanks and more men—men who had been in the army during the
> war and who knew how to shoot to kill; and he said they would
> be the right men in the right place.[35]

Tudor's chat with Sir Henry did little to diminish Wilson's hostility toward the RIC and the Black and Tans in particular. Afterwards, he noted in his diary that reprisals, like the one in Galway, "must lead to chaos and ruin." If anything, his chats with the police chief only made him more aggressive.

On September 21, Churchill came alone to see Sir Henry. Wilson warned him that "those 'Black and Tans' of Tudor who are carrying out very indiscriminate reprisals will play the devil in Ireland, but he won't listen or agree." Even as they spoke, the devil was making his presence felt in Balbriggan, a town about twenty miles from Dublin.

In the early morning hours that day, an estimated two hundred policemen had rampaged through Balbriggan, burning four pubs, a stocking factory and nine private homes, and vandalizing thirty other houses. It was a reprisal for the murder, some hours earlier, of an Irish-born RIC officer named Burke who had been celebrating a promotion with his brother in a local pub.

There were other policemen from Balbriggan and Dublin present. The celebration became rowdy. The woman behind the bar tried to cut the policemen off, but they ignored her. If she wouldn't serve them, they'd serve themselves. Hearing of the commotion, two local IRA gunmen entered the pub, guns drawn, and ordered the policemen to leave. One of the Burke brothers ran at the intruders and was shot dead.

There was a police barracks three miles away in Gormanstown, a training base for Black and Tans. The reprisal rampage started there, though General Tudor would, years later, deny that the Black and Tans had anything to do with it. His denial, however, was contradicted by a police commander in the RIC barracks at the time, who reported that he "had personally sent a detachment of Black and Tans to Balbriggan to reinforce the local police."[36]

A British army veteran led the police to the homes of local IRA men, suspects in the policeman's death. The houses were then burned. Two known Volunteers were dragged out of bed in one house and interrogated at the Balbriggan RIC station. There was evidence that they were tortured. A local policeman who knew them swore that the men were innocent, but they were taken to the street, bayoneted and shot to death.

The next day the IRA tracked down the British soldier who had identified the IRA homes for burning and, after a brief court martial, shot him dead.[37]

The "sack of Balbriggan," a town close to Dublin, was the talk of Dublin Castle almost as it was happening. Mark Sturgis, the assistant undersecretary, reported in his diary the next day: "Balbriggan was sacked yesterday by Black and Tans . . . in reprisal for two police officers shot." He was mistaken, in that it was only one officer shot.

The incident was unusual only in that it had happened almost on the doorstep of Dublin Castle and would inevitably attract media attention far beyond the shores of Ireland. The torture and murder of two men who were probably innocent was less outrageous to the British authorities than the property destruction. In the Dublin Castle version of the rampage, the victims were "prominent bad men" and "the reprisal would have been not so bad—but burning spoilt the whole thing."[38]

On September 24, Castle officials briefly considered, then scuttled, a plan to hold a public inquiry on Balbriggan. As Sturgis wrote, "How the devil can we round up and try 50 policemen when we know that they know that the bulk of their officers up to the top agree in principle with their action even if they prefer shooting to burning (as I do if we must have either)."[39]

On September 22, 1920, Balbriggan would be only one of many problems on the mind of the police chief. That day five RIC officers died at Rineen in County Clare, after they were attacked by about forty members of the 4th Battalion of the Mid-Clare IRA Brigade. A sixth RIC officer later died from wounds he'd suffered in the ambush. An eighty-year-old farmer who'd been working in a nearby hayfield was caught in the crossfire and also died.

The "Rineen ambush," as it would be known in history, was followed by revenge attacks by "uniformed men" in three nearby villages—

Ennistymon, Lahinch, and Miltown Malbay. Eighteen houses went up in flames.[40] In Ennistymon, Helena Connole would later describe "how the police ordered everyone out of her house, shot her husband dead in front of her and their young children, and then set their home on fire, throwing the body into the flames."[41] Three other men died in those reprisals, one while helping a neighbour put out a fire. One of the three had actually participated in the ambush and had been hiding in the upper storey of a pub when the police raiders burned the building down.

That same day, intelligence officers in the Dublin District Special Branch shot and killed a lawyer from Limerick named John Aloysius Lynch, whose law firm did legal business for Sinn Féin. He was in bed asleep when DDSB raiders broke into his hotel room. That he was in bed, apparently unarmed, didn't stop the officers involved from insisting that he'd shot at them before they killed him. One of the raiders was believed to have been the young army major who had recently arrived from Egypt, Osbert Smyth.[42]

16.

THERE WERE ALWAYS questions after a reprisal. There were meant to be questions after a reprisal, especially in the minds of the instigators of the outrages that had provoked the retaliation. Reprisals were supposed to be educational—and questions are a necessary part of education. The answers were supposed to be plain and simple.

If you keep fucking up, this is what will happen. Every time.

Your house will burn down. And if your neighbour's house burns down too, it will be your fault. We will destroy your workplace. Your job will disappear. And if your neighbour's job disappears, that, too, will be your fault.

If you kill one of us, we will kill as many of you as we can get our hands on. And we hope the last thought going through their pathetic rebel minds before they die will be that this is also your fault.

Most of the reprisals, and the questions they posed and the answers they were supposed to elicit, were in places far from Dublin. But Balbriggan was nearby and soon the story of the reprisal there was in the papers—and not just the Irish papers. The press on Fleet Street, in London, noticed too.

Journalists were now the ones asking questions. Parliamentarians too, on the floor of the House of Commons. And, most alarming to British politicians, people in the vast and influential Irish diaspora in America. Wishy-washy official answers were only raising other questions, especially among senior military officers.

Two days after Balbriggan, Sir Henry Wilson noted in his diary, "Winston Churchill saw very little harm in this, but it horrifies me." The historian Paul Bew would one day write that, after Balbriggan, "a terrible war on the Continent had been fought with decent national honour, but now that honour was being destroyed in the villages and hamlets of Ireland."[43]

Ironically, many of the men destroying Ireland's villages and hamlets were British veterans of that honourable war, led by a distinguished general who had fought in it with courage and professional creativity and who was now taking his cues directly from the British cabinet and, in particular, from the minister for war.

The RIC had ceased to be what it had been for most of the last century of its existence, a sleepy, mostly rural and small-town police service. By autumn 1920, it was equipped with military weapons and military transportation but defined by attitudes that were the antithesis of military discipline. Irish RIC policemen who had endured a year of torment, intimidation and assassination now harboured a bitterness that, in a crisis, turned to hatred of "the enemy," Sinn Féin and the IRA. They were reinforced in numbers and in attitude by the

Black and Tans, mostly Englishmen working for the money, fundamentally contemptuous of Ireland and the Irish, volatile when aroused
by a predictable hostility among the civilians they encountered. The
Auxiliaries were mercenary soldiers, working without rules in a place
they thought of as a foreign country, among people many of the Auxis
considered to be sub-human.

General Tudor's job was not so much to be their leader as to be their
manager, coping and channelling as best he could their needs, their
energy, their careless ruthlessness, the consequences of their violence. It
would be a mostly friendless job. Potential friends and allies in the military, men who knew his background, his brilliance on the battlefield,
the innovative leadership of his artillery commands, were puzzled—
some openly dismayed—by his willingness to take on and carry out a
job that should have been repugnant to any military officer.

It is impossible to know what Tudor thought, but there is little
evidence of hesitation in how he did what he perceived to be his duty
while in Ireland. The unloved child of introspection is self-doubt.
There is nothing we can learn about the mind of Major General Hugh
Tudor in 1920 to indicate that he was handicapped by either quality.
He was in Ireland to do a job. He could not have seen the job in
Ireland as a war. The only thing that Ireland had in common with war
in his experience was that people on both sides were being killed.

For Tudor, the miseries of past wars had been mitigated by the fel-
lowship of other warriors and by the intoxicating reassurance of patriotism. He had none of that to help him through the stress of what he
had to do in Ireland. He was a professional, a man of discipline, and
respectful of tradition. Much of what he saw in Ireland would have
rankled. But he was, above all, a man of loyalty, of loyalty to institutions and to friends. The higher institution in 1920, higher even than
the military, was the British Empire. The higher friend was Winston
Churchill.

Tudor's task in Ireland was deliberately flexible and vague, and that, in the short run, made his assignment easier. In the long run, it would create huge challenges for Ireland, for Britain, and for Tudor.

By the late summer of 1920, the "bad guys" in the Irish conflict were, in the public imagination, the Black and Tans. The reprisals might have been carried out by Irishmen, by soldiers, by Auxiliaries, but in the telling of the stories, the villains were the Black and Tans. And General Tudor was forever, after 1920, the leader of the Black and Tans.

At some point, Tudor came to understand that what was going on in Ireland was more dangerous than war. It was to war what an alley fight is to a boxing competition. He was good at war and he had once been good at boxing, but he was destined to find out how competent he was in a dirty street fight where there were no rules, no courtesies. Had he been of a more reflective tendency, he would have realized by the end of September 1920—after Galway, after Balbriggan, after the chaos that followed the Rineen ambush—that there was something going on in Ireland that was larger than the familiar Irish itch for independence.

In the past, the Irish wars had been little more than desperate disturbances. Rebels were considered traitors. The best of them were shot as warriors and the others hung as common criminals. Even as recently as Easter 1916, the majority of Irish men and women were uncomfortable with the word "rebellion."

The ferocity of the British attack to take back control of Dublin in Easter week was understandable when it was happening. The British army won that Easter skirmish in 1916. But there was evidence of cruelty in the punishment inflicted afterwards, and gratuitous cruelty can be evidence of panic.

The executions by firing squads were overkill. It was as if the army officers and the politicians had seen the Easter Rising as a virus that, if unchecked, would consume their empire, their certainties and their privileges. The firing squads and the internments were supposed to be the antivirus. Instead, they nourished the infection and it spread swiftly.

And now, in 1920, the word "rebellion" was respectable, heroic, among most Irish nationalists. As it persisted and metastasized throughout Ireland, it was possible to see the signs of a similar infection in the British labour movement, in the rise of socialism in Britain and in Europe, and in the embrace of nationalism in populations recently released from imperial hegemony in Asia, the Middle East, the Balkans.

Even in the absence of deep introspection, General Tudor would have been aware that Ireland was a small vessel riding on a rising tide of history and that his effort to suppress the inevitable outcome would be futile. But his loyalty to the past and to his friend Churchill was, like the rising tide, irreversible. Caught between the force of duty and a normal fear of the inevitable, faced with the murder of men he considered friends, General Tudor would begin to feel the hatred that he knew to be a crucial factor in determining the successful end of any war.

Churchill, being both introspective and self-critical, with a generous reserve of ruthlessness, would have understood the trend of history, an insight that inspired the strategy he helped devise for Ireland—get the violence and the hatred over with as soon as possible. Having lost a struggle to preserve the past, prepare for the battle to design a peaceful place for Ireland in Britain's future.

Tudor's task was to achieve the first phase in Churchill's vision, hanging on to Ireland as a semi-independent British asset. But after four months on the job, Tudor needed help, if only in the form of some explicit reassurance from his friend. And he got it. On September 22, Churchill accompanied Tudor on a visit to the prime minister's office. The gist of the discussion they had there has been preserved in the diaries of Sir Henry Wilson. That night, Wilson wrote, "Winston told me . . . that LG [Lloyd George] told Tudor that he would back him in this course through thick & thin."[44]

The next evening, September 23, Tudor and Churchill dropped in on Sir Henry to continue the discussion of reprisals. "Tudor made it very clear that the police and Black and Tans and the 100 [military and police] intelligence officers are all carrying out reprisal murders," Wilson recorded. "I am glad that I am in no way responsible for Tudor and that I have protested for months against this method of out-terrorizing the terrorists."

Churchill also seems to have gone to bat for Tudor with senior people in the War Office. On September 23, General Percy Radcliffe, director of military operations, wrote to Wilson to give his imprimatur for reprisals. In Sir Percy's view, "the only solution to this [reprisal] problem is to institute the system of *official* reprisals and to impress on the troops that by taking the law into their own hands they damage the cause instead of furthering it." In other words, if the behaviour offends discipline and the law, the obvious solution is to relax the disciplinary standards and to change the law.

Wilson agreed. "I am all in favour of reprisals," he wrote in his diary, "but these shd be done on the Govt's authority & shooting should be done by roster drawn up officially & publicly posted."[45] Memorably, in private, Wilson had earlier asserted to Lloyd George that if rebels "ought to be murdered, the government ought to murder them." What he opposed was a clandestine assassination campaign supervised by a policeman operating with no formal government authority. "Lloyd George danced at all this, said no government could take this responsibility."

On September 25–26, Sinn Féin sent out tentative peace feelers. Andy Cope, assistant undersecretary of state at Dublin Castle, had a secret mandate from Lloyd George to develop contacts in the top ranks of Sinn Féin, and he'd been making headway. His best hope for productive negotiations for a ceasefire was the Sinn Féin vice president, Arthur Griffith. The president, Eamon de Valera, was on a prolonged mission to America, seeking friends and raising money, and so out of the picture.

Griffith had agreed to a face-to-face conversation with John Anderson, the undersecretary for Ireland, that was tentatively arranged for September 26. The planning was so sensitive and secret that there is still debate about whether it ever happened. In any case, the initiative went nowhere.

The government now had the wind at its back, stirring embers of confidence that the war policy was on a successful track and that there were greater gains to be made by continuing the gunning. Talking truce was premature, according to the generals. Peace feelers were withdrawn as quietly and unexpectedly as they had arrived. The war intensified.

Twenty-one-year-old James Brady had been a member of the RIC since only February 1920. Even so, it was obvious he was highly regarded by the police hierarchy, because he was immediately appointed district inspector and assigned to Tubbercurry, County Sligo.

On September 30, he was in Sligo town for most of the day. Late that afternoon, on his way back to Tubbercurry, he was ambushed by the IRA on a stretch of country road well known to the police as "a death trap." The wounds that killed him were so gruesome that it would be alleged the attackers had used dum-dum bullets, outlawed by international convention because of how they mutilated victims. Two constables were also wounded. All three were rushed to the Tubbercurry barracks.[46]

An RIC official from Sligo described the scene when he arrived at the barracks later that night with a twenty-six-man police and army team:

[Brady's] naked body was lying on the kitchen floor, being washed
by one of his comrades. The three ghastly wounds made by the
shots were in full evidence. Head Constable O'Hara was lying in a
room nearby moaning and suffering intense pain. Police Constable
Brown was wandering about the room in a state of pain.[47]

The contingent of soldiers and police then went on a rampage
through the town, shooting and hurling hand grenades. They burned
three shops and wrecked as many as eleven others. They set fire to the
local creamery, then went looking for the manager, a known supporter of Sinn Féin. Arriving at his house, they called his wife outside,
demanding to know where he was hiding. "They all seemed to me to
speak with an Irish accent," she said later. "The swearing was awful.
The men asked me where my husband was and I asked what they
wanted him for. They replied, 'to shoot him.'"[48] When they couldn't
find him, they returned to finish the destruction of his creamery, then
moved on to a nearby village and burned down another one.

Tubbercurry was a long way from Dublin but, like Balbriggan, it
soon became famous among stories of 1920 police rampages. Government reprisals were becoming sensational news outside Ireland. Within
days, British reporters were in town. One of the more famous corre-
spondents, Hugh Martin of the London *Daily News*, vividly described
the scene before him:

Little spires of smoke were twisting up from three jagged stone
skeletons . . .

Many shops—I counted eleven, and there may have been
more between and beside the burnt-out buildings—had their
fronts battered and broken so that the whole triangle had the air
of having barely survived an earthquake.[49]

In the weeks and months ahead, media attention and public opinion would begin to play a defining role in the conduct and the outcome of the Irish conflict.

General Tudor took part in another, larger, reassuring meeting with Lloyd George the day after Tubbercurry, a conference that included the senior advisers on the Irish file in Dublin—Hamar Greenwood (chief secretary for Ireland), John Anderson (his undersecretary), and GOC General Macready. Greenwood was upbeat, reporting impressive progress "in the efficiency of both the military and police sides of the Irish executive." There was acknowledgement that "hot blood" had to be reined in. At the same time "unauthorized reprisals . . . unquestionably had a visible effect both in enabling the Executive to obtain information about ambushes and plots and in driving a wedge between the moderates and the extremists in the Sinn Féin camp."

Greenwood asked for assurance that the British government was "entirely behind" Dublin Castle's strategies. According to the minutes of the meeting, "The Prime Minister stated that there was no doubt of this. The British Government considered that the Irish Executive was tackling a very difficult task with great courage."[50]

Greenwood's wife, the chatty, charming Margo Greenwood, seemed to have at least as much influence with Lloyd George as her husband. (There were persistent rumours they were lovers.) Two days later, she wrote to Mark Sturgis, the Irish assistant undersecretary in Dublin, that "the PM 'is immensely pleased with the trend of events.'"[51]

The prime minister would soon thereafter confirm Margo Greenwood's observation in a major speech in a historic corner of his homeland, Wales. On October 9, in Carnarvon, Lloyd George publicly supported the practice of reprisals by the RIC and, by implication, the management tactics of the police chief, General Tudor.

One week later, Churchill, speaking in Dundee, Scotland, his parliamentary constituency at the time, took an equally hard line on the Irish conflict. Ireland was "tearing herself to pieces," he declared, and it was Britain's duty as "the stronger island and nation" to "help" Ireland through her troubles. The help, he made it clear, was coming in the form of tough love.

Churchill vowed to keep the tough love coming. "Already 115 policemen and 22 soldiers have been killed and not a single person brought to justice. I am told by those who have gone through it that the strain on a man's nerves far exceeds the bombardment of the trenches. Assassination will not be allowed to change the history of the British Empire."[52] He clearly wasn't ready to admit, if he ever would be, that assassination was and would remain an essential element in suppressing independence movements like Sinn Féin.

17.

HAMAR GREENWOOD'S ASSERTION that reprisals were, among other benefits, generating information "about ambushes and plots" was at best an optimistic overstatement. An early casualty of the IRA war against the RIC had been the crucial link between the Irish policeman and the people he served in the country's small villages and countryside.

Neighbourhood policing, where people know and trust the cop, is generally regarded as an ideal model for law enforcement, whether in a rural village or an urban ghetto. The relationship produces knowledge—clues about what might be happening, might be going to happen, and what has already happened.

But even before the end of 1919, neighbourhood policing in Ireland was already dead. The policeman, rebranded by the IRA, was no longer a neighbour but now an enemy, a spy for Dublin Castle. The army, through its remote outposts, managed to maintain a flow of information to the capital. But it lacked the substance and authenticity of the intelligence once collected by the "peelers" in casual encounters with friends and neighbours speaking in familiar accents, sometimes in a language that was gibberish to English ears.

Ormonde Winter, since General Tudor had appointed him director of intelligence in June 1920, had been working with the army to build an undercover system, part military and part civilian, that could fill the void, recruiting agents who had been trained by Britain's elite spy services. Like his boss, Winter was resented by the army. He was mysterious, which was acceptable. But his methods were unconventional, his bureaucratic style was devious, and the systems he devised made sharing information with the military cumbersome.

One Dublin soldier who was especially dubious about Winter was the head of the Dublin District Special Branch, General Walter Wilson. As an experienced military intelligence officer, Wilson resented having to collaborate with an unconventional novice, an odd hybrid policeman with no police experience and a peculiar personality.

Winter was, however, Wilson's boss and would soon officially integrate the military and civil intelligence branches. This was a development Wilson found frustrating and would eventually lead to his departure from the Dublin team.

But in the meantime, through the summer and the fall of 1920, they kept the friction under wraps and worked aggressively, conducting raids, seizing arms and documents, arresting suspected rebels. At least weekly, if not every night, Wilson's crew would find a suspicious house to visit, a suspicious door to knock on or knock down. It was to Walter Wilson's team that Winter, on the advice of General Tudor, had assigned Major Osbert Smyth when he arrived from Egypt in August to avenge his murdered brother.

Military intelligence had been successful in pestering, arresting and occasionally imprisoning medium- and low-level rebel activists. But the combined resources of the army and the police had never come even close to catching the biggest prize of all—the IRA's Michael Collins, who, among his many responsibilities, was Ormonde Winter's opposite number as director of intelligence for the insurgents.

The most wanted men in Ireland seemed to come and go and to spend long periods plotting with impunity in Dublin. Two of the most notorious, Dan Breen and Seán Treacy, the killers of the two RIC constables in Tipperary in January 1919, had acquired mythic reputations in nationalist circles, accused (or credited) for murders they probably didn't know about. (Breen had been erroneously linked to the murder of Colonel Gerald Smyth.[53]) Significant rewards were offered for their capture, dead or alive. By October 1920, both were believed to be living underground in Dublin, but Crown forces couldn't find them.

On the night of October 11, General Wilson had a tipoff that both Breen and Treacy were in a safe house in Drumcondra, a north Dublin suburb, guests of a prominent Sinn Féin sympathizer, Professor John Carolan, who was a lecturer at a teachers' college. Early on the morning of October 12, a ten-man DDSB team surrounded Carolan's house. When the professor answered a knock on his front door, several of the officers crowded past him, demanding to know who else was in the house.

The professor stalled as best he could, but when the officers noticed three overcoats hanging in the foyer, two of them rushed upstairs, guns drawn, to check the bedrooms. The occupant of the first room told them there were two strangers in the room across the landing.[54] When they pounded on that door, the men inside responded with a fusillade. The locked door offered no protection, the bullets splintering the wood. The two army officers fell instantly and died on the floor. One of them was Major Osbert Smyth.

A post-mortem examination revealed that a bullet had passed through Smyth's chest and liver, exiting through the right side of his back. A second bullet entered the left side of his back, hitting a vertebra and his right lung. He was thirty years old.

Breen and Treacy fled through a bedroom window. Breen fell and was injured, but he got away. Treacy, uninjured, disappeared into the night.

There would be conflicting stories about what happened that night. Dan Breen later wrote an account that could serve as a template for a Hollywood movie shootout—furious gunfire against overwhelming odds, multiple casualties, two heroes taking on the British army and escaping. Thirteen British officers dead and mysteriously hauled away in ambulances.

In his book *My Fight for Irish Freedom*, Breen recounts:

When [Osbert Smyth] heard that I had been traced to a house in Drumcondra, he called to his braves to help him "capture Breen alive and skin him." He had been warned that I was quick on the draw. "Not quick enough for me, the rat!" I'm still in my skin. He was the first to be killed that night.[55]

Ormonde Winter, the head of RIC intelligence, a man with a colourful imagination of his own, wryly described Breen's version of the Drumcondra incident as "Hibernian romance." His own account of the shootout is also less than truthful, but appropriately understated. He wrote cryptically that "in the turmoil . . . one or two shots were fired, one of which struck Prof. Carolan and killed him."

Carolan was, in fact, shot by the soldiers in retaliation for the death of Osbert Smyth. The professor lingered in hospital for sixteen days before he died on October 28. The story of what happened to Professor Carolan is probably best told in his own words in a statement he made, under oath, after he'd been shot:

> Immediately the firing ceased I was marched upstairs by an officer who kept a revolver pressed against my back. I was brought to the front room, where I saw a man in uniform lying on the floor, apparently dead. I was then brought out on the landing to the door of the back room, which was open, and I was able to see that there was no person in the room.
>
> One of the officers who was with me then went into the back room and I was told to turn my back towards him which I did. I immediately heard the report of a shot, and was shot through the back of the neck. I fell on my face on top of a man who was lying, apparently dead, on the landing. I was unable to move, but quite conscious.
>
> I tried to call my wife, and heard one of the officers say to the other, "I thought he was dead."[56]

Professor Carolan died shortly after swearing, in the presence of a lawyer, to this version of his own murder.

Coming less than three months after the assassination of Gerald Smyth in Cork, Osbert's death was a devastating blow to the prominent Ulster family. A cousin saw the news of the Drumcondra shootout posted outside a shop on Oxford Street in London that day—"Major Shot in Dublin." Osbert's mother, Helen, was also in London at the time. For her, it was "a family tragedy she did not recover from," as a relative would write years later.[57] The family talked her out of going straight to Dublin to view the body of her son, so instead she immediately returned to Banbridge.

On the day of Major Osbert Smyth's funeral, October 15, the Banbridge shops were closed. The funeral procession set out for the cemetery along a route that was lined by thousands of Ulster men and women. There was a guard of honour and a marching band from the Duke of Cornwall's Light Infantry regiment.

The coffin was on a gun carriage, and an army sergeant walked behind it, leading Major Smyth's dog. A laurel wreath with white lilies, placed on the coffin by his mother, bore the inscription "To the most devoted and loving son that ever lived." The regimental band played the death march from Handel's oratorio *Saul*. The honour guard fired three salutes across the grave. A bugler played the Last Post.[58]

General Tudor, given this tragedy for which he was, indirectly and unconsciously, the author, would badly have needed the morale boost he received the next day in a militant speech by Winston Churchill to his constituents in Dundee, Scotland:

> Are we now, fresh from victory in the great war, fresh from
> the sacrifices of the greatest of all wars that men ever fought,
> having struck down the most terrible antagonists that ever
> marched forth in strife in the whole history of mankind—
> are we now to collapse miserably and impotently before the
> meanest, basest, cruellest yet, and if they are only stood up to,
> the feeblest of all foes?

General Tudor might have answered: *Not on my watch.*

There would have been some welcome consolation in the news that he'd received as he arrived in Banbridge on the day of Osbert's funeral. Seán Treacy had been killed in a shootout with soldiers and Auxiliaries the previous afternoon on Talbot Street in Dublin.

But it was not enough for satisfaction. Breen was still out there somewhere. Treacy, now a martyr, was even more deadly as a symbol.

General Tudor was in a war that now, and for as long as he would survive in it, was personal.

Banbridge was quiet after Osbert Smyth's funeral, unlike in July, when his brother Gerald was buried and there had been rage and riots and pogroms against Catholics throughout Ulster. This time the north was almost calm.

Dan Breen described a similar atmosphere of dignified grief in Tipperary as Seán Treacy's coffin slowly travelled the five miles from Solohead to Kilfeacle cemetery. There was "a solid phalanx" of republicans along the road. As in Banbridge, shops and banks were closed in Tipperary for a day of mourning.

British forces tried to diminish the occasion by limiting the funeral procession but, in the end, the Volunteers "evaded" the restrictions, Breen wrote. And with what was possibly a touch of "Hibernian romance," he claimed that "British soldiers openly paid tribute to a gallant opponent by saluting as the hearse passed by." The funeral ended "when the green sod was rolled over the grave [and] three volleys were fired by Volunteers who melted away into the crowd."[59]

With Seán Treacy's death, General Tudor might have felt, at least for a day or two, that he was in control of his assignment. But almost immediately after the funeral in Banbridge, the Irish drama took another nasty turn. Daniel Roche, a forty-five-year-old RIC sergeant from Tipperary, had been summoned to Dublin to confirm Treacy's identity after he'd been killed. While alive, Treacy had been heroic. Now he was iconic. Dublin IRA leaders were soon aware of why Roche was in the city, and members of the Squad were told to kill him.

Even after being hit by at least six bullets, one newspaper reported, Roche ran from his assassins and almost got away. He finally fell dead after he was shot in the face as he turned a corner onto Little

Strand Street in Dublin's city centre.[60] The man who shot him, Joseph Dolan, was perhaps more accurate: "I took out my revolver and put six bullets into Roche when he was just in front of me . . . Tom Keogh and Jim Slattery put a few more bullets into Roche."[61]

A police reprisal followed swiftly.[62] On October 19, brothers Ned and Francis O'Dwyer were shot and killed in front of their sister in Bansha, Tipperary. She said the killers were wearing "military uniforms," but they were Tudor's officers, probably retaliating for the killing of Sergeant Roche—which had been an IRA reprisal for the death of Seán Treacy, and would be avenged in Bansha nine months later when two members of the RIC team that had killed the O'Dwyer brothers would themselves be killed.

On October 17, the day the Squad killed Sergeant Roche in Dublin, Michael Fitzgerald, thirty-nine, died in Cork, one of more than a dozen prisoners in Cork jail who had been on a hunger strike after mass arrests in August under the new Restoration of Order regulations. The best known of the Cork hunger strikers was the lord mayor, Terence MacSwiney, who had been wasting away in Brixton Prison, London, for more than two months when Fitzgerald died.

British government officials had been cynical at the outset of the hunger strikes, regarding MacSwiney's fast as a publicity stunt. In his August diary entries, the usually good-natured Mark Sturgis sarcastically refers to MacSwiney as "the Cork Martyr" and laments that the Irish Catholic hierarchy had announced that "if he dies, they will hold it a sacrificial not a suicidal death—damn them." The distinction was significant. In Roman Catholic doctrine, suicide was deemed to be a mortal sin that deprived the deceased of any sacramental recognition, including a funeral and burial in consecrated ground. In essence the influential Irish clergy had endorsed an act of extreme political resistance.

By the first of October, Sturgis had come to believe that the hunger strikes had "faded into insignificance as a topic beside reprisals." Government retaliation had the headlines now. Churchill, on October 16, called the hunger strikes a product of the "silly season." MacSwiney, the most high-profile of the hunger strikers, truly "didn't want to die," Churchill declared. "The government didn't want him to die but he had many friends in Ireland who wished he would die. Now, after nine weeks of fasting, he is still alive."[63]

The wishful thinking in Dublin Castle persisted—the mayor's condition was exaggerated, he was eating secretly, his jailers were slipping protein into his drinking water. Then, the day after Churchill's mocking speech, Michael Fitzgerald died of starvation. And on October 25, Terence MacSwiney, by now an international celebrity, died in Brixton Prison.

As expected, there was an uproar in Ireland and abroad, charging that MacSwiney's death could have been prevented. On August 25 senior government officials, meeting at 10 Downing Street, had seriously considered recommending his release for valid reasons. He was a political prisoner; his crime was innocuous, involving possession of "seditious" documents; he had recently developed full-blown tuberculosis. The group of six prominent Tories considering "the Irish situation" seemed to be leaning toward a merciful and prudent political decision. A former Liberal prime minister, H. H. Asquith, had publicly called for his release. Then Churchill, who was at the meeting, warned about the perception of an "apparent climb-down of the government."

In the end, the politicians passed the buck to a soldier, General Nevil Macready, who wasn't there. According to minutes of the meeting on August 25, "It was decided that if General Macready expressed strong views against his release, then the cabinet decision should stand." For once, Macready and the police chief were on the same page politically. They owed it to the soldiers and policemen under their command to let nature take its course.[64] And so the cabinet decision stood.

When MacSwiney died on October 25, after ten weeks without solid food, even Churchill was humbled. When challenged by an artist who was, at the time, painting his portrait, he walked back his earlier cynicism, saying "[MacSwiney] was a brave man. They are a fine people; we cannot afford to lose them. We shall be shaking hands together in three months."[65]

The controversy over MacSwiney's death swept through England. A British member of parliament, one of thousands of Londoners who viewed his corpse in Westminster Cathedral, described "a wizened little monkey" who had before imprisonment been "a robust man."

History has, without confirmation but persuasively, attributed a prediction to a young Vietnamese restaurant employee who was working in France at the time of MacSwiney's death: "Such a people will never be defeated." His name was Nguyen Ai Quoc. In his later years, he would be more widely known as Ho Chi Minh.[66]

In the end, as the historian Peter Hart has observed, "the government may have blunted the hunger weapon and buoyed the morale of its men in Ireland, but it had achieved nothing in military terms and had produced only despair and enmity among the population at large."[67]

The timing couldn't have been worse. MacSwiney was radical but reasonable. In his inaugural speech as Cork's mayor in March that year, after the murder of his predecessor, Tomás MacCurtain, MacSwiney had defined the independence struggle as a moral contest. "This contest of ours is not on our side a rivalry of vengeance but one of endurance—it is not they who can inflict the most, but they who can suffer most, will conquer."

A rebel comrade, Ernie O'Malley, described MacSwiney, who was forty-one and had been mayor for only seven months, as an example of "a young courage which death would hand on to the generation that would see this struggle through."

On October 21, just four days before MacSwiney's death became an international sensation, a British military court handed Sinn Féin another propaganda gift by sentencing a member of that courageous generation, an eighteen-year-old Dublin medical student, to death by hanging. Kevin Barry had been captured in September after a raid to steal weapons from British soldiers while they were picking up supplies at a Dublin bakery. Three soldiers, one of them even younger than Barry, died in the shootout. Private Harold Washington was listed by the army as being nineteen. He had, however, lied about his age when enlisting and was actually a month short of his sixteenth birthday.[68]

There was no evidence to indicate conclusively that Barry had killed anyone. But his trial was by military court martial, under the new Restoration of Order legislation that allowed the death penalty for any mortal crime. He was, to no one's great surprise, found guilty and sentenced to hang.[69]

There was an immediate and widespread public demand for clemency, and much debate within the British cabinet. The politicians, in the end, knowing that both General Tudor and General Macready were strongly in favour of hanging Barry as a gesture of support for soldiers and policemen, agreed to let the sentence stand. Tudor had made it clear to the politicians and bureaucrats, "vigorously," according to his deputy, Ormonde Winter, that failure to proceed with Barry's execution would "seriously undermine the morale of the RIC."

The execution order would have to be confirmed by the viceroy in Dublin, Sir John French. But Macready, who was at the meeting that decided Barry's fate, left little doubt about what he would recommend. Death by hanging. Sturgis was present when French gave his final judgment. His diary entry noted Macready's rationale, that "the soldiers and police rightly expected us to exact the full penalty."[70]

On November 1 at 8 a.m., six days after Terence MacSwiney's gruesome end, and one day after his politically charged public funeral in Cork, Kevin Barry went quietly to the gallows in Mountjoy Prison in north Dublin. His death was "one of the most holy," according to the priest who walked him to the scaffold. The priest would reassure Barry's mother, herself a staunch republican, that even while facing death her son was "one of the bravest and best boys" he had ever known.[71]

Mark Sturgis had noted solemnly the night before: "I hear Barry is quite calm and unrepentant, not at all like a boy driven into a deed by the orders of others. Rather a pity no one noticed it is All Saints' Day."[72]

In an unsurprising display of British cultural insensitivity—or indifference—Barry died early on one of the holiest days in the Catholic liturgical calendar. It was a day on which all the Catholics in Ireland were obliged to go to Mass, and a day on which most of the Catholic clergy in Ireland would use their pulpits to denounce Britain's obvious contempt for Ireland, her people and her faith. Two names— those of Kevin Barry and Terence MacSwiney—would ring through churches all over Ireland on that holy day, and from that day forward in the legends and poetry and history of Ireland's struggle to be free.

18.

MUCH OF WHAT was happening in Ireland was a propaganda war, a manipulative competition for public approval. In his prior life General Tudor had been able to assume that his deeds would be appreciated. In his military experience, propaganda was a faithful ally, a natural by-product of patriotism. The most ardent patriots in British wartime history had been newspaper proprietors and, often, war reporters, the custodians of political opinion.

Generals who won wars almost always became public heroes. Even honourable failures could be celebrated. But in this Irish war, General Tudor risked ending up a villain even if he won it. Stories of atrocities by Crown forces troubled even many unionists in the south and west of Ireland. The hard-edged patriotism from civilians that Tudor would normally have relied upon for moral sustenance could only be found among loyalists, most of them in Ulster.

That such Orange patriotism was tainted by the stain of radical religious bigotry should have bothered an Anglican like Tudor, who was moderate in matters of religion. But as he had learned from experience in Asia, the enemy of his enemy was, if not his friend, at least a potentially friendly ally when he needed one. In the Irish war, he and his political masters needed all the allies they could find.

The deaths of Terence MacSwiney and Kevin Barry had delivered a propaganda victory to Sinn Féin at a crucial moment in the war. Patriotic British propagandists worked to blunt the impact by emphasizing the reality that MacSwiney had been an IRA commander and that Barry was part of an IRA operation that had killed three young soldiers, one of them, it would emerge, significantly younger than he was.

But the coverage of MacSwiney's slow death, monitored by sympathetic media around the world, had emphasized his moderate political beliefs and religious piety. Executing Barry on the Feast of All Saints, the morning after MacSwiney's funeral, guaranteed a special place in Irish history for another martyr.

To preserve this propaganda windfall required an unusually level-headed response by Sinn Féin. Their first impulse was anything but level-headed. The night before Barry went to the scaffold, IRA leadership in Dublin ordered a campaign of mayhem. But then they reconsidered and cancelled it. Murdering British soldiers and policemen randomly would dilute the political impact of the two high-profile patriotic sacrifices.

The best of intentions, however, can be sabotaged by failures of communication. IRA units in County Kerry clearly didn't get the second memo, launching a wave of attacks on RIC officers with devastating consequences. In the previous four years, the Kerry IRA had murdered four policemen. In the twenty-four hours following the execution of Kevin Barry, sixteen policemen and a British navy radio operator were shot, seven of them fatally.[73]

But if the attacks in Kerry diminished public sympathy for Sinn Féin, the countermeasures by Crown forces there and elsewhere soon restored the republican advantage.

The carnage started swiftly, shortly after MacSwiney's funeral and the night before Barry's execution. After two RIC constables, returning from a date with two Irish women at about ten o'clock on the night of October 31, were shot dead on a roadside just outside Killorglin, Kerry, their colleagues dragged a Sinn Féin supporter from his bed, marched him outside and shot him four times. Somehow he survived, but the violence in Killorglin didn't stop there. The police then burned the local Sinn Féin hall, a garage, a temperance meeting place, and the home of a known Sinn Féin supporter, and they continued shooting wildly in the streets until about five thirty on the morning of November 1.

In Ballyduff, Kerry, at about one that morning, three RIC officers were ambushed while on patrol. One of them, twenty-three-year-old George Morgan, died instantly. His two fellow officers, though wounded, managed to survive.

A few hours later, eight RIC lorries arrived in town and went straight to the home of a thirty-year-old local IRA member, Seán Houlihan, and forced him and his parents out of their beds and outside. They made Houlihan's horrified parents watch while they beat, bayonetted and shot their son to death. Then they burned Houlihan's hay shed and a local creamery and set several nearby private homes on fire.[74]

At about the time Constable Morgan was killed in the attack in Ballyduff, two RIC officers, Ernest Bright, thirty-four, and Patrick Waters, twenty-four, were taken prisoner and killed just outside Tralee, about twelve miles away. There was a gruesome rumour, later proven to be false, that the constables had been thrown into a furnace at the Tralee gasworks while they were still alive. Their bodies were actually buried on a nearby beach but were never found.[75]

Tralee would suffer official retaliation during more than a week of terror that paralyzed the town and captured headlines around the world. While local citizens were attending Mass in Tralee on the morning of November 1, Black and Tans drove up and down the streets in lorries, shooting wildly as people emerged from St. John's parish church, forcing them to run back inside for safety.

Soon journalists were arriving in Tralee from the United States, France and England; the reprisals would become front-page news in newspapers as distant as the *New York Times* and the Montreal *Gazette*. Hugh Martin of the London *Daily News* had been covering the Irish war for months, and the RIC were unhappy with what they saw as a pro–Sinn Féin bias in his writing. They let it be known that they were "looking for him," which was immediately reported in stories written by his colleagues as intimidation.

The coverage of the "Siege of Tralee," which had been damaging to the British government before the threat to Martin, now became sensationally critical as the reprisal went on for nine days. Shops were closed on orders from the police, market days were cancelled, the town almost paralyzed. A French reporter wrote that it was "as if the Angel of death had passed through."[76]

The siege had started on Monday, the day of Barry's execution. By Thursday, international media were reporting that the police were firebombing the homes and businesses of known Sinn Féin sympathizers. In the House of Commons, there was a question about the death of

Seán Houlihan in Ballyduff. The Irish secretary, Hamar Greenwood, acknowledged that Houlihan had been shot but said the culprits were anonymous "masked men." When asked about John Conway, fifty-seven, shot dead in Tralee while on his way to church, Greenwood claimed that an inquiry had revealed he had died "of natural causes." But the London *Times* reported that a journalist had viewed Conway's body and had seen the obvious bullet hole in his temple.[77]

A nine-day siege in Tralee could hardly have been called hot-blooded and spontaneous. Dublin Castle had to know that it was going on. General Tudor, conflicted though he might have been, was either actively or passively responsible. The fact that he faced no consequences indicated that his support in the British cabinet was still firm.

Churchill was almost hysterically belligerent in a public speech in London on November 4. Ireland, he declared, was part of an international conspiracy, a rehearsal for all-out war against the Empire. "The rascals and rapscallions of mankind are now on the move against us," he warned. And he promised that whether it was "the Irish murder gang, or the Egyptian vengeance society, seditious traitors in India, or the arch traitors we have at home—they will feel the weight of the British arm."[78]

But, notwithstanding the encouraging political rhetoric, Tudor's critics in Dublin Castle were becoming restless.

On November 3, General Macready sent a memo to Sir John Anderson advising him that he had asked General Tudor to bring a halt to "promiscuous firing in the air" by RIC policemen as they raced through towns and villages and along country roads in their military vehicles. "When there are rebels in sight, I am all in favour of killing as many as possible," he wrote. But promiscuous firing "doesn't do any good and is very subversive to discipline."[79]

Macready could have made a stronger argument if he'd known about an incident two days earlier, on November 1, when gunfire from a passing lorry full of drunken Black and Tans killed Ellen Quinn, twenty-three, who was sitting on a stone wall near her home in Kiltartan, Galway, with an infant in her arms.

W. B. Yeats would immortalize Ellen Quinn. Though he doesn't name her, she was clearly in his mind when he composed a poem called "Reprisals"—a lament addressed to a dead military friend, Major Robert Gregory of Kiltartan:

> *Where may new-married women sit*
> *And suckle children now? Armed men*
> *May murder them in passing by*
> *Nor law nor parliament take heed.*

The British historian Charles Townshend, who has written seminal studies on the Irish fight for independence, declared that, for Yeats, "the autumn of 1920 and in particular the murder of Ellen Quinn, seemed to herald a new barbarism."

On November 5, Teresa O'Connell, fifteen, was shot dead while standing on the doorstep at her father's home in Ardfert, County Kerry, during a gunfight happening five hundred yards away between Crown forces and an IRA unit. Allegedly, she died because two Black and Tan policemen had placed a bet on which of them was the better marksman.[80]

Tudor finally issued a memorandum on discipline on November 11. It was, to say the least, ambiguous. "Firearms should never be fired except with the intention of hitting the object aimed at." His senior commanders distributed the instructions to the police the next day.

Noting their "unparalleled fortitude" in standing up to "a diabolical murder campaign," General Tudor paid tribute to the police for the fact that "discipline has been maintained at a very high level." He renewed his standing promise that "the RIC will have the fullest support in the most drastic action against that band of assassins, the so-called IRA." He instructed that "these murderers must be pursued relentlessly and their organization ruthlessly suppressed . . . the ambushers must be ambushed . . . The leaders and members of the criminal gang are mostly known to us. They must be given no rest. They must be hunted down," adding the caveat that the hunting down must be accomplished "with the highest discipline."[81]

By then neither police nor soldiers were paying much attention to the formal admonitions of their commanders. On November 13, Annie O'Neill, eight years old, was playing with a friend on a street near her home in Dublin when a military patrol shot at someone who was trying to run away from them. A stray bullet killed Annie and, passing through her body, seriously wounded six-year-old Teresa Kavanagh.

Edwin S. Montagu was British secretary of state for India, but in November 1920, it was Ireland that was perplexing him. He worried that dissidents in India would adopt "the methods of the Sinn Féiners." And he was even more alarmed by the British strategy to combat Sinn Féin's "detestable outrages" by "acquiescing to unlawful and often vicarious punishments" in response. In a memo to the cabinet dated November 10, he singled out "the 'black and tan' officers as being wholly undisciplined, shooting and burning indiscriminately." What was the rationale behind indiscriminate retaliation? Where was the honest logic in the posture that reprisals were "hot blooded" and principled on one side, but barbaric on the other?

Sir Edwin understood the moral contradiction in preaching discipline to policemen and soldiers when "they have every reason to believe that the government has encouraged them in the action they feel justified in taking." He wrote, "I hear and read stories, not of vengeance in hot blood, but of deliberate outrage without authoritative and definite permission by uniformed men as an answer to outrage. Terror is answered by terror, crime by crime, blood by blood."

Montagu wasn't buying the political rationale that the ends justified the means. His ambivalence was rooted not so much in ethics as in common sense. He wrote that "even if the murder gang in Ireland can be destroyed by this process—which I doubt—the younger generation in Ireland is being educated in murderous thought and is entering upon manhood and public life with murder and revenge in their hearts."[82]

He issued a warning which, from the perspective of the next century, was prescient: "For myself, I see nothing but an unconquerable hatred between the two countries."

To Churchill, Montagu's perception of the perils for both Ireland and Britain would have seemed naive. It is possible to imagine eye-rolling by Churchill and a heavy sigh from the prime minister as they read his earnest Irish memorandum at a time when they were ramping up the violence. It was now too late for second-guessing, for self-doubt. And General Tudor knew more clearly than anyone in London that there was no way to prettify the quotidian reality of the conflict to which he was now committed.

19.

GENERAL TUDOR AND Colonel Winter might have raised a glass of cheer on Tuesday, November 9, after receiving a political high-five from Lloyd George in a high-profile speech at the Guildhall in London. The government, the prime minister declared, finally had "murder by the throat," thanks to dogged work by the police. Of course, he acknowledged, getting murder by the throat had required some rough policework.

There is no doubt that at last their [RIC policemen's] patience
has given way and there has been some severe hitting back . . .

[But] let us be fair to these gallant men who are doing their
duty in Ireland . . . it is no use talking about this being war and
these being reprisals . . . we had to reorganize the police. When
the government was ready, we struck the terrorists and now the
terrorists are complaining of terror.

The message from Lloyd George was clear—the Black and Tans
and the Auxiliary Division were getting the job done. He would have
more to brag about just one week later. On the night of November
15–16, Ormonde Winter's raid bureau produced a windfall of crucial
information about the structure, the people and even the firepower at
the heart of the IRA insurgency. Included among secret IRA documents their raid produced were detailed plans for arson and bombing
campaigns in England.[83]

Mark Sturgis was ecstatic. "The papers collected in the Mulcahy
raid are absolutely smashing and should practically kill the English
support of SF."

Lloyd George had been encouraged by fresh peace feelers from Sinn
Féin. His Castle peacemakers—Andy Cope and William Wylie—
sensed that Michael Collins was, at last, truly interested in a ceasefire. For moderates, a softer Sinn Féin stance was evidence of progress.
For Lloyd George it was evidence of weakness. In the murky realm
of intelligence, the government was finally catching up, and Collins
obviously knew it.

Sinn Féin spies were everywhere—inside the police, the army, the
Castle, the railway system, post offices. Every Irishman, it seemed, was
a part-time spy. But now, thanks to Winter's Raid Bureau and careless-
ness by Richard Mulcahy, the IRA chief of staff, the government had

the names, addresses and occupations of two hundred of the most committed rebels in the Dublin region. They narrowly missed arresting Mulcahy himself, but his files would enable other key arrests in the coming weeks.

Collins now had to be aware that British spies were penetrating his defences. He would have known that Winter, working closely with the London Special Branch, MI5 and other British agencies, had planted trained intelligence officers in Dublin, maybe as many as a hundred of them. Soon they'd be all over Ireland, with a special emphasis on Munster. The enemy was obviously making headway. Several senior IRA officers had been picked up by the DDSB in October. The seizure of Mulcahy's files was a coup that couldn't go unanswered. Maybe it was time to remind the hawks in Dublin Castle who they were up against.

The IRA had been preparing a list of the new British undercover agents and already knew the names of many, where they lived (most of them in south-central Dublin) and where they socialized. It was time for action—a mass-execution of "spies" in one brief and savage operation, quickly planned and precisely coordinated. The plan would involve a simultaneous invasion of seven private homes and a hotel precisely at nine o'clock on a Sunday morning, November 21. It would go down in history as "Bloody Sunday."

A telephone call just after noon that day advised officials at the Castle that, hours earlier, there had been "a wholesale shooting of British officers."[84] By mid-afternoon Castle officials had been informed that ten British military officers, two civilians and two Auxiliary policemen had been killed. Details were still emerging, but they had a fairly accurate picture of the morning's bloodbath. It was spectacular and gory, but not especially successful as a military operation. The IRA teams didn't kill as many spies as they had hoped for. And in the final tally, some of the victims weren't spies at all.

Even in the violent context of November and December 1920, the operation was shocking in its gratuitous brutality. Men in bed alone or with their wives on a lazy Sunday morning. One man in bed with another man. The owner of a house where officers were living, killed in the presence of his shrieking family.

Two Auxiliary officers, part of a patrol that stumbled on the massacre and were sent back to base for reinforcements, were captured by an IRA team of lookouts. Francis Garniss, thirty-four, and Cecil Morris, twenty-four, had joined the Auxiliary Division together one month and three days earlier. They were escorted into a nearby backyard and shot.

There was widespread panic in the city. In the Castle there was chaos as British officials and their families fled there for sanctuary. That afternoon there would be grim conferences with input from military and police officials, including General Tudor and Colonel Winter, and an ex-reporter, Basil Clarke, the Castle specialist in spin control. They were dealing with a human tragedy, but one that was also rich in possibilities for political advantage. There could no longer be any doubt in the minds of reasonable people about the real nature of the Irish "fight for freedom" and the ruthless enemy that the Crown was up against.

A conference at half past three that afternoon was meant to be constructive, exploring strategies to own the moment, to convert what was a devastating setback into a propaganda victory. If there was a sour note at the conference, it was the mood of the police chief, General Tudor. Mark Sturgis, who was at the meeting, summed it up in his diary entry for what he called a day of black murder. "Tudor didn't shine. He doesn't on these occasions."

General Tudor might have been in shock. He seemed to be confused, and confusion can be a symptom of either shock or guilt. Perhaps he was aware of aspects of the Bloody Sunday carnage that he didn't want to share. As police commander, he knew about a raid that afternoon. Even as officials were meeting in Dublin Castle, his Black and Tans and Auxiliaries were crashing a Gaelic football game at Croke Park, north Dublin.

Violent reprisals by his policemen after recent IRA outrages had redefined the Irish conflict. What had happened Sunday morning was an outrage on an unprecedented scale: mass murder of British servicemen. A reprisal should have been predictable for the police chief who had allowed the practice of retaliation to escalate in recent months. And the crowd in the Croke Park stadium would have been almost entirely republican—Gaelic football, like hurling and the Gaelic language, was part of the cultural bedrock of the Irish independence movement.

The original plan to raid the football game had been set days earlier—probably a follow-up to the successful seizure of Sinn Féin files by the DDSB and the RIC on the night of November 15–16. Black and Tans and Auxiliaries would surround the football field with assistance from the army, block the exits and search all male spectators as they were leaving. They would arrest anyone with a weapon or suspicious documents, shoot anyone who resisted.

There had been aerial reconnaissance of the crowd before the game began. It was an unusual sight in November 1920. An airplane circling Croke Park twice, then heading off in the direction of Phoenix Park, the RIC main depot, about two miles away.[85]

What could go wrong? Squads of armed and angry British peelers and mercenaries confronting thousands of Irish patriots just hours after an attack that had killed a still-unknown number of British officers. The images were already vivid—unarmed men, some still in bed, some standing helpless, hands up, in their pyjamas, some beside their wives. Images that, properly framed and circulated, would sicken decent people everywhere.

But it could so easily be undone. One careless move by a Black and Tan or Auxiliary on Sunday afternoon could negate the moral value of the morning's sacrifice. No wonder their commander, General Tudor, didn't shine that afternoon—perhaps he knew that a situation that was already horrifying was about to worsen. Perhaps he could foresee the consequences of what was about to happen at Croke Park.

His deputy and head of intelligence, Ormonde Winter—usually talkative, invariably exhibiting a cool, somewhat theatrical appearance—was, as Sturgis noted, "distinctly nervy and over-wrought" that afternoon and evening. Winter, like Tudor, would have been well aware of perils in the scene that was unfolding in Croke Park. He would also know, and would certainly have shared with his commander, that, in a Castle guardroom where F Company Auxiliaries were holding three suspected IRA conspirators, the horrors of the day were still unfolding.

General Frank Crozier, commander of Tudor's Auxiliary Division, had stumbled into the morning carnage as it was winding down. It is unclear what Crozier might have contributed to the deliberations in the Castle that day. He wasn't at the planning conference. But he did have first-hand information.

Crozier had arrived at Lower Mount Street, central Dublin, in the immediate aftermath of three murders and just in time to prevent another. He had seen the body of a dead British officer. He also knew that two of his Auxiliaries had been caught by the IRA and executed. He got there just as one of his men was about to shoot Frank Teeling, the only IRA gunman they had managed to capture at the crime scene. Teeling was wounded. The Auxiliary had a gun pointed at his head and was counting to ten, demanding the names of other IRA men involved. Crozier knocked the gun aside, arrested Teeling and ordered that he be taken to a military hospital.

But Teeling wasn't the only IRA man in the hands of the Auxiliaries that day. The lists of names and addresses in General Mulcahy's files had already led to raids in the days and hours before Bloody Sunday morning.

Late Saturday night, Richard Mulcahy and Michael Collins had been in the smoking room at Vaughan's Hotel on Parnell Square, completing plans for the Bloody Sunday operation. The meeting ended quickly when word came from an informant that a raiding party of Auxiliary and military officers was bearing down on the hotel. The big fish all escaped. The only catch at Vaughan's was a young Gaelic-language scholar visiting from out of town. He happened to be in the vicinity of the high-powered meeting, but not a part of it.

His name was Conor Clune, a twenty-seven-year-old co-op society manager from County Clare. He had no known IRA connections. He was a nephew of the politically active bishop Patrick Clune, who had been working quietly behind the scenes to broker a ceasefire. On that Saturday night, young Conor happened to be in the wrong place at the wrong time, and he soon found himself in custody and on the way to a lockup in Dublin Castle.

Hours after Clune's arrest, another raid, presumably inspired by the intelligence windfall of November 15–16, caught two senior IRA men—Dick McKee, commander of the Dublin IRA Brigade, and his second-in-command, Peadar Clancy—each of them deeply involved in planning the Sunday morning murders. Both had been present at the planning meeting at Vaughan's Hotel with Collins and had managed to escape. They took refuge in a private home not far away but were caught a few hours later. Both were in custody, along with Conor Clune, in a Dublin Castle lockup when the Sunday assassinations happened later that same morning.

Ormonde Winter would have known that the men were being interrogated while he and Tudor sat quietly through a conference on

public relations strategies elsewhere in the Castle that Sunday afternoon. He would also have known that the interrogations were under
the direction of two notorious government enforcers, Captain J. L.
Hardy, who reported, through Winter, to the head of London Special
Branch, and the Auxiliary F Company intelligence officer, W. L. King.

Hardy and King were two of the more infamous police enforcers
in Dublin Castle.[86] The interrogation in the Auxiliaries' guardroom
would continue until it reached a bloody and still controversial climax
shortly before midnight.

Where questions about Bloody Sunday would remain unresolved,
potentially forever, would be in the bloody muddle of that Sunday
afternoon when Crown forces descended on the football game at
Croke Park. Before the afternoon was over, there would be sixteen
more victims of the Bloody Sunday violence.

Was Croke Park a deliberate reprisal? If so, it brutally exposed the
fundamental weakness in what had apparently become an official
strategy for defeating Irish separatism. Fighting fire with fire predictably created an inferno.

There would be no doubt about the vital facts: eleven people,
including three children and a football player, were dead. Dozens
were injured—five more civilians would die from their gunshot
wounds within the week. Psychological and emotional wounds would
fester for decades afterwards.

The best account of what happened at Croke Park was delivered to
General Crozier by one of his senior officers, Major E. L. Mills, late
on the afternoon of Bloody Sunday. Mills had led a joint force of
Auxiliaries and Black and Tans to the stadium and was probably the
most authoritative witness to what had happened shortly after their
arrival. He was obviously still shaken when he briefed his boss. The
operation by the police at Croke Park had been "a rotten show" that,

he said, had quickly turned into a rampage by "excited" RIC officers.

Crozier told Mills to write down what he had seen in a report and he would make sure it got to the proper authorities in Dublin Castle. Mills followed up that night and handed in his version of events the next day. If officials in the Castle saw his report, they ignored and ultimately buried it. Dr. David Leeson, a Canadian, found the report by Major Mills in the British Public Records Office in November 1999 and became the first historian to report the find.

Major Mills had written that, on arrival at Croke Park with his mixed squad of Auxiliaries and RIC policemen, he saw RIC men in vehicles in front of him scrambling out of their cars and rushing toward the football field.[87] "I stopped my car, jumped out and went to see what was the matter. At this moment I heard a considerable amount of rifle fire." He managed to stop the first barrage of shooting but there was still "firing going on in the football ground." He wrote, "I ran down into the ground and shouted to all the armed men to stop firing at once and eventually the firing ceased. The crowd by this time was in a state of panic."

Major Mills took part in a careful search for weapons but "found no weapons on the people attending the match . . . [He] did not see any need for any firing at all and the indiscriminate firing absolutely spoilt any chance of getting hold of any people in possession of any arms."

Crozier, Mills's commander, would later write:

The military surrounded the Hurley ground according to plan and were to warn the crowd by megaphone to file out of the gates where they would be searched.

Well, would you believe it, suddenly the regular RIC from Phoenix Park and the Black and Tans arrived up in lorries, opened fire into the crowd without warning.[88]

The official version of events, when finally available to scholars in 1999, would perpetuate a lie:

> The firing was started by civilians unknown, either as a warning of the raid or with intention of creating a panic . . .
>
> Injuries on deceased persons [were] inflicted by rifle or revolver fire . . . by members of the RIC . . . and by civilians in the football ground.

Part of the hidden official file would be the eyewitness account prepared by Major Mills, discovered nearly seventy years later by Professor Leeson and other scholars.

There would be one factual admission in the official story: "The firing by the RIC was carried out without orders and was in excess of what was necessitated by the situation." That finding would be spun as a kind of absolution for the military and the Auxiliary Division. The shooting was a spontaneous reaction by hot-blooded policemen, presumably outraged by the murders that morning.

The official story would insinuate that the bloodshed at Croke Park was an understandable consequence of another horrifying outrage by the IRA. Hamar Greenwood would confidently tell the House of Commons two days later that the police had acted in self-defence. That many innocent people had died was "entirely" the responsibility of "those assassins whose existence is a constant menace to all law-abiding persons in Ireland."[89]

Part of what Greenwood described as "indisputable evidence" was a false claim that thirty revolvers were found scattered on the ground in the aftermath of the killing, presumably discarded by the men who had initiated the deadly gunfight. But there were no discarded guns. The only firearms on the field, according to the evidence available, were the rifles and revolvers in the hands of the police. The only shooting anyone credibly reported was by members of the RIC.

Neither General Tudor nor Colonel Winter would be asked to officially testify in the aftermath of the Croke Park debacle.

General Tudor and his deputy would also escape accountability for a final atrocity near the end of an already bloody day—the violent deaths of three prisoners who were in the hands of Auxiliary police-men in Dublin Castle. The three suspects picked up by the Auxiliaries late Saturday night and early Sunday morning—Clune, Clancy and McKee—were killed in a Castle guardroom late Sunday night "while trying to escape."

Ormonde Winter knew that they were there, and given the events of Sunday morning, had to know that they were in mortal peril. He knew the reputation of the man he'd left in charge, J. L. Hardy, an officer with a widely known reputation for inflicting sadistic torture on prisoners. Winter's version of what happened to the prisoners in a Castle guardroom steps away from where he lived and worked is either egregiously wrong or deliberately falsified.

In *Winter's Tale*, his memoir published in 1955, he claims to have first heard of the killings at "10.30 a.m." without specifically noting what day it was, Sunday or Monday. He was told that the men had been shot while attempting to escape "a few minutes after 10 o'clock" while all but one of their guards were at breakfast. He wrote that he immediately investigated and spoke to the guards, who described a furious struggle in which the three prisoners were killed, and imme-diately reported to the deputy undersecretary, John Anderson, who accepted his account. The sentry left in charge

> was attacked by the three men, so he fired a shot to alarm the guard, and had then had his rifle seized.

The remainder of the guard then rushed into the guard-room, where one of the three men attacked an Auxiliary with a spade, while another prisoner fired a shot from the sentry's rifle which missed . . . The guard then opened fire.[90]

There is no longer any doubt that the killings happened late Sunday night or early Monday morning. The vagueness in Winter's account might have been intended to somehow diminish his personal responsibility for the safety of the prisoners while they were in the Castle, in the custody of his officers. If the killings happened Sunday morning, he couldn't have been expected to be aware of their extreme vulnerability. Word of the murder of British officers elsewhere in the city hadn't reached the Castle yet. As director of intelligence, by Sunday afternoon Winter should have been aware of what was happening with the prisoners—two of whom were high-value IRA commanders. At least six published references to the incident state specifically that the men were tortured and killed Sunday night, possibly near midnight.[91]

A crucial source of information for the IRA was a Castle spy believed to be an F Company Auxiliary officer who reported to the IRA that the prisoners were "kicked and beaten" before they were shot to death on Sunday night.[92]

People who saw the bodies of the dead men on Monday would insist the three had been "interrogated, tortured and executed as a reprisal for the Sunday assassinations."[93] Medical examinations would reveal broken bones and abrasions "consistent with prolonged assaults, and bullet wounds to the head and body."

Patrick McCrae (member of the Squad, Dublin IRA) viewed the bodies at a local morgue: "Clancy had a large hole in the temple between the eye and the ear . . . [and was] badly wounded about the throat . . . badly marked."

John Fitzpatrick, who owned the house in which Clancy and McKee had been captured, was arrested with them but taken to a different lockup. He later viewed the bodies. "McKee's face was battered up a lot. He had big marks all around his face. Some marks looked as if pieces of flesh was knocked out of them. He had bayonet wound in [his] side & his fingers were all cut where he had grabbed [the bayonet]."

Clancy's face, according to Fitzpatrick, "looked as if it had got a good beating. His forehead was marked over the eye. Also it stuck out well over his face & it looked as if it was burnt. His face was all yellow."[94] And Conor Clune's body showed what appeared to be nine wounds caused by seven bullets.

20.

AMONG POPULAR PERCEPTIONS about power, there is the notion that the buck stops at the top of a pyramid of authority. The two officers at the top of the pyramid of tactical authority in Ireland in November 1920 were General Nevil Macready, of the British army, and General Hugh Tudor, who was in charge of the police.

The raid on Croke Park was an operation by the police—the RIC and Auxiliaries—supported by the army. In his diary entry for November 21, Mark Sturgis noted that the raid had been "arranged some time ago between Dublin District [Special Branch] and the RIC." At a Sunday conference, however, the head of DDSB, General Wilson, "tactfully" made clear "his junior position vis a vis Winter," who was Tudor's deputy and head of intelligence. In his account of Bloody Sunday, Ormonde Winter makes no mention at all of the shooting at Croke Park, although it cost the lives of sixteen people. His account of the murders of Clune, Clancy and McKee that night is a possibly deliberate distortion of what really happened.

On Bloody Sunday, General Macready was on holiday in France. His professional background as a military officer with police experience might have given him the credibility to investigate the circumstances that led to the atrocity at Croke Park. Instead, his military title, general officer commanding, and his absence from the country gave him an excuse to sit out the search for understanding and responsibility. Two inquiries, conducted simultaneously, were led by officers under his command. Crucial questions remained unasked or, if asked, the answers went unchallenged.

The decision to dispatch the Auxiliaries and RIC to raid Croke Park that Sunday afternoon would have been a provocation with little prospect of catching anyone responsible for the morning outrage. If the Croke Park operation had been planned before Sunday, should it not have been reconsidered in the light of the altered circumstances of Sunday morning?

General Tudor's version of the Croke Park story, shared privately with Mark Sturgis on Monday, November 22, confirms that Tudor was part of the planning for an orderly search for fugitives and weapons. But the plans all fell apart, according to an unsubstantiated diary entry for the day, "when three men on the grandstand whipped out revolvers and fired in the air, an obviously pre-arranged signal."

But who, ultimately, was responsible for the decision to proceed that afternoon? Considering the explosive volatility in Dublin as the day unfolded, a raid by rowdy armed policemen on a Gaelic football match might have seemed to be another Black and Tan reprisal, on an epic scale. The perception, right or wrong, would be irresistible in a crowd of nationalists, and the response of normally non-violent men and women, numbering in the thousands, would be unpredictable.

Crown forces—the Auxiliaries—already had two of the masterminds behind the Sunday morning assassinations in custody in Dublin Castle.

Perhaps they didn't know the value of their catch. But they had the legal authority to hold Peadar Clancy and Dick McKee indefinitely; they had the legal flexibility and means to investigate aggressively for proof of their involvement.

Instead, according to the evidence available, Auxiliary officers beat Clancy and McKee to a pulp, more out of vengeance than a thirst for justice, then shot them dead with the flimsy excuse that they'd been trying to escape. Whatever information they might have contributed to history was lost. But neither General Tudor nor his second-in-command would be invited or obliged to answer questions by the official inquiries into Bloody Sunday.

The outcome was predictable. The inquiries pointed fingers at "police"—without attributing specific responsibility to either individual policemen or their leaders. The Anglo-Irish propaganda war would soon leave Bloody Sunday in the dust of ambiguity, ambivalence and spin. Within days it would be overtaken by another outrage.

On Sunday, November 28, an attack on an Auxiliary patrol left seventeen British officers dead and one missing. Sixteen policemen were killed in a brutal shootout on a country road in County Cork; one who escaped was captured and killed the next day by members of the IRA. The missing officer survived, but he was so severely injured he had no useful memory of what had happened near Kilmichael Cross, about seven miles from an Auxiliary barracks in Macroom. The victims were all former army officers, all veterans of the recent war. Two of the dead Auxiliaries had won the Military Cross for "exemplary gallantry" under fire in the First World War. The lone survivor, H. F. Forde, had also won the Military Cross in the Great War.[95]

The Dublin Castle version of the event, known as the Kilmichael ambush, highlighted treachery, claiming that IRA fighters dressed in

"British army uniforms" tricked the Auxiliary patrol into slowing down until their vehicles were almost stopped within a hundred feet of hidden riflemen. Auxiliary policemen were shot down in cold blood as they attempted to surrender after a brief firefight.

The leader of the attack, Tom Barry, had served in the British army during the Great War. He later claimed that, of the attackers, only he wore a military uniform, a tunic used occasionally by senior IRA officers, and he had done so deliberately to confuse the enemy. In his opinion, it was a legitimate deception to gain the tactical advantage of surprise. It worked.

The details of what followed are uniformly ugly in all accounts. Post-mortem examinations confirmed that some victims were shot while their arms were raised. Some bodies bore evidence of battery, probably by rifle butts.

The Kilmichael incident, so soon after Bloody Sunday, rattled senior members of the British government because it had the appearance of a competent military operation. The planning, the discipline and the ruthlessness were a departure from the ragtag ambushes and assassinations that were primary rebel tactics in the early stages of the conflict.

In November, the government had continued to receive encouraging peace feelers from Sinn Féin moderates. Churchill and Lloyd George, even after Bloody Sunday, seemed hopeful that the enemy was growing weary of the fight, looking for an honourable pathway to at least a conversation about peace. But within days, Kilmichael opened a new phase in the war. In the aftermath, martial law was formally declared through most of Munster province. The viceroy, John French, cited Kilmichael as the main reason for the drastic move.

Martial law was swiftly followed by a unilateral decision by senior military officers to round up and intern five hundred Sinn Féin activists—including Arthur Griffith, potentially Lloyd George's best prospect for productive peace talks.

The martial law decree issued on December 10 had only a limited effect on the role of the police. Tudor's friend, the "wild" divisional commissioner in Munster, General Cyril Prescott-Decie, shared authority with his military counterpart, General Peter Strickland. Tudor remained responsible for discipline among policemen and Auxiliaries—in effect, granted the authority to continue his reprisals.

General Strickland would have to "watch the police very carefully," General Macready warned in a note to another army general. Prescott-Decie would consider martial law to mean that "he can kill anybody he sees walking along the road whose appearance may be distasteful to him."[96] Macready and his officers were becoming weary of the police chief and his fighting men and the fiction that reprisals by the RIC were unavoidable.

Indiscipline by the RIC and the Auxiliaries, in Macready's estimation, was a product of either incompetence or policy. Tudor was violating principles of military leadership by ignoring rogue behaviour. He had either been corrupted by his job in Ireland or was dutifully following corrupt instructions from his political superiors.

On December 11, the day after the official declaration of martial law, the IRA ambushed another Auxiliary patrol, this one just outside their barracks in Cork city. An officer was killed and several were wounded. So soon after Kilmichael, it was a provocation that was guaranteed to generate reprisals. Just hours after the attack on the patrol, Auxiliary police and Black and Tans swarmed through downtown Cork, and soon the commercial centre of the city was ablaze.

An inventory for General Tudor, prepared on December 15, listed fifty-seven destroyed buildings, twenty badly damaged and twelve houses "wrecked and looted." The British army launched its own inquiry. The cabinet discussed the army's findings on December 29.

While blaming a specific unit of the Auxiliary police for starting the fires, General Strickland, senior army officer in Cork, singled out "the higher authority who ordered a unit in so raw a state" to move into Cork so soon after the massacre at Kilmichael. Tudor, who, along with General Macready, was at the meeting, bristled at the accusation—in his opinion, Strickland's focus on discipline reflected on him personally. He had a manpower problem after the Kilmichael massacre and had done his best to cope. Strickland replied that he should have asked the military for assistance.[97]

General Macready raised the heat: police discipline was always challenging because policemen "had no code to work under" and RIC leadership that was not "the standard of men who could enforce discipline." Tudor shot back that, according to former military officers now serving in the RIC, discipline on the police force was "stricter than the army."

Lloyd George weighed in diplomatically. He simply wanted an assurance that Tudor would "deal strongly" with indiscipline. He appreciated "the fine work" that Tudor and his men had done. He only hoped the police chief could "prevent further incidents of the kind" that generated scandals—like torching major cities.

The government, under pressure, had promised that General Strickland's arson investigation would spare no effort in the search for truth, and that the findings would be published. But Strickland's pointed criticism of the "higher authority" in charge of the RIC compelled a change of heart when it came to sharing his analysis with the public. Debate on how to handle it went on for months.

Within days of the Cork inferno, the Auxiliary section most responsible for the burnings had disappeared from Cork. K Company soon reappeared in Dunmanway, about forty miles to the west. They weren't there long before they handed the expanding ranks of their critics another propaganda coup. A double murder—two civilians, one of them a priest.

There are several accounts of what happened on a roadside just outside Dunmanway on December 15, but all agree that two innocent civilians were murdered in cold blood by an apparently drunk Auxiliary policeman. In the most persuasive version, a priest, Thomas Magner, seventy-three, and Timothy Crowley, twenty-four, the son of a local farmer, were helping a local magistrate whose car had broken down.[98] As two Auxiliary lorries were passing the disabled car, one pulled over. An officer named Vernon Harte climbed out and began to question the priest aggressively. Without warning, he ordered Magner to kneel and shot him dead. He then turned to Crowley and killed him with a single shot.

Lloyd George knew the killing of the priest could become a political disaster. It could validate the psychopathic image the Irish police had earned through their reprisals and generally wild behaviour. He insisted on a swift response to the murders. General Tudor, however, stood behind his policemen. The prime minister was rattled. He thought the declaration of martial law would mean swift military justice in which the murderous officer would be swiftly tried and executed. "The PM is furious," wrote Mark Sturgis, the assistant undersecretary at Dublin Castle, "and the whole cabinet has been badly frightened."

The Castle, however, also seemed to have some sympathy for the accused killer. Policemen, Sturgis wrote in his diary, "have undoubtedly been influenced by what they have taken to be the passive approval of their officers from Tudor downwards to believe that they will never be punished for anything." Should the killer escape the gallows on grounds that he was "raving mad," Sturgis wrote, "surely those responsible for leaving him loose on the world in charge of a party armed to the teeth should take his place in the dock."[99]

Harte eventually did stand trial for murder. The military tribunal found him guilty but insane. He escaped the gallows. "Those responsible" walked away again unscathed.

As the bloody year ended, whispers about a potential truce were becoming speculation in high places. Bishop Clune seems to have taken the murder of his nephew philosophically and continued his quiet peace diplomacy. Lloyd George summed up the options facing his government with uncharacteristic candour in cabinet: reject peace feelers and continue the campaign to "crush the embers" of revolt or, when there is an opening for peace, take it. As a bonus, talk of peace was another indication that his policy was working.

The prime minister was clearly in a relaxed frame of mind, demonstrated by his reaction to an incident while he was waiting for a train in Westminster Station one afternoon around that time. Two young men who were racing to catch the same train dashed around a corner, didn't notice he was there and flattened him.

They seemed like nice young chaps, apologizing profusely, brushing platform dust from his clothing as they helped him to his feet. Then they recognized him. Lloyd George? *Jesus Christ!* Suddenly, the prime minister's two bodyguards had their guns out, warning him to step away from the young men who'd knocked him down. These two strangers were, by their accents, Irish. Lloyd George instructed his bodyguards to put away the guns. "Irishmen or no Irishmen, if they were out to shoot me, I was shot long ago."

He might have been less sanguine had he known that the two Irishmen were IRA men visiting from Dublin. Frank Thornton, a member of the IRA assassination team, the Squad, and Seán Flood, from a Dublin active service unit, were in London laying plans to kidnap a dozen members of the British cabinet. The abduction plan collapsed and the two hit men returned to Ireland unscathed. Thornton wrote about the incident decades later. Lloyd George probably never knew how close he'd been to a personal calamity on that train platform.[100]

But the potential opening for peace talks closed quickly following the swift round-up and internment of five hundred Sinn Féin and IRA activists, including moderates like Arthur Griffith, shortly after Bloody Sunday. Lloyd George saw Griffith as an enemy that he could trust, but he hadn't been consulted before the arrests. Locking up a moderate like Griffith at such a crucial moment without prior political approval was "a piece of impertinence," and he would have "repudiated" it but for the implied insult to the military, which had done the rounding up.

It was a reminder to everyone involved that the road to peace was long and rocky and would eventually bear a price that was still impossible to calculate. After the First World War, peace had been a reward for a victory achieved at an unprecedented human cost. How much would the British people pay in blood to end the Irish War of Independence? How much would the Irish people pay to sever their connection to the British Crown, the British Empire? In fact, how much was the imperial connection worth—to anyone anywhere any more?

Part IV

WHIRLWIND

For my enemy is dead—a man divine as myself is dead;
I look where he lies, white-faced and still, in the coffin—I draw near;
I bend down and touch lightly with my lips the white face in the coffin.

WALT WHITMAN, "RECONCILIATION"

21.

THEY WERE SOLDIERS when they first met in India, and on that foundation, they built a lifelong friendship that transcended their differences. Churchill was irresistibly attracted to political intrigue. Tudor seemed to be repelled by the duplicity of politicians. The enduring mystery of the bond was that the friendship survived the complicated politics of the Anglo-Irish War and the challenges that followed it for both.

By the end of 1920, public attitudes about the struggle for Irish independence, in Ireland and in Britain, were unsettled and politically unsettling. The Archbishop of Canterbury, one of England's leading moral voices, was privately describing Ireland as "the worst sore on our body politic." In a November speech in the House of Lords, he specifically denounced reprisals. On April 6, 1921, twenty British Protestant prelates would denounce the government's reprisals policy in a letter to the *Times*.[1]

A commission of inquiry created by the British Labour Party to investigate the government's handling of the Irish conflict was preparing a report, to be released in January 1921, that would describe reprisals as "a cruel and inhuman policy." The Black and Tans and the Auxiliary police, according to the Labour Party, were out of control. They had become "a weapon which [the government] cannot wield . . . undisciplined and virtually uncontrolled."[2] The report concluded: "Things are being done in the name of Britain which must make her name stink in the nostrils of the whole world."

Photographs of Cork's commercial and administrative centre after the inferno of December 11–12 brought back scenes from the Great War. That British officers had turned the core of a major Irish city into a smouldering ruin was shocking, even for hard-liners, and another serious public relations setback for British policy in Ireland.

Questions screamed for answers and critics screamed for accountability, and the government had made a reckless promise to investigate the Cork fires and to make the findings public. The cabinet was now dithering because the army officer handling the inquiry had been bluntly critical of police leadership. He didn't name the name—but he didn't really have to. Even though General Tudor didn't light the match in Cork, he was the man in charge of the Auxiliaries who did. And to make matters potentially more serious, Tudor was, as usual, standing firm behind his officers.

In his own "supplementary report" on Cork, Tudor pointed out that no one claimed to have *seen* Auxiliary officers actually setting fires; or maybe some unknown person set a small fire that just spread and grew because of gas explosions; or maybe "Sinn Féiners" set the fires themselves, confident that "Crown forces" would be blamed.[3] But the official finding, based on an investigation by an army general, Peter Strickland, was unambiguous. Policemen set the fires. Police leaders were ultimately responsible.

Lloyd George and Churchill cringed. The reckless promise to make the findings public now had to be reconsidered. Even more politically sensitive was the murder of a seventy-three-year-old priest by the drunk Auxiliary on that roadside in Dunmanway. The image of an old priest bleeding on a roadside, a victim of a rogue policeman, had universal resonance that could shift political opinions. Especially in the United States.

British policy in Ireland was now threatened by a hovering American reality—the agitated interest of a large and influential

Irish migrant population. It is unlikely that Tudor considered the influence of the American diaspora to be significant, but the politicians, Churchill and Lloyd George, saw it as a major threat to the British strategy. Churchill even contemplated the possibility that the Irish war could escalate into a major international confrontation. A recurring nightmare for Lloyd George was that by continuing with reprisals like Cork and Dunmanway, the Irish conflict would eventually "create unpleasantness with the United States where feeling was dangerous." As he reminded members of the cabinet and his military and police commanders on December 29, "these were the kinds of incidents that drove a country like the United States to do something beyond discretion."[4] And he wondered, hypothetically, if it was time to throttle back the violence. What about a truce?

In a rare show of unanimity, the generals of the army and the police told him a truce was a bad idea. The reprisal strategy, controversial though it was to many, was delivering results. In the most likely scenario, the IRA—considered by the generals to be stumbling—would use a pause in the war to recover and reload, which was a bad idea when a clear-cut victory could be just around the corner.

Lloyd George wanted to schedule an election in Ireland as soon as possible. Home Rule—the Government of Ireland Act—was on the books and there were two new Irish parliaments waiting to be born. Ulster was anxious to elect members to a new parliament; the Ulster unionists wanted a vote as soon as February. The south of Ireland was ambivalent. Two parliaments in Ireland meant de facto partition, which the nationalists were dead set against. But it was crucial to persuade Sinn Féin that political partition, and the new Irish parliaments, north and south, represented the only hope for an honourable exit from a war that they were, inevitably, going to lose. Could there be an election with a war on?

The generals told the prime minister they were confident the war would soon be over. General Tudor, and Greenwood too, argued that southern Ireland might be sufficiently pacified to enable a free election by the end of February, and they put their optimistic prediction on the record.[5] But Tudor was certain that the enemy would be on its knees in four months, by the end of April.

The senior army generals agreed that a clear victory in the armed struggle was a realistic possibility. Just keep the pressure on. The chief of the imperial general staff, Sir Henry Wilson, was sure that if the government had the guts to extend martial law to all of Ireland, "the decent peasant" who made up "eighty to ninety percent" of the Irish population would be on side within six months.

General Macready, who was usually in agreement with Sir Henry, was also confident of victory but would not commit to a specific timeline, only that "the terror would be broken if martial law was spread all over the country." Hamar Greenwood was convinced there could be free elections in the spring—in May, at the latest. After that, the Irish and the British politicians could get down to serious treaty talks, and there seemed to be little doubt where that would lead. A ceasefire was a bad idea and, more to the point, unnecessary, in the view of Lloyd George's warriors. The alternative was an escalating war. Temporarily, of course.

Backing up his Black and Tans, Tudor now had eighteen companies of Auxiliary policemen, all seasoned combat veterans, all commissioned army officers in their past careers, patrolling the Irish countryside in the service of the Crown. His people were more mobile now, with trucks and cars soon to be joined by eighty armoured vehicles. "Six months ago," he told the cabinet on December 29, "the police were living behind sandbags and wire entanglements, they were boycotted and life was altogether intolerable; but now things were quite different and they could move about freely, and with the exception of ambushes, they were practically out of danger."

The military and the chief of police were ready to do more to get this miserable conflict over with. The overarching policy was working. Persuaded by his top advisers that the good guys were winning on the ground, Lloyd George was able to defer his political anxieties.

22.

THE OPTIMISM OF January 1, 1921, had evaporated by January 24, when Hamar Greenwood ruefully reported, in a weekly summary of "outrages," that it had been "one of the worst on record." There were forty-two attacks on police and soldiers that week, eleven policemen killed, five of them in "cold-blooded, cowardly assassinations."[6]

On January 20, at Glenwood, County Clare, about thirty Volunteers ambushed ten RIC policemen and killed six of them. Two were wounded and two escaped. The IRA men gathered up all the weapons and ammunition and fled into the surrounding countryside. The retaliation came swiftly: that night Michael Brennan, one of the attackers who was hiding on a mountainside, counted thirty-six burning houses in the district.[7]

Earlier that day, in Listowel, three IRA men had shot Tobias O'Sullivan, the RIC district inspector, just outside his home in sight of his wife and a child. He was on his way to lunch.

O'Sullivan had impressed the police chief when, as a sergeant in charge of the RIC barracks in Kilmallock, he had fought off a prolonged assault by five IRA units in which two policemen were killed. He and five other officers were wounded. One IRA man, Liam Scully, was shot to death during the siege. General Tudor awarded O'Sullivan a medal and a promotion for his bravery. The IRA marked him for assassination to avenge Scully's death. Two earlier attempts to shoot him failed before they brought him down in Listowel on January 20.[8]

The late December predictions of swift victory had been blithely premature. As historian Peter Hart has written, the IRA was shaken by martial law but "recovered by tightening its security and its hold on host communities. Lost leaders were replaced, activists still at large went on the run and went further underground (literally where dugouts were built), arms were moved and better hidden, larger and more vulnerable flying columns were broken up and a savage war was launched on suspected spies and informers."[9]

Both sides wanted peace. But both believed a precondition for even talking about peace was more bloodshed—victory through violence.

In theory, martial law in Munster should have meant a lower profile for the police, less focus on Tudor's leadership, less attention to the lack of discipline in the Black and Tans. But the martial law in force in January 1921 was a far cry from what the army generals had hoped for. The police and the army had almost equal status. Police discipline was still the responsibility of senior police officers in the RIC and the Auxiliary Division. The police could still launch independent operations. Black and Tans and Auxiliaries were still conspicuous and still "wild" on raids.

General Tudor had no plans to change his fighting style, taking note of but then ignoring the prime minister's implicit instruction to avoid the messier reprisals. From Tudor's point of view, the messages about discipline would have seemed to be political performance. The officer who had gained renown as one of Britain's most effective "fighting generals" either didn't understand what the prime minister had said on December 29, or he understood it better than anyone else. As Tudor heard Lloyd George, the prime minister wasn't asking for a change in tactics, only suggesting that the Black and Tans should be more aware of the political consequences of their enthusiasms.

While Lloyd George still seemed to be a fan, Tudor must have felt a growing chill from his Dublin colleagues. There was now a palpable squeamishness among his critics in the Castle as they learned more about the realities of fighting guerrillas with tactics the RIC had borrowed from them. Fire with fire. Ambush with ambush. Terrorism with greater terror. And yet, General Tudor seemed to be unwilling to rein in the violence lest too much "discipline" compromised the safety and effectiveness of his policemen.

"Stories are buzzing about as usual of the almost childlike simplicity of Tudor," Mark Sturgis wrote in his diary on January 13. "He does not consciously deceive but his belief in all that's good of his Black and Tans and his inability to believe a word against them is super human." Tudor, seemingly insensitive to squeamish politicians, carried on, supporting RIC officers with a zeal approaching moral blindness.

When a Black and Tan was accused of killing a civilian while robbing a pub in Balscadden, County Dublin, in February, Tudor seemed indifferent. "Curiously," David Leeson, the Canadian historian, would write years later, "the highest-ranking police officer in Ireland, the chief of police, Major General Henry Hugh Tudor, seems hardly to have concerned himself with such matters, despite being responsible for the recruitment of thousands of Black and Tans and Auxiliaries."[10]

The case was straightforward. The accused policeman was identified by witnesses and arrested shortly after the killing. He was tried by a military tribunal and sentenced to death. The sentence was, however, soon commuted to life imprisonment. After serving less than nine months of his life sentence, he was released.

By comparison, the case of an IRA Volunteer named Patrick Casey, who had killed no one, was prosecuted with chilling speed. Casey was caught with weapons near the scene of a bungled ambush in County Cork on the afternoon of May 1, 1921. By dinnertime next evening Casey had been charged, tried and convicted by a military tribunal, sentenced to death and shot by firing squad.[11]

Martial law, in theory, would deliver unity of command in Munster and clarity of legal jurisdiction. But the political designs of Churchill and Lloyd George guaranteed that no aspect of the Irish War of Independence was ever straightforward.

Martial law had cleared the way for a more aggressive role by the military in the martial law area—the six counties of Munster province, and two in neighbouring Leinster. Official reprisals by the army were now allowed in these counties, and military officers were quick to take advantage of their new authority. On December 29, 1920, in Midleton, County Cork, soldiers destroyed six houses in retaliation for an earlier ambush there.

The Lloyd George cabinet had been uneasy about "burnings," preferring "gunning" as punishment for IRA outrages, viewing scenes of smouldering homes and businesses as potentially more offensive to liberal sensibilities than the cold-blooded murder of suspected terrorists. Nevertheless, between January and June 1921, there would be 150 such reprisals in the martial law area—the bombing and burning of homes suspected of providing cover for attacks on British forces. At the same time, the army was stepping up the gunning.

On February 20, near Clonmult village, County Cork, members of an IRA active service unit found themselves surrounded in a rural cottage near where they'd been training for about a month. Security was lax. Two of the men, sent to a nearby spring to fill water bottles, spotted soldiers, tried to run back to the farmhouse and were shot down as they ran. Five rebels later burst out through the one door of the house and tried to shoot their way to safety. Three were killed, one got away, one ran back inside.

The soldiers were soon joined by a contingent of twenty-five Black and Tans. After an hour-long siege, the soldiers set fire to the house. Fifteen men inside the cottage soon surrendered, dumped their weapons and walked outside, hands up—according to their version of events. "We were lined up outside an outhouse with our hands up," one survivor reported years later. "The Tans came along and shot every one with the exception of three." An army officer, belatedly but firmly, put a stop to the massacre.

The Tans actually shot seven of the men, point blank, in the face. Six died instantly. One, shot through the mouth, survived. An army officer took charge of eight survivors, all of whom would soon be tried in military courts and sentenced to death by firing squad. Two were shot months later. Delays and legal complications would eventually save the lives of the other six.[12]

In Dublin Castle, preliminary reports from Clonmult were a cause for celebration; it was considered "a very nice bit of work," as Mark Sturgis heard the story. The murder by the Black and Tans of six prisoners was either omitted from the narrative or buried in the details. The shootout was a welcome army victory at a time when wild policemen were too often dominating news about the war.

In mid-February another Black and Tans atrocity was raising eyebrows in Dublin Castle. It was a relatively old story by then, but Tudor's critics were now noticing events that a few months earlier would have been considered sketchy sidebars in the larger drama of the war. His Castle colleagues were now wondering how long the police chief could survive the behaviour of his men.

On January 5, people in the village of Clondulane, on the River Blackwater, downstream from Fermoy, had noticed a body tangled in debris on the riverbank. The corpse was badly decomposed but soon identified as Nicholas Prendergast, a former British soldier who, with his wife, owned the Blackwater-on-Vale Hotel in Fermoy. He had been drinking in a local bar on December 1, 1920, when he became involved in an argument with Auxiliary policemen who were also drinking there. They accused Prendergast of being an IRA supporter. He denied it but it didn't save him.

The Auxiliaries dragged Prendergast out to the street, battered him with rifle and revolver butts, knocked his false teeth down his throat, then threw him in the river, where he drowned.[13] His body vanished in the darkness. It would take two months for his story to become public.

Mark Sturgis described the incident in his diary on February 11 (misidentifying the Auxiliaries as Black and Tans):

> I have read today the account of the murder of an apparently
> inoffensive ex-soldier called Prendergast at Fermoy by unidentified
> Black and Tans—can see nothing against him except that he
> sometimes got drunk which I didn't know was a crime.
>
> A nasty rotten business—Hope to Gawd we get the fellows
> who did it and make an example.

It shouldn't have been difficult to get "the fellows who did it"— they'd been part of an escort travelling with General Tudor when a military vehicle broke down while passing through Fermoy. According to a local witness, many of the Auxiliaries were already drunk when they arrived in town. Tudor left them there while the lorry was being repaired and carried on to Cork. He would have had no problem identifying the culprits. Two Auxiliaries, A. K. Watson and E. S. Radford, were later charged with murder but were acquitted. As was frequently the case in military courts, being drunk or crazy was often an acceptable excuse for homicide.

———

A minor scandal on the night of February 10 offered a rare moment of amusement in the Castle—a team of Black and Tans raided and looted a prominent Dublin public house and stole liquor and cigars. The loot included three dozen bottles of champagne that had been consigned to Neary's pub for resale—by the Irish viceroy, Sir John French. The King's representative in Ireland was "in a black rage" over the loss and even more alarmed that the story of the theft might surface publicly. He gave instructions to Macready and Tudor to identify the culprits, but in total secrecy.[14]

The levity didn't last long. Castle officials also learned that day that one of General Tudor's senior Auxiliary officers, Captain W. L. King—who, along with Captain J. L. Hardy, had been implicated in the Bloody Sunday deaths of Clune, Clancy and McKee—was at the centre of another violent incident. He was the accused in two horrific murders in Dublin on February 9.

Patrick Kennedy, eighteen, had no apparent political affiliation, but when Auxiliaries stopped him that evening outside a Dublin Cinema, they found a poem in his pocket, allegedly about the death of Kevin Barry, the eighteen-year-old hanged by the British on November 1, 1920.[15] The Auxiliaries arrested Kennedy and another young Dubliner, James Murphy, twenty-five, whom they had stopped outside a nearby poolroom, and took them both to the Castle for interrogation. Officially, they were questioned, then released. The truth, when it emerged within days, would horrify the country.

Because they were released during a curfew, Captain King and two other Auxiliary officers volunteered to drive them home. They set off in a military vehicle but then stopped near Clonturk Park in Drumcondra. The officers led Kennedy and Murphy into a field, placed them up against a wall and shot them both.[16]

Kennedy died almost immediately, but Murphy lived long enough to give a statement to a Dublin Metropolitan policeman and, later, just before he died, to his brother, who swore an affidavit based on what he had been told. His affidavit was raised and read aloud in the House of Commons eleven days later.

According to Murphy's dying statement, the Auxiliaries brought him and Kennedy "into the field, put old tin cans over their heads, put them up against the wall, and fired a number of shots at them." The affidavit continued: "I believe Patrick Kennedy was killed almost instantaneously. My brother was hit through the tin can in his mouth on the right cheek, on the left cheek and through the breast. Having done this the soldiers [i.e., Auxiliaries] left them and went away."

In Dublin Castle, Mark Sturgis recorded in his diary, on February 12, that he had reliable information that independent witnesses were ready to come forward. "K [Captain King], an auxiliary Co Commander is said to have been there and a man in civilian clothes with two revolvers who did the principal shooting. I don't know but if true it should go near to breaking poor Tudor."

General Frank Crozier, senior commander of the Auxiliaries, was faced with two horrendous challenges on the evening Kennedy and Murphy were murdered. He was already on his way to Trim, County Meath, about thirty miles northwest of Dublin, to investigate another rampage by his men. It was also about an incident of looting in a pub, but this one wasn't funny.

A large contingent of Auxiliaries had appeared in Trim earlier that evening and invaded a shop, ostensibly in search of hidden ammunition. The business happened to be owned by a unionist couple, until then sympathetic to the British cause. The Auxiliaries found no ammunition but "helped themselves liberally to the drinks in the shop, then stripped the counters of a side of bacon, ten chickens, two bags of candles, a quantity of condensed milk, two hundredweight of sugar, bottles of milk, whisky, rum, ale, champagne and twenty-three bottles of brandy. They also robbed the till of five sovereigns."[17] Then they moved upstairs, where they stripped the beds and pillaged dressers for jewellery, dragged the loot outside and loaded it into military lorries. Before leaving, they insulted and abused the owners and their staff and, for good measure, damaged their pony cart and shot up their water tank.

When Crozier confirmed the details, he immediately dismissed twenty-one Auxiliaries and ordered five others to be charged and held for trial. But after reviewing Crozier's disciplinary action, General Tudor reinstated the twenty-one dismissed men.

Crozier threatened to resign, but someone in authority (whom he didn't name) assured him that the Auxiliary Division would be reorganized to make sure that he would never have to deal with the offending officers again. If Crozier went ahead and quit, he'd ignite a political scandal that would be damaging to everyone. The unnamed person also made a vague promise that when this little war was over there would be large rewards for the winners. Possibly a knighthood.[18]

Crozier never specified the source of the pressures and inducements, but it is not unreasonable to assume they came from his commander, the police chief. In any case, he was unpersuaded, and he quit. Then he blew the whistle. He made inflammatory statements to the London press. He spoke with an opposition politician, Joseph Kenworthy, a Liberal critic of the Lloyd George coalition. In the aftermath, major newspapers called for Hamar Greenwood's resignation.

This public controversy reflected badly on Dublin Castle. Even if General Tudor was unable to control the wild men, he was obliged to seem to try.

The top bureaucrat in Dublin Castle, John Anderson, was outraged by what he was now hearing—stories, like the murders in Fermoy and

Drumcondra, that he had never heard before. He admitted to Mark Sturgis that he had only recently discovered that "such things . . . went on in more than very isolated cases."

Anderson was so unsettled he was thinking about resigning. And he seems to have wasted no time making his displeasure known to the police chief. Sturgis reported in his diary the next day: "[Tudor] is really hard hit, poor devil. Jonathan [Anderson] gave him an awful doing last night after we got back . . . and told me he hadn't a word to say."

Sturgis, in his diary, fretted on February 25: "L'affaire Crozier almost monopolizes attention. This beauty who is, I am sure, more truly responsible for indiscipline in the Auxiliaries whom he commanded than anybody else, has seized a golden opportunity to resign posing as . . . a glorious martyr. Poor simple Tudor has been carted again."

There was a note of sympathy in the reference to "poor simple Tudor"—implying that he was becoming a victim of rogue policemen and deceitful politicians. He was, in fact, caught in an impossible conflict of loyalties—to the officers under his command and to the minister for war who, in an act of faith based on long-standing friendship, had entrusted him with a mission that might have been too much for anyone.

From General Tudor's point of view, the timing was potentially disastrous. As the controversy in the second half of February threatened to consume him, his friend Winston Churchill, his political protector, was no longer British minister for war.

Churchill's change of jobs in mid-February had by then been in the works for six weeks. Early on the morning of New Year's Day, Lloyd George had asked him if he would accept a new portfolio. The country needed a stronger hand in the Colonial Office, and the prime minister wanted him in the role. Churchill was uncertain, but six days later he agreed to take the job.

Churchill would remain part of a high-level cabinet committee on the Irish "situation," but Tudor's personal connection to the War Office was now broken. He didn't know the new war minister, Laming Worthington-Evans, a political nonentity compared to Churchill. Before his promotion to the War Office, Worthington-Evans had been secretary for pensions, then minister without portfolio. General Macready was quick to seize the moment.

On February 14, the day Churchill moved on to his new assignment, Macready wrote to the undersecretary, John Anderson. "I saw Tudor last night and I think it would be wise if you made sure that he now cuts himself adrift from Churchill, now that the latter has left the War Office, and can have no connection of any kind with him."[19]

Macready complained that in the Military Law Area, the police were supposed to be under the control of the military but persisted in behaving as though Munster had become a kind of shooting gallery for "their amusement." A week later, he wrote the War Office about police indiscipline, renewing his long-standing arguments for martial law throughout all of Ireland.

Macready's conversations with Tudor also seemed to have a sharper edge. Macready told the police chief he was aware of efforts by a prominent policeman to undermine the prosecution of the Auxiliary officers who had murdered Kennedy and Murphy. Captain Jocelyn Hardy, who reported directly to London Special Branch intelligence officials, was attempting to "intimidate witnesses" in the murder trial of his friend, the Auxiliary commander W. L. King. Tudor's reply to Macready was defensive.

Macready grumbled that Tudor, once again, was irresponsibly attempting to excuse criminal behaviour by his men. "Tudor, of course, has a cock and bull story about the two men who were killed being rabid S.F.s [Sinn Féin members] but I have very grave doubts on that point."

The case against King and two other Auxiliaries seemed solid
until military judges declared Murphy's statement to the Dublin
policeman who found him near death in Clonturk Park to be hear-
say and inadmissible. Murphy's brother's affidavit was contradicted
by obviously perjured testimony from Auxiliary policemen who
swore that Captain King was somewhere else when Kennedy and
Murphy were shot.

Their evidence was implausible, and it contradicted earlier sworn
statements, but it was sufficient to save King from a firing squad. He
and the other Auxiliaries were eventually acquitted of the charge that
they had murdered James Murphy. There were no charges brought in
the death of Patrick Kennedy. It was a blunt message to the army and
the bureaucrats in Dublin: King and Hardy, through their connections to the deep intelligence establishment in London and the police
chief's office in the Castle, were untouchable.

On his last day in the War Office, February 14, Churchill wrote to his
closest friend and confidante, his wife, Clementine, that "the Irish
question . . . has been getting more grave in the last few weeks, and
the confident assertions of Hamar Greenwood and the military do
not seem to be borne out by events."

Clementine was on a holiday in France and replied two days later
with advice that would, in the months ahead, inform a fundamental
change in her husband's attitude toward the Irish struggle. She wrote,
underlining several words for emphasis:

Do, my Darling, use your influence now, for some sort of
moderation or at any rate justice for Ireland.

Put yourself in the place of the Irish. If you were their leader,
you would not be cowed by severity and certainly not by reprisals
which fall like rain from Heaven upon the just and the unjust.

You say that the confident assertions of Hamar do not seem
to be borne out by events. It makes me blush to think that men
of the calibre of yourself and the PM should have listened to a
man of the stamp of Hamar who is nothing but a blaspheming,
hearty, vulgar, knock-about colonial.

It always makes me unhappy and disappointed when I see you
inclined to take for granted that the rough iron-fisted "hunnish"
way will prevail.[20]

The impact of her words would soon become apparent inside the
Lloyd George cabinet, where her husband would continue to exert a
powerful but gradually moderating influence on Irish policy.

23.

BY FEBRUARY 28, the reality of martial law was unmistakeable for
anyone who heard the crash of gunfire inside the Victoria military
barracks in Cork in the early hours of a day that would begin and end
with violent death.

Churchill and Lloyd George had frequently complained that
rebels all too often got away with murder. They once found it dis-
graceful that there had been no "hangings" as punishment. As of
February 1921, that a firing squad would now be substituted for a
hangman, and for crimes far less egregious than murder, might have
reassured impatient politicians, but the executions would resonate
more deeply among ordinary people.

Cornelius Murphy, thirty-one, convicted by a military court for
possession of a loaded gun, was the first to step before a firing squad
that month, on February 1. On the morning of February 28, six men,
one by one, would follow in his footsteps. The executed men were all

in their twenties, the eldest twenty-six. Seán Allen, a twenty-four-year-old shoemaker, had been convicted and sentenced by a military tribunal for carrying a revolver and incriminating literature. The other five had been caught while preparing for an ambush near the village of Dripsey, in County Cork, in late January.

Cork came to a standstill on February 28. Crowds gathered early outside the walls of the military jail while grim British soldiers stood watching. Women, including the mothers of the condemned, huddled in a cold drizzle, kneeling before a makeshift altar propped against the prison wall, their prayers interrupted six times by fusillades from just inside. The executions fuelled emotions beyond grief for the loss of sons, husbands and comrades, inspiring a kind of rapture as new martyrs entered Irish history.

Mary Collins, an activist in the women's movement, Cumann na mBan, and sister of the IRA leader Michael Collins, would later try to describe the "wonderful patience and heroism, almost to the point of elation, displayed by these bereaved mothers . . . The reaction no doubt came later but that day they each felt it a privilege to have raised a son for God and Ireland."[21]

The condemned men went to their deaths, according to the priest who accompanied them, "like schoolboys to a holiday."[22] Their comrades in the IRA were less rapturous and forgiving. That evening, in a ninety-minute shooting spree in Cork, IRA Volunteers killed six members of the British army in retaliation for the six executions.

Before martial law, being arrested, for most, meant being inconvenienced. Perhaps a thrashing or, at worst, internment. New penalties under martial law meant that possession of a weapon or a seditious document, or being caught in an act of rebellion, like an ambush, almost inevitably meant death. In consequence, the stakes for Sinn Féin and the IRA were significantly higher. A betrayal, always risky for a traitor when discovered, now sparked a merciless response as both a punishment for the accused and a warning for the unwise and the misguided. The incident at Dripsey, on January 28, became a graphic lesson for anyone in any doubt about the cost of treachery, no matter how well intentioned the betrayal.

The Dripsey operation had been carefully planned and involved about sixty IRA fighters who undertook two weeks of practice near where it was supposed to happen. Because of its scale, the operation was soon common knowledge locally. Mary Lindsay, the sixty-year-old widow of a local businessman, who was both a Presbyterian and a staunch loyalist, decided to prevent it. She first told the military. Then she told a local priest to inform the ambush team that the military knew what they were up to and they should just pack up their weapons and go home. "You save your people, and I'll save mine," she told the priest, at the end of a discreet discussion in the back seat of her car.[23]

The military listened to Mrs. Lindsay. The IRA brushed off the warning from the priest, whom they didn't like. He was known to preach against the rebel cause, so they considered him a closet unionist. They should have listened. By the time they realized that the warning had been genuine, the soldiers were all around and all over them. One IRA man later died of wounds he received that day. The military captured eight others, six of whom were sentenced to death.[24]

When the IRA discovered the full story behind the failure of their ambush, they kidnapped Mrs. Lindsay and her fifty-year-old chauffeur/butler, James Clarke, and offered to exchange them for the lives of the condemned Dripsey prisoners. The military ignored them. The hostages, Mrs. Lindsay and her driver, were doomed.

When Frank Busteed, the IRA officer who had overseen the aborted Dripsey ambush, told Mrs. Lindsay that she and Clarke were about to be shot, she was dismissive. He offered a five-minute reprieve for them to say their prayers. She replied, "We do not want any favours from you . . . We have made our preparations before now."

Mrs. Lindsay was, Busteed reported later, "physically exhausted," but when told she was about to die, "she never blinked an eye . . . I'll say this for her," he said, "for bravery, she was excellent."

Her employee wasn't as resigned to death as she was. As Mrs. Lindsay stumbled bravely through the darkness of the night toward a shallow grave, James Clarke could barely walk. Busteed forced Clarke to drink *poitín* (homemade whiskey) to calm him down. Even then, Clarke was unable to stand and had to be propped up on his knees to be shot.[25]

On March 12, Frank Busteed led the IRA team that burned down Mrs. Lindsay's house in the village of Coachford, County Cork.[26] Possibly in an act of retribution, on March 14, four British intelligence officers raided the home of Busteed's mother, Nora, in Blarney. They dragged her out of bed and threw her down a flight of stairs. Nora Busteed was found the next morning on the floor of her living room, having suffered a broken back. She told the servant who found her, "Tell Frank one of them was a man with one arm." She died the next day.[27] (In 1974, Busteed would claim that he'd eventually tracked down and killed three of the men believed to have caused his mother's death.)

Since the Restoration of Order in Ireland Act, proclaimed in August 1920, the gallows and the firing squads were now part of the official government response to outrages by the rebels. In Cork, under martial law, the condemned were shot. Elsewhere they faced death by hanging. For many of the people facing trial and, potentially, death, reasonable doubt was no sure guarantee of an acquittal.

On March 14, six IRA men were hanged in Mountjoy Prison in

Dublin between 6 and 8 a.m. One, Patrick Moran, a thirty-three-year-old bartender, was accused—wrongly, he would claim up to the end—in one of the Bloody Sunday murders. Moran could have escaped with two other prisoners in a breakout on February 14 but was so certain that he would be acquitted that he stayed behind and let another inmate take his place. He fatally misjudged the unilateral finality of most military trials. He and Thomas Whelan, twenty-two, who was also implicated in the Bloody Sunday killings and who also had a persuasive alibi, were hanged together, the first of the six to die on the gallows that day.

Patrick Doyle and Bernard Ryan had been picked up with two other Volunteers, Thomas Bryan and Frank Flood, after a failed ambush in Drumcondra on January 21. The only fatality in the ambush was another IRA man. The four were charged with high treason, found guilty and condemned to death. Doyle and Ryan were hanged together at 7 a.m., March 14. Flood and Bryan followed them to the gallows one hour later.

Even when the lives of high-ranking military officers and policemen were at stake, the military justice system was impervious to persuasion, prayers and threats. On April 16, 1921, Major Geoffrey Compton-Smith, thirty-one, an army officer stationed in County Cork with the Royal Welch Fusiliers, was buying a newspaper and a package of cigarettes in Blarney when he was spotted by some IRA men, one of whom was Frank Busteed. They seized him and for two weeks shuttled him around the countryside, finally settling in a remote hideout known to rebels as "the cottage"—or to the bloody-minded Frank Busteed, as "the death chamber." The IRA offered to release Major Compton-Smith in exchange for the lives of four Volunteers scheduled for execution on April 28. The army refused to bargain.

Compton-Smith didn't seem surprised. When his captors told him that he would be shot, he thanked his executioners for their hospitality. He and his guards had passed the weeks they'd been together chatting about history and politics. They had a singalong one night and he amused them with a rebel ballad.

In a letter to his regiment, Compton-Smith wrote that he wanted his death to "lessen rather than increase the bitterness which exists between England and Ireland." And, he assured his army comrades, he had been treated "with great kindness."

Maurice Brew, a member of the firing squad that shot Compton-Smith on the morning of April 30, described the major's final moments in a statement decades later.

> When removed to the place of execution, he placed his cigarette case in the breast pocket of his tunic and asked that, after his death, it should be sent to his regiment.
>
> He then lighted a cigarette and said that, when he dropped the cigarette, it could be taken as a signal by the execution squad to open fire.

After several puffs, he held the cigarette up briefly, then dropped it. As instructed, the firing party shot him.[28]

Gilbert Potter, forty-three, had joined the RIC at the age of twenty-two. He was captured during an IRA ambush in April 1921. Thomas Traynor, a thirty-nine-year-old shoemaker, had been arrested on April 5 after a Dublin City shootout and was accused of murdering a policeman. He was tried by a military court and sentenced to hang on April 25. The IRA offered to exchange Potter for Traynor. The military refused. When the IRA man died on schedule in Mountjoy Prison, Potter was informed that he, too, must die.

James Kilmartin, second-in-command of the unit holding Potter in the Waterford countryside, had grown fond of him.

He was a very gentlemanly, nice kind of man and though he seemed fanatically attached to what he considered to be his duty, he also admired our adherence to duty and the service of our country as we saw it.

We put it to him unofficially that we would allow him to escape provided he gave us his word of honour, in which we trusted, that he would take no further action against us. He appreciated our reliance on his honour . . . yet he would not give his word as required by us, but said he must do his duty as he saw it.

On "the dark night" of his execution, Potter was "marched up to where the newly opened grave was on the hillside." A two-man firing party shot him. Potter fell. There was silence for a moment, then Potter called out, "I am not dead." One of his executioners then "stepped over to him and administered the final shot."[29]

General Macready and his senior commanders had achieved what they'd been asking for, martial law in Munster, military justice everywhere. But it didn't change much on the ground, where paramilitary policemen and republican guerrillas were engaged in what amounted to a murder competition.

The army, however, seemed to be having significant success in military courtrooms, enforcing extraordinary laws as judges, juries and executioners. Kevin Barry's execution, in November 1920, had been shocking because death, as a legal penalty, was still unusual. Between February and June 1921, there would be twenty-three such deaths.

For the hard-liners, like Tudor and Macready, Churchill and Lloyd George, the executions were reassurance to soldiers and policemen. In Dublin Castle, Mark Sturgis hoped that the executions would now proceed "with greater despatch," avoiding delays that gave enemies "time for all sorts of petitions and propaganda." He wrote, "It seems to me the most curious attitude of mind of these people that while it is their proudest boast that they repudiate British authority and that they are fighting the tyrant, no sooner is anyone of 'em caught than the prayers that he may be let off pour in without shame."[30]

"Due process" in military courts was meant, theoretically at least, to take the place of rough justice in the Irish countryside. In the public mind, however, deaths by firing squad and hanging were merely added to the list of government reprisals.

24.

THE END OF February 1921 marked the halfway point on the schedule promised as the new year began by Tudor and Greenwood—a clear military victory by the end of April. But peace on Britain's terms seemed ever more elusive. Public opinion was shifting as outrage and reprisal blurred in the public mind into a dismal spectacle of colonial violence on England's doorstep.

There was more muttering in the Castle. The comments were prudently non-specific, but General Tudor was obviously being talked about in private. Mark Sturgis felt sorry for him ("he is such a nice fellow"), presumably believing the general had been led astray by the prime minister's macho notions about how to fight the IRA. Tudor, the good soldier, listened to Lloyd George and did as he was told, but maybe too enthusiastically.

February 15 was the beginning of a new parliament, with the reading of a throne speech; Lloyd George could expect a grilling in the House of Commons afterwards. So the day before, he sent for Tudor to help him prepare for questions. After Tudor showed up, they huddled and then, a few hours later, with the police chief watching from the Commons gallery, Lloyd George gave a master class in obfuscation when he was, as expected, asked about Ireland. High on the list of questions: the December fire that wiped out central Cork, and a rampage by policemen in Mallow, County Cork, a few weeks later.

On the night of January 31, an IRA team accidentally shot and killed the wife of a police inspector at the Mallow railway station instead of her husband, whom they'd been aiming for. Local RIC constables rampaged through the town, descending on the station, where they rounded up suspected perpetrators who were actually railway employees just coming off shift. They immediately killed an eighteen-year-old locomotive cleaner. Three other railwaymen died later of their wounds. Another six were wounded but survived.

Lloyd George, coached by his police chief, managed to deflect questions about Mallow. He quibbled about the gory details and claimed that the dead and wounded men were all likely supporters if not members of the IRA. He emphasized the tragic death of the police inspector's heroic wife, who, he claimed, had thrown herself in front of her husband to save his life. On the subject of Cork, he denied that there had ever been a promise to make public the official report on the causes of the fire. There had merely been a promise to consider it, and it had been considered. On the plus side, the Auxiliary company blamed for starting the fires had been dissolved, with seven officers dismissed and a senior man suspended. End of story.

No questions were raised about the criticism in the report about the police chief, because, at that point, no one knew about it. Instead, Lloyd George praised the efforts of the police force. People were "delighted to see this reign of terror being broken up," he declared.

Ireland wants it. Ireland needs it . . . I know there will be
unpleasant incidents, but I have seen the men who are in charge,

and I have great confidence, not merely in their courage, their capacity, their determination—I feel confident that order will be restored to Ireland, and, with order, liberty.[31]

Perhaps a more accurate version of political reality had unfolded earlier that day at a private club not far from parliament where the Irish undersecretary, John Anderson, was having lunch with Lloyd George's confidant and fellow Welshman Tom Jones, who was also deputy secretary to the cabinet. Jones was closer to Lloyd George than anyone else around him, with the possible exception of Frances Stevenson, the prime minister's secretary and mistress, and in later life his wife. Jones and Lloyd George shared a deeper bond than politics or love—an intense consciousness of their common ethnicity as Celts. When unusual discretion was required, they would communicate in Welsh, a Brythonic Celtic language that was impenetrable for anglophones and even Gaelic-speaking Irishmen.

Tom Jones seemed to understand the fragility of the relationship between Lloyd George and General Tudor. He understood how swiftly political support for the policy of reprisals could change to disapproval when aggression no longer served the larger political objective—negotiation and reconciliation on British terms. From Anderson's point of view, talking to Jones was as good as talking to the boss.

Anderson was frustrated with the continuing political management of the Irish conflict. Among his frustrations was that senior politicians, such as Hamar Greenwood, Winston Churchill and Lloyd George, seemed indifferent to all misgivings about Tudor and the RIC.

Jones's written recollections of the noontime conversation confirm that he privately agreed with Anderson. In his eyes, Tudor had a talent for double-talk. While he said he agreed with official criticism of indiscipline among the Black and Tans and the Auxiliaries, it seemed clear that he was privately encouraging their bad behaviour.

At least he wasn't doing much to stop it. Jones wrote: "Tudor would agree that steps ought to be taken to deal with these [disciplinary breaches] but Anderson's advisers were satisfied that he took another line when he met his men."

It was beyond frustrating for the bureaucrat who was officially responsible for the behaviour of the police, Jones noted. "Anderson had the feeling that whenever Tudor came over to see the P.M. he returned very much strengthened in his policy—that even if not in words yet by atmosphere and suggestion the P.M. conveyed his encouragement to Tudor."[32] Significantly, Tom Jones didn't disagree with anything he was hearing from the senior bureaucrat in Dublin.

As Anderson and Jones expected, General Tudor went back to Dublin much encouraged by the time he'd spent with the prime minister, and even more committed to his heavy-handed mission. The general might have been less cheerful, however, if he'd been able to see just a few days into the future when, on February 25, Lloyd George would give a more candid political evaluation of the police in a stern private letter to the Irish secretary, Hamar Greenwood.

The prime minister was blunt. He was unhappy with the state of discipline in the Royal Irish Constabulary and its auxiliary force. "Accounts reach me from too many and too authoritative quarters to leave any doubt in my mind that the charges of drunkenness, looting and other acts of indiscipline are in too many cases substantially true."

The public, he wrote, were shocked and sensed that "there is something wrong." He didn't mention Tudor, but for now, he was holding Hamar Greenwood responsible for finding a solution for the most conspicuous problem. Discipline. The Black and Tans.

As you know, I have given to yourself and to your subordinates my full and unswerving support. But it is vital that the violence and indiscipline which undoubtedly characterises certain units of the RIC should be terminated in the most prompt and drastic manner. It is weakening the hands of the executive.

It was conventional political protocol to delegate an awkward job to someone lower in the pecking order, another politician who was under one's control. And that's what Lloyd George did, explicitly assigning ownership of the problem to Greenwood.

I rely upon you to take such steps immediately as will convince both public opinion here and in Ireland that you are determined that the RIC shall recover that great reputation for discipline that it has always held, and which is essential if your policy is to continue to receive the support of Parliament and public opinion.[33]

Greenwood would now have the daunting job of reining in the RIC, leaving the prime minister, for the moment, with the flexibility to shift and shuffle and, when necessary, reassure the police chief as the situation on the ground evolved.

Tudor, insensitive as he was to political subtleties, continued to assume that the rough behaviour of the Black and Tans and the Auxiliaries was exactly the strategy that senior members of the cabinet required, even if they were frightened by the messy details.

One of Greenwood's solutions, implemented a few days later, would be a mysterious new appointment to the Dublin Castle team—an official who would be sarcastically described by Mark Sturgis as "a tutor for Tudor." Colonel Ralph Umfreville would become the RIC's "discipline officer," whose duties seemed to be defined entirely by his title. Discipline. How he might achieve the elusive outcome that everyone claimed they wanted would be up to him.

The "tutor" was a political compromise—General Macready had suggested the position and the man who filled it. Macready had been lobbying for overall control of the Irish war—martial law for all of Ireland, his panacea for all strategic challenges. Unity of command would give him the clout to deal with the discipline problems that, in his mind, were undermining the entire British war effort. He wasn't going to get it. But, sensitive to rising public criticism, the cabinet consented to installing a Macready surrogate in Tudor's office.

Umfreville's success at improving discipline is probably best measured by the unfolding of events in Ireland afterwards. There is no evidence to indicate that General Tudor was even aware of his existence.[34] Even as Umfreville was moving into Dublin Castle in early March, Black and Tans were rampaging through Carrick-on-Shannon in retaliation for an IRA ambush. They trashed the offices of a local newspaper that was considered too sympathetic to the independence movement and burned a building used by a local rowing club. Two nights later, on March 7, masked men believed to be Auxiliaries murdered three Sinn Féin supporters in Limerick. Two of the victims were moderate Sinn Féin politicians—Mayor George Clancy and ex-mayor Michael O'Callaghan—in a community that had already been largely "pacified" by force under Tudor's chosen RIC commissioner, General Cyril Prescott-Decie.[35]

Asked, in the House of Commons, about the Limerick murders, Lloyd George repeated speculation that the victims died at the hands of the IRA because they were too moderate. But the killers were unwise enough to leave witnesses—including the victims' wives. Máire Clancy had seen one of the death squad members on previous police raids at her house and at the home of O'Callaghan.

On the night of the murders, the killers had moved freely through the streets of Limerick after curfew, unchallenged by the policemen who saw them before and after they had methodically dispatched three unsuspecting enemies. The third victim was a well-known IRA activist. A British journalist and author, Richard Bennett, investigated the Limerick murders decades later and managed to contact two former Auxiliaries who had known and worked with the alleged leader of the death squad.[36]

Just past midnight, March 10, in Thurles, County Tipperary, masked policemen killed two IRA men in a reprisal for the deaths two days earlier of two suspected police informers. One of the victims of the police reprisal, Laurence Hickey, suffered a broken neck when thrown down the stairs before a policeman shot him dead. William Loughnane was still in bed when shot. A third IRA man survived multiple bullet wounds that night.

And there were disturbing signs that Macready's soldiers were now openly adopting some of the terror tactics of the Black and Tans. Also on March 10, in Nadd, County Cork, the army captured five IRA men while they were sleeping in a local "safe house" and decided to shoot them without the formality of a court martial. The army officer in command selected a firing squad, then told the captives they could make a run for freedom. Two managed to escape, but three were shot dead running for their lives.[37]

In mid-March, General Tudor blatantly overstepped what seemed to be his limitless authority by approving reprisals in Westport, County Mayo, and in Clifden, Galway—both outside the martial law area. The reprisals, inconveniently, happened at a time when tentative conversations were once again under way between the Castle and Sinn Féin moderates about how to end the conflict, perhaps by starting with a truce.

Retaliating for the murder of two policeman in Clifden on March 16, the next day a raiding party made up of police and soldiers from Galway swarmed into what was ordinarily a quiet town well beyond the battlegrounds of Munster province. They burned sixteen houses and dragged a local Sinn Féin supporter from his bed, escorted him outside and killed him.

Moderates in Dublin Castle saw this reprisal as an outrageous vigilante incident. The Sturgis diary entry for March 31 reads: "Personally I know of no law, other than Martial Law, which does not obtain in Galway, under which this can be done and I have referred to London for instructions."

March was shaping up to become the bloodiest month so far in the Irish war. On March 11, at Selton Hill, County Leitrim, a joint force of police and military caught an IRA ambush team by surprise and killed six of them as they tried to run away. A rebel survivor described "the enemy as they swarmed over the place pounding our dead or dying men . . . with the butts of their rifles."[38]

Tudor was asked by London "somewhat tersely," according to Sturgis, "to explain the reprisals in Westport and Clifden." There is no surviving record of his response, but by the end of March, Lloyd George obviously realized that his political exposure to the behaviour of the Black and Tans was becoming perilous. Even King George V had joined the growing ranks of critics of the RIC.

On March 28, Sir Henry Wilson noted in his diary, after speaking with the King, that His Majesty clearly wanted to eliminate the Black and Tans entirely and, based on conversations with senior army officers, he had a negative opinion of the police chief. King George wanted to know who had appointed Tudor anyway. The criticism of the police and specifically of General Tudor must have been music to Sir Henry's ears: General Tudor, he told the King, was "a man of no balance, knowledge or judgment and therefore a deplorable selection for his present post." But Sir Henry assured His Majesty that Tudor was, nevertheless, "a gallant fellow on service."[39]

King George was also critical of General Macready, but Wilson wasn't going to let that negative opinion stand unchallenged. He blamed Macready's deficiencies on the politicians, a class of people he contemptuously referred to as "the frocks."

In a matter of days, it would seem, the King's critique had registered with Hamar Greenwood, who arranged his first frank discussion with Tudor about the state of discipline in the RIC. Before the conversation ended, Greenwood, presumably with the blessing of the prime minister, threatened to fire the police chief. On April 3 he was able to assure Lloyd George, "I've told Tudor that discipline must be maintained or he and certain subordinates must go. He is a gallant man and it is hard to be blunt with him, but he appreciates the position."[40]

Tudor took Greenwood's lecture calmly because he knew that, notwithstanding threats and political uneasiness, his job was safe. Lloyd George was struggling to manage two competing strategies, talking peace while making war. The war was messy, but it was the messiness that was motivating reasonable people to look for ways to end it. On the war front, for the time being, it would be business as usual.

The fragmented and supposedly undisciplined performance of the RIC might have been horrifying to vulnerable politicians and even the King, but the reality was that the policemen had learned the worst of their offensive tactics from the enemy, and those tactics were undeniably effective.

Before long, Tudor would be obliged to accommodate political squeamishness. But not just yet. The Irish War of Independence was a "guerrilla war," and Tudor had learned the hard way that a response to a guerrilla enemy requires guerrilla thinking and guerrilla tactics. General Macready's unity of command was a recipe for failure. Discipline rooted in orthodox obedience was often fatal for any soldier or policeman facing an opponent whose discipline was an implacable extension of personal idealism.

On March 19, Tom Barry, the rebel commander at the Kilmichael massacre of Auxiliaries four months earlier, and himself a veteran of the British army, was leader of an IRA active service unit preparing for action near Crossbarry, County Cork. He had 104 fighters but not much ammunition—about forty bullets for each rifle. He had recently recruited a piper to raise martial enthusiasm and morale during combat.

Barry had decided to ambush a British army force nearly three times the size of his own. By daybreak on St. Patrick's Day, March 17, he'd had his men in place. The enemy, however, had somehow got wind of what he was up to, and so he had to call the ambush off. But Barry kept his men together, waiting for another opportunity to strike.

He was still in the area on the morning of March 19 when scouts informed him of large troop movements nearby—a total of 1,200 soldiers and 120 Auxiliaries, not only heading in his general direction but clearly looking for him. Barry now had to make a choice: cut and run or stand and fight. He was outnumbered ten to one, which, in his mind, seemed a reasonable ratio.

Before dawn, a motorcade of military lorries crept slowly along country lanes as troops on foot searched houses, barns and bogs, hassling sleepy citizens, arresting anyone who raised suspicion. The troops were soon coming at Barry and his men on three sides. A normal impulse would have been to scatter, run, hope for a miracle. Tom Barry decided to attack the encirclement. He found the weakest point and caught the army by surprise.

Under a barrage of IRA gunfire at close range and assaulted by screaming Irish battle music from the bagpipes, the soldiers broke and fled, running for their lives. Barry could then have safely withdrawn his force. Instead, he gathered up the weapons and ammunition left behind by the retreating soldiers, deployed his men in defensive positions, and waited.

The soldiers returned in three more waves, fought briefly, then withdrew. When Barry tallied the results, three IRA men were dead and several wounded. In the official British record, eight soldiers died and four, including two officers, were wounded. In the heat of victory, Tom Barry surveyed the aftermath; he later wrote that "British corpses were strewn" on the Crossbarry road and crumpled in the fields around him.[41]

The most successful guerrilla leader of the century, Mao Tse-tung, compared guerrilla fighters to "innumerable gnats which while biting a giant both in front and in rear ultimately exhaust him. They make themselves unendurable as a group of cruel and hateful devils, and as they grow and attain gigantic proportions, they will find that their victim is not only exhausted but practically perishing."[42]

In March 1921, General Tudor would have grudgingly agreed with him, as would, no doubt, Winston Churchill. Later in life, as prime minister during the Second World War, Churchill would embrace Mao's basic guerrilla strategy, instructing subordinates to "pester, nag and bite" to break down their adversaries, and to "improvise and dare" in the relentless pursuit of victory.[43]

25.

BY APRIL 1921, Lloyd George had a daunting to-do list on his desk. The war was getting in the way of governance. He had to activate two new parliaments in Ireland: one for six of Ulster's counties, another for the remaining twenty-six. He hoped the parliaments would establish mature, enduring dialogue and eliminate the ever-present spectre of civil war. To achieve this, there had to be an election to fill the seats created in the two new legislatures. But could there be an election in the middle of a rebellion?

On March 8, Lloyd George had been cautioned by Lord Midleton, a prominent southern unionist, that an election during the revolt would have "gravest consequences" for southern Ireland. Having studied the situation on the ground, Midleton could report "no progress in restoring order." If anything, the violence was three times worse than it had been eight months earlier. "If the resistance in last July is indicated by 100, the resistance can now be put at 300," he warned. The fighting, in the estimation of Hamar Greenwood, was "ferocious."[44]

Still, an election was a necessary starting point for a long-term solution to the Irish problem. But which should come first—an election or a ceasefire? The British prime minister's acute political instincts were telling him that it was time to shift from coercion to persuasion. But the transition had to be gradual, accomplished subtly. Premature persuasion could be interpreted as weakness. A temporary pause in the bloodshed to enable an election could give the enemy an opportunity to recover their diminishing enthusiasm for the fight.

Maybe back in December 1920 there could have been an honourable ceasefire that would have set the stage for a peaceful settlement. But British bravado had eliminated that possibility. Now the war was probably unwinnable for both sides without a terrible and politically unpalatable escalation. The British had the military muscle. Under Tudor, the RIC had proved that the police force had the manpower and the nerve to outlast the IRA in the ugly struggle that, from his perspective, the republicans had started.

If they wanted an assassination contest, Lloyd George now had his own team of competent assassins. If they wanted war by ambush, his Black and Tans and Auxiliaries would give them ambush. And, slowly, the army was learning guerrilla tactics too. His military courts were dispensing heavy-handed justice, turning the death penalty into another weapon. Nothing gets the attention of an Irishman like a gunshot or a noose.

At the same time, the nagging about RIC discipline was beginning to show some results. By April, Greenwood was able to report a dramatic change of attitude in the RIC. "I saw all the heads of the police . . . from all parts of Ireland. They report that both Auxiliaries and RIC are cheerful and working well. I made it plain to each that his personal position depended upon the discipline of his men."[45] He insisted that the RIC was actively culling officers "on the grounds of their unsuitability."

Perhaps the threat to fire the police chief was having an effect. Or perhaps General Tudor could now appreciate that there were limits to the public's tolerance of violence, and that tolerance was wearing thin with death squads active on both sides and the killings seeming more gratuitous and more frequent. It had become a ghoulish competition over who had the greatest appetite for murder, the greatest tolerance for grief.

Finally, Lloyd George and his cabinet decided: there would be an election in May, a critical first step toward either resolving or redefining what a previous prime minister was now referring to as the "loathsome war" in Ireland. Even the Castle was now in favour of the vote.

There were risks in allowing a free campaign for a democratic mandate. Sinn Féin would make unreasonable demands that would be popular with both the radicals and moderates. A republic. Complete independence from Great Britain and her Empire. Wild financial demands. What if Sinn Féin swept the south of Ireland?

The most dramatic sign of a change in the political environment was Winston Churchill's retreat from his customary belligerence. In a cabinet meeting on April 27, perhaps with Clementine's reasonable voice still resonating in his head, Churchill made the most persuasive point in favour of proceeding with a May election. "How are you worse off if all returned are Sinn Féiners than you are now? If Sinn Féins are returned," he argued hopefully, "a wave of feeling will sweep over the nationalist world that the movement is passing from murderous to non-murderous, from non-constitutional to constitutional."

The prime minister was skeptical. "There is a hard side to the Irish nature," he lamented. "They are greedy beyond any other part of the United Kingdom. They will drive a hard bargain."[46]

But discussion of the pros and cons of holding an election was academic now. There were other, more consequential issues to talk about. On May 12, the cabinet came to grips with the contentious question of when or whether to negotiate a ceasefire. A former prime minister, Arthur Balfour, concisely spelled out one side of the prevailing disagreement: showing a desire for peace would be "a sign of weakness," he argued. "Naturally we should wish to end this uphill, sordid, unchivalrous, loathsome conflict—we are sick of it. [But] I want no further concessions made, for if made they'll only strengthen the Republicans."

Lloyd George was opposed to truce talks. And it was the almost unanimous view of Dublin Castle that truce talks would only embolden the enemy. Surprisingly, the most powerful advocate for a ceasefire during what would be a long and often passionate debate was Churchill. He saw no downside. Truce talks in December 1920 might have been a tactical mistake. But not in the spring of 1921. "Now our forces are stronger and better trained; auxiliaries are stronger; the police are extending their control over the country." The government's position was "vastly better," he declared. But the government advantage might be temporary.

A prolonged conflict would be "very unpleasant . . . we are getting an odious reputation; poisoning our relations with the United States; it is in our power to go on and enlist constables and Black and Tans; but we should do everything to get away to a settlement. An offer by the government to take off pressure is an act of good faith."

In the end, they voted. Churchill was one of five cabinet members who voted for a truce. Lloyd George was among the nine who opposed it.[47] The shooting would continue even as the politicians planned for voting.

Candidates were chosen on May 13 and 14 and, as expected, the only people nominated in 124 of 128 constituencies in southern Ireland were members of Sinn Féin. In the days leading up to the election, to be held on May 24, fears that political violence would disrupt the process seemed well founded.

Ominously, on May 14, the IRA shot and killed ten soldiers and eight policemen in various, largely spontaneous, encounters. On May 15, in Gort, County Galway, an ambush by Volunteers killed four people, including the RIC district inspector, Cecil Blake, and his wife, Eliza, who was nine months pregnant. But it was significant that neither outrage resulted in reprisals by either the RIC or the army.

Election day was quiet. There were four killings, but none by the IRA. (In one, a jealous Black and Tan shot his Irish girlfriend dead in a drapery store in Monaghan. He was charged with murder, tried by a military court and acquitted.) As predicted, Sinn Féin swept the south, claiming 124 of the available 128 seats. The other four, a block assigned to Trinity College Dublin, went to unionists. The election in the north was also quiet, the outcome dominated by Ulster unionists.

The day after the election, May 25, was not so quiet in the south and would be remembered for an IRA attack that, while it succeeded in its main objective, would be recorded as a rare triumph for the Auxiliary Division of the RIC—and for their commander. It was an attack conceived by the Sinn Féin president, Eamon de Valera, who, after spending most of the war in the United States making friends and raising money, was anxious to prove his worth as a military strategist. De Valera didn't think guerrilla warfare was sufficiently spectacular. He wanted a display that everyone would notice, and on May 25 he got it, with an attack that destroyed the

Dublin Custom House, an ancient symbol of Britain's imperial prestige in Ireland, a repository for government documents dating back to the seventeenth century.

Mark Sturgis watched the fire from Dublin Castle: "[To] burn the finest building in one's own capital city simply because the hated Saxon uses it as a government office and as an anti-British propaganda stunt seems sheer lunacy."

It was a coordinated effort by at least 120 of the IRA's best fighting men in Dublin, including the entire Squad, the IRA's assassination specialists, and a large part of the city's #2 IRA Brigade. It was supposed to be a twenty-minute operation. Last-minute complications added another five minutes, and that slowdown proved disastrous for the IRA.

They intended to clear the building of employees, set fires in offices on every floor, and be out the door by 1:20 that afternoon. They were still inside the Custom House at 1:25, when two companies of Auxiliaries and a military unit, alerted by gunshots, arrived outside, guns blazing at rebel sentries. The Custom House was quickly surrounded.

When the siege was over, five IRA men were dead and three wounded. Several civilians died in the crossfire. Worse for de Valera, between eighty and a hundred of the IRA's most effective warriors were arrested, and most of them remained in jail for the next six months—effectively out of action for the remainder of the war against the British.[48]

On June 1, Sturgis reported that, according to people he was speaking with, "the anti-extremist feeling in all classes in Dublin has grown very strong" since the burning of the Custom House. And it was growing even stronger because of a bloody incident in Youghal, a seaside town in east Cork.

On May 31, British troops in Youghal were marching to a local firing range for target practice. Their regimental band had been in the area on a goodwill visit for the previous two weeks and had performed daily concerts for appreciative civilian audiences. The "band boys," as they were known, were marching with the soldiers, playing martial music, when a roadside bomb exploded. The musicians took the main force of the blast. Seven of them died almost instantly. Twenty-one musicians and soldiers were wounded. The youngest fatality was a fifteen-year-old bugler. The attack soon became a sensational news story all over Britain.

Now there was a legitimate "Shinner" government, an official entity that British politicians could talk to, face to face. No longer did they need to communicate through surreptitious back-channel nods and winks and nudges. It was time for a serious attempt to end the conflict by negotiating an honourable exit for both sides. There was one practical problem, though—an obvious lack of enthusiasm among the republicans for constructive dialogue. At least not yet.

The Irish had a strategy for war. But planning for a ceasefire and negotiation raised a basic political dilemma. Sinn Féin leaders had sworn allegiance to an ideal, an autonomous republic; peace talks would present them with an implacable demand for a binding oath of loyalty to the British Crown. Hanging over the political conundrum were inescapable existential questions about the IRA's readiness for all-out war if Sinn Féin diplomacy should fail.

In June, the Lloyd George cabinet set a deadline calculated to accelerate the process—July 14, Bastille Day in France, potentially provocative for revolutionaries but less inflammatory than his cabinet's first suggestion of July 12, a day of triumphal Protestant celebration in Ulster. If, by July 14, there had been no progress toward a ceasefire and real peace negotiations, there would be all-out war in Ireland.

26.

ON THURSDAY AFTERNOON, June 2, 1921, somebody shot Ormonde Winter as he drove away from Dublin Castle. He was about to take a puff on a cigarette when it happened. From the trajectory of the bullet, he calculated that it was aimed at his head. The bullet struck his hand. It hurt like hell, but it also seemed to cheer him up.

Mark Sturgis went to see Winter in the hospital that evening and found him to be "still cheerful," though "he expressed regret that . . . his hand hurt most damnably . . . [and] that he hadn't killed the man who shot him." He told Sturgis that the crowded streets "seemed to empty by magic when the shots and a bomb or two began to fly."

For Winter, who thrived on peril, the episode would have been a welcome break from the tedium of recent weeks, when, like almost everyone in Dublin Castle, he had seemed uptight or, as the always merry Sturgis remarked in his diary, "nervy." Winter would have been further cheered by a meeting at Downing Street earlier that day to discuss the Irish situation.

The Irish Situation Committee session at the cabinet conference in London had been a round of "what if . . ." speculation. What if Sinn Féin refuses to play ball? What if Sinn Féin's newly elected politicians decline to participate in the government's effort to find constructive solutions to the interminable hostility between Britain and Ireland? What if they flatly refuse to swear allegiance to the British Crown?

For almost everyone in the room at 10 Downing Street, the answer was simple: there will be more hostility. Hostility as the Irish had not seen it since Cromwell. Or since the Viking raiders. The hostility would continue until there was an unequivocal win for the British Crown and Empire. And to make the prospect very clear, Lloyd George emphatically and, for him, unequivocally spelled out a crucial feature of a future war. The next Irish war would also be "a policeman's job supported by the military and not vice versa. So long as it becomes a military job only, it will fail."[49]

He was responding to a theoretical question: how to resolve a perpetual conflict in relations between the military and civil arms of government in a state of martial law. Lloyd George was clear. Tudor's fighting style during the past year had won the confidence of the prime minister. The police, under Tudor, had done an effective job against the IRA, he declared, and there was no reason to believe the police could not do an even more effective job if the conflict were to go on indefinitely.

Lloyd George was growing weary of the constant complaints by army officers about the Black and Tans, the RIC and Tudor. "Every time I have seen Macready," he declared, "he is rather disposed to crab the police." According to the minutes from the meeting, "The P.M. expressed his strong resentment at the animus against the police constantly shewn by Macready . . . He went on to pay a tribute to the auxiliary police during the fire of the Custom House."

Churchill was listening carefully and couldn't resist throwing in his personal opinion as former minister for war and a friend of the police chief. He felt the army had let the country down. "Tudor and his men," on the other hand, had proven their abilities at "getting to the root of the matter quicker than the military." Lloyd George agreed with him.

It would take five more weeks of political manoeuvring, patient waiting and diplomatic pressure to get the Irish to the table, and it would require the ceasefire that the hawks on Downing Street and in Dublin Castle had resisted.

Plans for peace and war progressed on parallel trajectories for most of June 1921. While Tudor and Macready watched and listened nervously, Andy Cope, the most persistent peace advocate in Dublin Castle, was relentless, shuttling between the Castle and various Sinn

Féin offices, with frequent trips across the sea to Downing Street. There was a heatwave in June and, after one impassioned performance at 10 Downing, Cope reported that he was "pouring sweat," which might also have been a consequence of the pressure he was feeling. It was worth the effort, though, because the top decision makers were now listening and many of them agreed with him.

On June 15, the cabinet's Irish Situation Committee discussed another memorandum, this one prepared by General Macready, laying out some hard truths about the road ahead in the absence of a settlement. He wondered how the government would react to the reality of all-out war. The bloodshed. How would they feel about charging Sinn Féin leaders with treason? Hanging them? Did the cabinet understand what was likely to happen in an all-out war? "Will they go through with it? Will they begin to howl when they hear of our shooting a hundred men in one week?" The backroom talks continued.

It was relatively quiet in the combat zones. There were shootings, but it felt like they were near the end of something. Perhaps a last chance for revenge or perhaps a reluctant sense of duty. Death near the end of conflict seems more poignant, more unfair.

That would have been a normal human response to the fate of three Englishmen out walking in the countryside near Clonmel, Tipperary, on June 19. Though they wore civilian clothes, they were unmistakably soldiers. They were carrying revolvers. They were unable to explain what they were up to, if anything. Ernie O'Malley, the senior IRA commander in the area, had to deal with them. He wrote about it later.

"Any officers we capture in this area are to be shot until such time as you cease shooting your prisoners," he told them.

"We have nothing to do with the shooting of prisoners," one said.

"This is not a personal question . . . my mind is made up about it. You will be shot at dawn tomorrow," O'Malley replied.

"Can you consider the matter?" one of them asked.

"You will have to consult your officers," another said. "You can't do it without authority."

"I happen to be in command of this area. This is my authority. It would be better to prepare your minds."

O'Malley described the scene as dawn arrived and they set out for the place of execution:

The sky lighted silvery grey, the wind dropped.

We reached the roadway. There was a wall in front of a church. The three officers were placed on the green grass edge of the dusty road. "Do you mind," I said, as I placed their handkerchiefs around their eyes. One handkerchief was of silk and claret coloured.

"No."

"This is good bye," I said.

They shook hands with the QM [quartermaster] and myself. Their hands were cold and limp. They shook hands with each other. The six men of the firing squad stood near the other side of the road.

"Are you ready?" asked the QM.

One of the officers nodded. They joined hands. "Goodbye old boy," they said, inclining their heads.

The volley crashed sharply. The three fell to the ground; their arms twitched. The QM put his revolver to their foreheads in turn and fired.

The bodies lay still on the green grass. We stood to attention. Then slowly we went up the hill across country . . . None of us spoke until we had crossed a good many fields where wind had snaked the rye grass.[50]

The bodies were discovered the next day. Their names, which O'Malley neglected to record in his account, were Robert Bettridge, twenty-one, from Devon; Walter Glossop, twenty-one, a vicar's son from Sussex; and Alexander Toogood, twenty, the son of a British army officer then based in India. Ernie O'Malley, a Dublin medical student when the Easter Rising broke out in 1916, after which he was forever politicized, was twenty-four.

Events moved quickly after June. Two new players became prominent in the conversations about a ceasefire: King George V and the prime minister of South Africa, General Jan Smuts. The King used his speech at the opening of the new Northern Ireland Parliament in Belfast on June 22 to appeal for all-Ireland unity and conciliation. The speech came as a tonic to a public wearied and depressed by centuries of anger.

Smuts, who helped draft the King's speech, opened talks with both sides. He had credibility with the Irish for having fought against the British as a commando in the Boer War. He was admired by the British for a relentless campaign against a German guerrilla leader in East Africa during the Great War.[51] He had made the difficult political transition from freedom fighter to imperial statesman. If the Boers could do it, there should be nothing holding back the Irish.

Smuts persuaded Lloyd George to talk directly to the Sinn Féin leadership. Then he went to Dublin on July 5 and persuaded the Irish leaders to listen to the English politicians. He spoke bluntly to Sinn Féin leaders, saying, "You have no force but a certain measure of public opinion and you will alienate it if you refuse this olive branch. For the first time, you have been invited by the P.M. unconditionally in the widest terms to explore conditions of settlement. It would be an awful blunder to refuse."

His second message was even more persuasive: The Boers had fought a three-year war because of perceived British "limitations" on their aspirations for national self-determination, for a republic. The outcome? "My country was reduced to ashes," he said. "If I can give you any warning it is to avoid that fate."[52]

The next day, July 6, in London, the cabinet once again considered the possibility of a ceasefire to enable direct talks with the rebels. Macready and Tudor were summoned to the cabinet room and asked for their advice. Both were adamantly opposed, arguing that a truce would be an admission of weakness. A truce would give the enemy an opportunity to refresh.

In the end, Macready agreed to "an open and formal truce." Tudor preferred a "tacit arrangement" rather than one formally declared. Lloyd George and Churchill agreed with Tudor that a "gentlemanly understanding" would be preferable.

Two days later, on July 8, General Macready ironed out the details at a meeting in the Mansion House in Dublin, with representatives of a new southern Irish government. The informal truce would start at noon on July 11.

Smuts warned Lloyd George that de Valera, president of the Irish parliament, Dáil Éireann, and president-in-waiting for a new republic, loved to talk and talk. De Valera would talk your ear off about Irish history, English perfidy, a millennium of Irish grievances. "My impression is they are people you can satisfy with phrases," Smuts said, perhaps to reassure the prime minister. Lloyd George said he wasn't looking forward to conversations with the Irishmen.

"The thing to do with people of this kind," Smuts advised, "is let them talk themselves out and then get to business. Let them talk themselves to the death."[53]

The two leaders met face to face for the first time on July 14. Much of their first conversation, as Lloyd George had feared, was focused on

Irish history. But the Welshman scored the first point in their cautious dialogue. On his arrival, de Valera had presented the British prime minister with a document whose title was an Irish phrase: *Saorstat Eireann*. When Lloyd George asked what it meant, de Valera could only reply, "Irish Free State."

Lloyd George agreed. Yes, but what does *that* mean? What is the Irish word for . . . *republic*?

While the Irish president was conferring (in English) with colleagues, Lloyd George launched a clearly audible conversation in Welsh with Tom Jones. He then turned back to de Valera and suggested they should agree that "the Celts never were Republicans and have no native word for such an idea."[54]

That meeting was the beginning of a graceful British exit from Irish politics. For Ireland, a new nightmare that would compromise the Irish dream of independence for generations was just beginning.

27.

THE CEASEFIRE PRODUCED a kind of limbo for both sides. People still died, from accidents, from suicide. There were still suspicious killings, but they were suddenly surprising once again.

IRA men got used to safety, to doing normal things. Sleeping in their homes, with their wives, their girlfriends. But there were provocations. The rebels unavoidably ran into people they had been keen to kill just weeks earlier. They encountered Tans and Auxiliaries in the streets. What then?

Michael Brennan, of the East Clare IRA Brigade, later described the unsettling sensations. "Meeting Black and Tans and Auxiliaries also armed was at first rather a nervy business and we circled rather than walked past each other, both parties becoming adepts at watching sideways and over their shoulders and keeping a right hand ready to pull a gun."[55]

What if they started shooting? Worse, what if they all started being friendly to each other?

The problem was unfamiliar and, at a deep level, it was unwelcome to the people who were looking after armies, the generals. The relaxation of vigilance made the generals uneasy.

Tudor might have been shocked to find a document on his desk on the morning of Wednesday, August 3, just twenty-three days after the beginning of the truce. The sixteen-page memorandum had been written by his secretary, William Darling, and described a chance encounter Darling had had with the enemy the night before.[56]

As he read, Tudor likely had to remind himself that the war was now in neutral. Hostilities on hold. But this sounded almost like sedition: Darling was describing an all-night binge with Michael Collins, the man who, just before the truce, had been the most wanted fugitive in the British Empire. Collins was officially Sinn Féin's minister of finance, but more importantly, he was the brains behind the armed struggle for Irish independence. Darling had to have been aware that Collins was also director of intelligence for the IRA. So, what the hell had Darling been doing in a well-known Shinner hangout, Vaughan's Hotel, in the wee hours of the morning? With Michael Collins?

Near the top of Darling's document, which he had dramatically titled "Night and Morning," Tudor saw a mention of Andy Cope. The "peace plotter," as Cope was being called around the Castle, was suspiciously cozy with dodgy people in Sinn Féin. Tudor continued reading.

"About 11.30 on Tuesday night," Darling wrote, "I was in my office when Mr. Cope came in and asked me if Colonel Elliott [RIC director of personnel and transportation] was about." Andy Cope wanted

Colonel Elliott to go with him to the scene of a car accident—a vehicle registered to the RIC had collided with a private car just outside Dublin. "I told Mr. Cope that Elliott was not in, or had gone to bed, but I offered to go with him. I got a gun and put on an overcoat and went downstairs."

The RIC car had "collided violently" with a taxi while driving on the wrong side of the road. The taxi was occupied by several Sinn Féin officials who were now stranded about two miles outside Dublin on the road to Naas. Cope and Darling found two badly damaged cars and half a dozen people standing on the roadside.

Cope agreed to drive as many as he could pack into his car to the city centre. Cope and Darling and four of the Sinn Féin people crowded into the police car. A "tallish man, clean shaven, wearing an overcoat," squeezed in beside Darling. On the drive, they spoke about the truce and "the great improvement" since it had begun, just three weeks earlier.

"As we drew near Dublin, his seat was uncomfortable, apparently, and he moved over nearer to me. As he moved, I said, 'Be careful, for I have a gun in my pocket.' It was then that he told me he was Michael Collins."

To maintain the truce, General Tudor, the police chief, had to keep reminding his people to stay calm. But he also had to keep them on their toes, alert, war-ready. The current atmosphere at Dublin Castle was making that last task difficult, given that Andy Cope was the senior bureaucrat in Dublin while Anderson was away in London, working with the government on a pathway to a treaty.

It was taking a long time to work out details. The generals were inclined to blame the doves in the Castle and the government for the slow pace. In persuading Sinn Féin to sit down at the negotiating table, they had raised false expectations. In late October, well on into the truce, Tudor complained to Mark Sturgis that peace was nice, but RIC "fighting efficiency" was being compromised by indecision. The war was only paused. It was more than likely that it would start up again.

It took the Irish until nearly the middle of October to send a team of negotiators to London. It came as no surprise that Collins was on that team. Less widely known was that he had to be practically dragged there, protesting all the way. He understood the challenge, the essence of negotiation, the likely need to compromise, the peril in concessions to Britain's adamant demand for continued Irish recognition of the Crown.

Darling seems to have been charmed by Michael Collins. The rebel had a sense of humour. He seemed to be fond of and knowledgeable about poetry. A poem that he especially liked was "Reconciliation," written by Walt Whitman after the US Civil War.

> On this subject he became very accessible, approachable,
> assenting to the suggestion that there might be brave and
> honourable men fighting in defence of what he believed to be
> tyranny, just as I might be prepared to admit that men who
> I thought were murderers and assassins might be misguided
> men believing themselves to be heroes and sterling patriots.

Collins had some surprising opinions about the British. He was bitter that Crown forces had abused his brother's wife, who he claimed had died partly because of the stress caused by harassment from the military and the police. Then, shortly after her death, during a reprisal on April 16, 1921, the army had burned down his brother's house, the home Michael Collins had grown up in, leaving John Collins and his eight children homeless.

He had "nothing very much against" the Black and Tans; "they did their business as they understood it. His quarrel was with their masters who kept out of the fight themselves but pushed the Black and Tans into it." But he seems to have excluded General Tudor from the category of those masters. Darling wrote, "He had no objection to Tudor except that he thought it a little hard that the British government should take one of their best fighting generals and put him up against the IRA."

The Auxiliaries, Collins declared, were "the finest fighting men in Ireland and . . . for them he had every respect. They fought hard but they fought fair and he admired them for it." Darling described Collins as, "on the whole, an agreeable, pleasant-looking man, full head of hair, fattish cheeks, general well-fed condition."

Darling continued, "When he speaks, he is very much moved, as for example, when he spoke of his brother's wife's death, his face assumed a very fierce expression. He purses his lips and half closes his eyes."

Collins had impressed him. "I am confident that he will be reasonable, clear-thinking, and quick to act," Darling wrote. "He certainly is much above the standard of the ordinary Member of Parliament in mental alertness and sagacity. He is nonetheless very young, not so much in years as in outlook."

As both Darling and Tudor had expected, when Sinn Féin and the government got down to hard negotiating on a treaty, Collins would be singled out for particular attention—and what seemed to be genuine respect—from both Churchill and Lloyd George. It wouldn't have surprised Tom Jones, the prime minister's friend and confidant, that the British negotiators quickly warmed to Collins. "I am sure the PM has a secret admiration for him," he had confided to a friend earlier that year. "He'll be canonised some day."[57]

As of November, negotiations were already bogging down. For the leaders of soldiers and policemen, it was enough to keep a man awake at night. The nightmare scenarios were unavoidable: resistance in the form of an endless guerrilla war in which the interests of nationalists and republicans would merge; a likely civil war between united Irish nationalists and an alliance of moderate unionists and hard-core Ulster loyalists backed by British forces. The cost in lives and property would be incalculable. The violence would inevitably draw international outrage and perhaps even intervention. The Irish diaspora was large, bitter, well-heeled and politically influential, especially in America.

At a cabinet meeting in September, Lloyd George had grimly commented that if war resumed, he hoped it would be "much more thorough than anything we have had yet and a complete smash-up of the revolutionists." By late November, it was looking like this dire outlook was turning into prophecy.

The elephant in the room was the Sinn Féin leader who wasn't in the room at all, Eamon de Valera, the president. The reason for his absence in London would feed speculation and controversy for years, maybe centuries to come. The reality was that de Valera had stayed in the game just long enough to realize—as Michael Collins had suspected—that the deck of cards on the negotiating table was stacked against the Irish from the start. So de Valera remained in Dublin, becoming a kind of backseat driver as a five-man team of newcomers to the arena of diplomacy, led by Michael Collins and Arthur Griffith, fenced with some of the sharpest minds and most experienced negotiators in the world. Griffith and Collins did their best.

Lloyd George had made it clear from the beginning that any treaty would require Sinn Féin to accept partition of the island. There were two political realities, north and south. To accommodate them both was a concession necessary to avoid a civil war involving Ulster. They all knew that, but a permanently fractured Ireland was still a bitter pill to swallow. Like it or not, Ireland would also become a member of the British Commonwealth, which would preclude its becoming a republic and would oblige the Irish to swear allegiance to the British Crown. But most other aspects of self-determination were up for grabs. Negotiations focused on finding a way around the two essentially symbolic requirements—partition and the Crown—while nailing down the fiscal and defence relationships essential for real nationhood.

There is no doubt that de Valera knew what they would be up against. Maybe if he had been there with Collins and the others, the Irish might have achieved more than they eventually got in the final treaty. But he wasn't. De Valera's absence from the London treaty talks was a decision, or a strategy, that future historians would call "bizarre" or, in one less restrained evaluation, "one of the most cowardly political acts in history."[58]

In the final hours of negotiation, members of the Irish delegation were faced with a grim set of options: accept an agreement that at best would offer a solid start on the road to republican independence or spark an all-out war. Talks reached an impasse on December 4. Lloyd George set a deadline: "war within three days" if the treaty wasn't signed by the night of December 5. It was a no-win prospect for members of the Irish delegation, who "had to sign and disregard whatever their Sinn Féin mandate said or, if they believed the Prime Minister, face the accumulated might of the British forces."[59]

There was even then the shadow of an outcome that would be worse—a civil war that would turn former comrades into deadly enemies and haunt the Irish independence struggle for generations. But at 2:10 on the morning of December 6, three of the five members of the Irish delegation signed the treaty.

In his comprehensive history of the process, *The Republic*, Charles Townshend summed up the political reality that was finally accepted by the key members of the Irish delegation, Michael Collins and Arthur Griffith: "The terms were disagreeable but they were not dishonourable—and there was no alternative."

Michael Collins would take the heat for the failure of the Irish delegation to win a total republican victory, and he knew it. As the ink dried on the document, Lord Birkenhead, lord high chancellor of Great Britain and one of the British signatories, turned to Collins and declared, "I may have signed my political death-warrant tonight."

Michael Collins grimly replied, "I may have signed my actual death-warrant."[60]

The deal left Ireland with basically the same national integrity as Australia, South Africa and Canada. As Collins would argue, it was a realistic starting point for future progress toward whatever status the Irish, as an independent people, wanted to achieve. Partition was a political reality, and it remains a flash point in relations between Ireland and Britain more than a century removed from the controversial treaty. The offensive but obligatory oath of allegiance to the Crown was, in the words of a later historian, "a mishmash of legal verbiage, making the oath almost meaningless."[61] Ireland would function as a "free state" until 1937, when a new constitution effectively established the status of a republic—though the Republic of Ireland would not become a political reality until 1949.

While the Anglo-Irish treaty was the best deal that anyone was going to get, it wasn't good enough for the hard-liners back in Dublin, among whom de Valera was soon a champion. His role would be to lead a violent struggle to destroy the treaty—a civil war with tragic consequences for Ireland and for Michael Collins, who would die in a shoot-out with anti-treaty forces, former comrades in the struggle against Britain, on August 22, 1922. Not incidentally, de Valera would survive to become perhaps the most successful Irish politician of the century.

On December 16, 1922, the British prime minister wrote a personal note to General Tudor, thanking him for his contribution to the satisfying outcome of the Anglo-Irish conflict. Lloyd George was effusive in his praise.

It is a great achievement that the Irish Free State is now a fact
and although they seem to be going through very difficult times,
I think they will make good.

It would not have been possible to bring the negotiations with
the Irish leaders to a successful issue had it not been for your
courageous fight for the Empire in Ireland.[62]

It was high praise, but also an acknowledgement that the government
strategy from the outset was not to defeat the rebels but to wear them
and the Irish people down until they could herd them into a diplomatic
arena where, in bloodless combat, the British diplomats would win.

Both sides left the War of Independence claiming victory, but
both sides were exhausted: the IRA physically, by the relentless ruthlessness of Tudor's forces; the British morally, because of the world's
response to British tactics. Both sides won and both sides lost. Ireland
would become a "free state." Britain, after centuries of strife, would
get out of Ireland but, at the same time, keep Ireland on a leash for
another generation, if not longer.

The hard reality was perhaps best expressed by the IRA commander
Florrie O'Donoghue, in a bitter retrospective contradiction of what
many Irish politicians called, at least in the early days, their victory.

British diplomacy had won what British arms had failed to
achieve. The dread shadow of disunity fell on a great national
movement. A chapter of heartbreak, bitterness, sorrow and
death was opened.[63]

For Ireland, for years to come, the British "victory" meant continued
conflict, the spectre of hostility that would linger over Anglo-Irish
politics for at least another century.

Lieutenant Tudor after service in the Boer War.
Courtesy John Davenport

Winston Churchill with his second-in-command, Archie Sinclair, in 1916, while serving in the 9th Scottish Division at the Western Front. *Churchill Archives*

Tudor at the end of the
First World War.
Courtesy John Davenport

King Leopold inspects the 9th (Scottish) Division.

Leopold, King of the Belgians.
Major-General H. H. Tudor, CB, CMG.
Flanders, November 7th 1918

General Tudor and the Belgian king, Albert 1, on November 5, 1918,
inspecting Tudor's 9th Scottish Division at Flanders. (The official
photo of the occasion incorrectly identifies the king as "Leopold"
and the date as November 7.)
The Rooms, Provincial Archives of Newfoundland and Labrador

General Tudor, at home with his family in England after the end of the Great War, demonstrates his fitness with a handstand in the garden.

Courtesy John Davenport

General Tudor in 1920, before he departed for Ireland and his most consequential war. His wife, Eva, clasps his forearm; his children are Helen, six, Harry, nine, and Margaret, twelve. His eldest, Elizabeth, is believed to have been the photographer.
Courtesy John Davenport

Harry, General Tudor's only son, was nine years old when his father left for Ireland.
Courtesy John Davenport

Black and Tans patrol, Dublin, 1920.
National Library of Ireland

Ormonde de l'Épeé Winter, deputy
chief and head of intelligence for the
RIC 1920 to 1922.

General Sir Nevil Macready,
General Officer Commanding,
British forces in Ireland.

Constable Jeremiah Mee led the "Listowel mutiny" of RIC officers protesting the recruitment of former British soldiers to bolster the ranks and fighting spirit of the Irish police. He later became a Sinn Féin activist, working closely with Countess Constance Markievicz and the Irish Republican movement.
Courtesy Fr. Anthony Gaughan

Col. Gerald Smyth, a close friend of General Tudor, and fellow officer in 9th Scottish Division on the Western Front—murdered in July 1920, by an IRA team in Cork.
Courtesy Fr. Anthony Gaughan

Tómas MacCurtain, Lord Mayor of Cork, and an IRA commander, shortly before his assassination in March 1920, in the early morning hours of his thirty-sixth birthday.
©National Museum of Ireland

Terence MacSwiney, his wife, Muriel, and their daughter, Máire, before his arrest and the beginning of his fatal hunger strike, in 1920.

Aftermath of a reprisal in Balbriggan, County Dublin, in response to the killing of a policeman in 1920. *©National Museum of Ireland*

Mourners praying at centre field, Croke Park stadium, where a player died, one of sixteen civilians killed by RIC Auxiliaries during a Gaelic football match, November 21, 1920. *American Commission on Conditions in Ireland, preliminary report, 1921.*

The RIC's notorious Auxiliary Company F lived and manned a guardroom near this area in Dublin Castle, the lower castle yard where three prisoners were murdered on the night of November 21, 1920, Bloody Sunday.
National Library of Ireland

Cork City business district on December 12, 1920, after it was burned and looted by members of the RIC Auxiliary Division in retaliation for an IRA ambush on December 11.
National Library of Ireland

On January 7, 1921, Miss Brown, of Meelin, County Cork, surveys the wreckage of her home after a reprisal by the Black and Tans.
National Library of Ireland

Tudor at Phoenix Park, Dublin, in 1921, with his policemen, including a company from the Auxiliary Division.

A nighttime British military patrol in Dublin, 1921.
©National Museum of Ireland

Policemen, Black and Tans and Auxiliaries mingle outside a Dublin pub after a rebel attack.
National Library of Ireland

The aftermath of an IRA attack on the Custom House, a repository of government records covering centuries of British rule, on May 25, 1921. *National Library of Ireland*

IRA fighters among nearly 100 captured by RIC Auxiliaries after their costly attack on the Custom House document centre in Dublin. *©National Museum of Ireland*

Elizabeth Tudor, eighteen, in 1923. A debutante who was presented to royalty a year earlier, she was coming to terms with the mysterious collapse of her parents' marriage.
Courtesy John Davenport

Lady Eva Tudor, estranged wife of Major General Sir Hugh Tudor.
Courtesy John Davenport

St. John's, Newfoundland, photographed from Signal Hill in October 1925, a month before Tudor's arrival.
The Rooms, Archives of Newfoundland and Labrador

Harry Tudor and his bride, Sonia Sawrey-Cookson, on their wedding day in 1945. Harry served in the RAF during the Second World War, with the rank of wing commander. In 1947, Harry and Sonia visited General Tudor in Newfoundland for a week-long stay.
Courtesy John Davenport

Tudor relaxing in St. John's in 1947. The photo was forwarded to Churchill by Sir William Darling who had served with General Tudor on the Western Front and later, at Churchill's urging, as Tudor's secretary in Ireland.
Churchill Archives

January 25, 1965. After three days of official mourning, Sir Winston Churchill is escorted through the streets of London for the last time by a military contingent including 104 Royal Navy sailors. An estimated 350 million people watched Winston Churchill's funeral on television.

A small graveside gathering after General Tudor's funeral in St. John's, in September 1965. The woman in black, fourth from the left, is Monica McCarthy, his companion-caregiver; the woman in front of her, speaking with the officiating clergyman, is General Tudor's friend, Carla Emerson Furlong.

Part V

THE
HOLY
LAND

"It is unlikely that the Arab, if handled firmly,
will ever do much more than agitate and talk."

TUDOR TO CHURCHILL, SEPTEMBER 21, 1923

28.

June 15, 1922, Victoria Station, London

IT WASN'T THE first time that Elizabeth, General Tudor's eldest daughter, had accompanied her parents to a railway station to say farewell to a father who was always on the move. But she found something ominous about this departure. Maybe it was just because she was older now, more aware of adult feelings.

Her parents seemed subdued. She could understand that. She could relate to the sense of loss that would wrap her mother in silence after her father had walked away, down the busy platform to the waiting train. Both mother and daughter would retreat into their own privacies as they watched him disappear yet again. But this time he seemed more vulnerable, perhaps burdened by the challenges of Ireland. He was limping, an old injury to his foot recently inflamed by a failed medical procedure. Maybe it was in that moment she felt the flutter of uncertainty: When, if ever, would he return?

Elizabeth Tudor, who had turned seventeen six months earlier, was at the beginning of her life as an adult woman. Or at least the beginning of the beginning. She was sure of that much. As of her birthday, she was now a debutante, which meant a year of celebration, marked by a formal introduction to the King and Queen near the end of June. She would spend the summer "doing the season"—being seen at events like the Royal Ascot races, the Wimbledon All England Tennis Championships, the Henley Royal Regatta, a series of formal gatherings, teas and luncheons, culminating in Queen Charlotte's Ball. She took these rites of passage for ladies of her social class seriously—as the highlight of her year, potentially of her life.

But by mid-June, a cloud of wistfulness was hovering, dimming all her happy expectations. Her father, barely home from Ireland, was needed in a place even more remote, a place she could barely imagine. Palestine. And he was leaving a week before her formal presentation to royalty. He couldn't wait. He had his marching orders, once again, from Winston Churchill.

The timing of his departure would resonate for other reasons, personal and historical. Within a week of the Tudors' sad farewells on the Victoria railway station platform, two IRA gunmen would assassinate one of Britain's most famous soldiers, Sir Henry Wilson, just outside his home in Belgravia. Elizabeth knew Sir Henry. Her father had introduced them. They'd occasionally had lunch together when she was attending school in London. She found him odd, eccentric, gruff but warm. The relationship between her father and Sir Henry was complex. She was in her teens and not all that interested in the politics, but she understood that much.[1]

The Tudors were a military family, accustomed to absences. But there was something unfamiliar in his absence after her father went to Ireland in the spring of 1920. The distance was more than geographical. It was existential. Elizabeth could feel it on his rare visits home. But she witnessed it, memorably, on an English golf course on a sunny springtime afternoon in 1922.

She'd shared her father's obsession with the game of golf from the time she could lift a club. And she had practised hard that spring so that she'd be ready to compete if and when he invited her to play. She was thrilled when he did invite her to join him for a round. The game was going well until they were on the fifth hole. There was a hedge to their right, and beyond the hedge, an open field. Suddenly a head popped up above the hedge, staring at them. In a flash, her father had drawn a revolver from his pocket and was aiming at the head, preparing to shoot, until she shouted that the head belonged to a worker at the golf course.

For her father, England was now as dangerous as Ireland. It would always be a place of peril for him, he explained, and unsafe for his family whenever he was present. On his advice, her mother kept a loaded revolver in her bedroom and, on one occasion, nearly shot her youngest daughter, Helen, who sometimes roamed around the house at night, walking in her sleep.[2]

Elizabeth didn't fully understand her father's role in Ireland, but she did know that the danger they were in was one of his reasons for going away again in the most important season of her young life. What she couldn't know was that this absence would last, but for brief interruptions, forever.

Ireland had changed her father fundamentally. Elizabeth could see it as clearly as anyone. He'd been a soldier when he'd married her mother, Eva Edwards, in late 1903, yet her parents had managed to create a family while accommodating the disruptions of colonial military service and then a four-year, all-consuming war.

While Tudor served in India and Egypt, his wife had made frequent extended visits. Elizabeth was their first-born. Their second child, another daughter, Mary Margaret, was born in India in 1907. By 1920, when General Tudor went to Dublin, Elizabeth was fifteen, his only son, Harry, was ten, and the youngest daughter, Helen, was only seven. But there were no family excursions to Ireland, and Tudor could only get leave to come home occasionally. And while he stayed in touch with Elizabeth, he was only rarely in contact with his wife and other children.

In later life, Elizabeth would have warm memories of a father she had known only sporadically. She remembered him giving her riding lessons on a pony when she was five, teaching her to swim, to dive. She remembered him busily taking notes in church during Sunday sermons, only to discover later that he was practising shorthand. Learning shorthand and foreign languages, she would discover, were initiatives he undertook to improve his prospects for promotion and, not incidentally, his army income.

For Tudor, his occasional encounters with his teenaged daughter would have underscored the sterility of life in Dublin Castle, where he was regarded as the leader of an organization that he was barely able to control. Or was he complicit in the behaviour of the Black and Tans and the wild Auxiliaries? Were their indiscipline and retaliation tactical? Was he truly a trusted friend of the minister for war, or was he being used by him and his shifty prime minister to front a politically unpalatable dirty war?

Too many people had to live in cramped accommodations in Dublin Castle, because it had become too dangerous for British public servants to live anywhere else in Dublin. The Castle was a place where people ate with weapons on the table; where at least five people in the police chief's office committed suicide under Tudor's watch;[3] where, for physical exercise, Tudor was limited to pacing back and forth in the shadows of the lower castle yard.[4]

The general would occasionally venture to a golf course, but only in the company of bodyguards. It was an indulgence he might have reconsidered after one of his Auxiliary commanders, John Alistair MacKinnon—who usually wore body armour and was accompanied by a bodyguard—was picked off by a sniper while putting on the third green at the Tralee golf course on April 15, 1921.[5]

The end of a war was always a time of great relief. In the general's professional experience, wars were over when someone, usually his side, won them. The Irish conflict was a confusing kind of war, one with no clear end and no clear winner. Even when the shooting was suspended, the diplomatic haggling left no opportunity for celebration, just anxiety, more uncertainty.

The question facing Tudor was where he could safely go after Ireland. What remained of the career he'd left behind in May 1920 and the life that he had put on hold? And then the man who had recruited him for Ireland surfaced again, with a scheme that would determine the rest of Tudor's life and the lives of the people closest to him.

29.

TUDOR ARRIVED AT Ramleh Aerodrome in Palestine just after noon on June 22, 1922. The last leg of his journey was by airplane. He was fascinated by flight. While in Palestine, he would be working closely with the British Air Ministry, the government department running the RAF, and he resolved to try to earn a pilot's licence.

His second-in-command, Colonel Angus John McNeill, a forty-seven-year-old career army officer, was waiting for him on the tarmac, studying the new commander as he alighted from the plane and hobbled awkwardly toward him on crutches. They didn't know each other well but had a lot in common. They were both veterans of large wars in South Africa and Europe. Both men had history with Winston Churchill. McNeill had more experience in the Middle East, but Tudor, having served extensively in Egypt, was fluent in Arabic. Under Churchill, they made a formidable leadership team, at least on paper. But paper, of course, rarely takes account of human nature, the most important factor in any fresh relationship.

The latest dramatic news from London—the murder of Sir Henry Wilson—had yet to reach them as they set out for the Arab village of

Bir Salem, which would be Tudor's main base of operations. By the time they met to talk business the next morning, June 23, it was the unavoidable topic of conversation.[6]

The murder shook everyone who knew Sir Henry, but General Tudor in particular. If Wilson had been targeted by the IRA, General Tudor wouldn't be far behind him on the list of people marked for elimination. Still, Sir Henry had been unafraid to speak his mind. Though he grew up in County Longford, in what was now the Irish Free State, he had strong political ties in the north. He'd always felt his hybrid status as a southern Irishman with credibility in Ulster entitled him to firm, sometimes extreme, opinions about how the whole country should be run. Republicans considered him a hard-line loyalist and a supporter of militant Protestants. And shortly before he was shot down on his doorstep in London, he had been linked to a plan to secretly enlist recruits from extremist Ulster paramilitaries for police work in the north, where a significant republican minority, mostly Catholics, remained militant.

General Tudor, unlike Wilson, had been wise enough to keep his mouth shut, at least in public, while he was in Ireland. Out of either modesty or prudence, he had suppressed his public profile. He didn't talk about Ireland. He didn't write about it either (and he never would). But he could not ignore his vulnerability as the commander of the hated Black and Tans.

There were angry, dangerous men, experienced killers, at loose ends in Ireland; many had already relocated to England. They didn't need permission to kill an enemy if they happened to bump into one, which is likely what had happened to Sir Henry Wilson. Random violence directed against people identified as enemies during the War of Independence was becoming commonplace. Two RIC officers had been murdered in Galway in mid-March 1922, while they were patients in a hospital. In April, in County Cork, it almost seemed like open season on Protestants suspected of having collaborated with the British. IRA gunmen tracked one suspected informer to New York and shot him down near Central Park.

But surely Palestine was far enough away from Ireland, England, even New York. Surely Tudor would be safe from Irish retribution here, surrounded by people like himself—British officers and bureaucrats, and nearly eight hundred of the best and bravest of his Black and Tans, who had accompanied him to serve in a new police force in the Middle East. Though there was some petty crime and random violence, and political tensions between members of the Arab majority and a growing Jewish population, compared to Ireland, Palestine was paradise.

In February 1921, only a week into his new cabinet posting as colonial secretary, Churchill was already floating the idea to create a force "very similar to the Royal Irish Constabulary" to replace British army units in the Middle East.[7] Britain had inherited Palestine from the old Turkish Empire after it was dismantled in the First World War. Britain had a mandate from the League of Nations to manage Palestine until its inhabitants could run their own affairs, which could take a while. The task was complicated by an official British undertaking in 1917 to help establish "a national home for the Jewish people" in Palestine, where the Arab population outnumbered Jews by more than five to one.

The Balfour Declaration predictably caused a stir in the non-Jewish world, and even among some Jews in Britain. Edwin Montagu, the only Jewish minister in the Lloyd George cabinet in 1917—and the secretary of state for India—had publicly declared Zionism, the force behind the creation of a Jewish homeland, to be "a mischievous political creed." It would, he believed, create an incentive for countries everywhere "to get rid of their Jewish citizens" by sending them to

Palestine. Which was also a problem because there were "three times as many Jewish people in the world as could possibly get into Palestine if you drove out all the population that remains there now."[8]

Of course, no one anticipated driving anyone out of Palestine, and the Balfour Declaration explicitly foresaw creation of a Jewish homeland while protecting "the religious and civil rights of the non-Jewish communities" already there. But anti-Zionist feelings ran deeply through British society and were blatant in the British army, now a mainstay of political stability in the Middle East. The general commanding British forces in the region, Sir Walter Congreve, had been bluntly critical, declaring Zionism a "detestable and odious policy."[9] He wrote:

> There are certain problems such as those of Ireland and Palestine
> in which the sympathies of the army are on one side or the other.
> In the case of Palestine, these sympathies are rather obviously
> with the Arabs . . . who have been the victims of the unjust
> policy forced upon them by the British government.[10]

The army wasn't the only source of anti-Zionist hostility. The Palestine police service was a predominantly Arab force and known to sympathize with Arabs when conflicts led to confrontations. Tensions were already growing before the Balfour Declaration sparked a sudden increase in Jewish immigration. Conflict was inevitable.

Churchill tackled the problem head-on. He would create a new Palestine gendarmerie with a better ethnic balance—one-third Arab, one-third Jewish, one-third other—and cut back the army presence. Churchill also had in mind a second paramilitary force, all-new and "all-white," to back up the Palestinian police. With Churchill at the wheel as secretary of state for the colonies, the British army and General Congreve would be out of Palestine. The system would run more smoothly and, most important, at a fraction of the cost involved in paying British soldiers to do police work in a place and among people they neither understood nor cared about.

Churchill pitched his ideas for a new security establishment in Palestine to Lloyd George on September 3, 1921. The prime minister optimistically approved the Churchill plan in principle, including the new all-British gendarmerie. It is likely that Churchill already had a plan as to where the new British police in Palestine would come from, given there was a paramilitary police force ready-made and soon to be redundant in Ireland.

On September 11, Churchill sent a telegram to General Tudor, informing his old friend that he was planning to assemble a new police force, modelled on the RIC and drawn mainly from the Black and Tans and the Auxiliaries, for law-enforcement duties in the Middle East. "Please begin to concert your plans accordingly and let me have proposals of a more or less detailed character," Churchill wrote. But he warned that Tudor should not yet raise the subject with his men, as it "might raise false hopes."[11]

Obviously eager for his next adventure, Tudor moved quickly. He was also keen to find safe employment for policemen who had served under him in Ireland. All he needed was a green light and he could begin recruiting.

By mid-November, Churchill was ready to inform Herbert Samuel, the British high commissioner in Jerusalem, of his plan to reduce the role of the British army, raise the profile of the Air Ministry—a key part of the Palestine security establishment—and create a bold new police presence in the region, a British paramilitary gendarmerie. He also promised that the new policing system would be run by a "pro-Zionist" commander.

Samuel, who had been one of the first observant Jewish cabinet ministers in Britain before he moved on to his role in Palestine, was all in favour of the Churchill plan. Unlike his Jewish colleague in the government, Edwin Montagu, Samuel had been an early advocate for a Jewish homeland. In 1915 he had written that "under the Turk, Palestine has been blighted . . . [and has] produced neither men nor things useful to the world." If it was designated a Jewish homeland, "Jewish immigration, carefully regulated, would be given preference so that in the course of time the Jewish people grow into a majority and, settled in the land, may be conceded such a degree of self-government as the conditions of that day may justify."[12] As the head of civil government in Palestine in 1921, Samuel was more subtle about such ends, but his appointment was a clear statement of British political intentions for the region.

By mid-December, Churchill's scheme had cabinet approval. There were political sensitivities from the start—the Irish connection would be controversial if the public knew about it, so official statements about the new police force would have to mute any references to Ireland or the Black and Tans.

The high commissioner acknowledged that including the Black and Tans could be problematic. "Their reputation, as a Corps, has not been savoury, and if any idea was created in the public mind in England or here that the Black and Tans, or any part of them, were being transferred as a body to Palestine, the new Gendarmerie might be discredited from the outset." But, "provided that the men selected were of good character," he saw no other problem with Churchill's plan.[13] On December 24, the Colonial Office Middle East Committee cautioned Tudor that while the new gendarmerie would be recruited and organized from RIC personnel, it was crucial that any "moral connection between the new force and the Black and Tans" be suppressed. They instructed him to avoid "the inevitable idea that we are importing into Palestine the traditions of recent Irish politics."

On January 5, 1922, members of the RIC were officially informed that their police force was about to be disbanded. Three weeks later,

RIC officers were told that applications for jobs with a new gendarmerie in Palestine would be welcome. Head constables and sergeants up to age thirty-five would be considered, though preference would be given to unmarried men under the age of thirty. They were looking for men "of superior education and first-class records."

As of May 16, General Tudor would be general officer commanding Palestine, for British and Indian military units. Wearing his military cap, he would be responsible to the high commissioner and the head of the British Air Ministry, adding the status of air vice-marshal to his army rank of major general. As director of public security, he would take charge of the new British Gendarmerie, drawn from veterans of the Irish conflict, of an existing Palestinian Gendarmerie, and of a conventional police force. He would, in this non-military role, report to the Colonial Office through the high commissioner in Jerusalem, Sir Herbert Samuel.

As military GOC *and* head of civil policing, he would have the "unity of command" he'd lacked in Ireland. The arrangement would, Tudor clearly anticipated, forestall bureaucratic complications. His relationship with Churchill was, as usual, the icing on the cake.

Samuel's reaction to Churchill's choice for the security czar for Palestine was cautious from the outset. In a telegram to Churchill dated February 26, he was lukewarm: "I do not know anything of General Tudor and can therefore form no opinions. He does not appear to have much experience in police work." General Tudor, Samuel told Churchill, would need the assistance of an officer "with police experience" to assist him and, he added, he had "someone in mind."

Tudor also had someone in mind: he wanted his second-in-command in Ireland, Colonel Ormonde de l'Épée Winter, to be commander of the new Palestinian police force. The Colonial Office swiftly vetoed that appointment. Winter's reputation, in the opinion of the bureaucrats, made him unsuitable. Churchill, however, had already picked the officer who would serve as Tudor's second-in-command and would run the British Gendarmerie.

Colonel Angus John McNeill was just three years younger than General Tudor, a career officer with experience in Africa and, significantly, in Palestine during the First World War. McNeill had been on the job since February 17, the day that Winston Churchill had summoned him to the Colonial Office in London and described the complicated scheme he had for maintaining peace as well as law and order in Palestine. McNeill didn't know much about Tudor but he admired Churchill. And he accepted the assignment, mainly because the charismatic Churchill was in overall control and had promised McNeill that anything he and Tudor recommended "after careful consideration would get done."

"A most satisfactory interview," McNeill wrote in his diary, but he would discover that his new job was even more demanding than he'd imagined. He soon found himself uncomfortably performing tasks he would normally have assigned to men of lower rank: "at one moment interviewing an officer and the next moment selecting frying pans for the cook-house and designing a badge for the officers' caps." But collaborating with a commander he would never really get to know would become the greater challenge.

Repurposing and rebranding the RIC was intense work, the pressure mounting and the pace accelerating when it became clear, by the end of 1921, that the Anglo-Irish War was really over. A new and bloodier chapter in the Irish conflict was coming, but it would be an Irish problem, handled by a newly formed Irish government and a Free State army generously equipped by the former British enemy. And it would be a civil war, with the Irish killing one another. As of

December 7, 1921, General Hugh Tudor and his RIC were effectively out of it, ready for new challenges—cultural, climatic and political. But compared to Ireland, Palestine was peaceful.

The efforts to conceal the Irish origins of the new British Gendarmerie were, in the end, futile. The Black and Tans identity stuck to the British police in Palestine for decades, thanks to what Tudor would dismiss as "Shinner propaganda." But that propaganda would work to the advantage of his new police force. The Black and Tans reputation, a stain in Ireland, soon became a badge in Palestine. In the early days, as one observer recorded,

> So fearsome was the force's prior reputation that when it was
> deployed, its mere presence, coupled with what [was] called
> "the moral effect" of the appearance of these men of "exceptional
> physique" on horseback or in armoured cars, was frequently
> sufficient to maintain or restore public order.[14]

In September 1922, in Nablus, a rowdy demonstration by local Arabs who attacked the police with "volleys of stones and bottles" was settled, according to Colonel McNeill, "in two minutes (literally)." The Irishmen were "ordered to unfix bayonets and clear the street," which they did by cracking skulls with batons and rifle butts, without firing a shot at the protesters. Arab disturbances were anticipated on November 2, which was the anniversary of the Balfour Declaration, but all was quiet. As McNeill recorded in his diary, "the Battle of Nablus is not yet forgotten."

Boredom became an unfamiliar challenge for members of the new gendarmerie. They spent a lot of time waiting in their barracks for the call to action. Sports events and inspections were contrived to keep them fit and disciplined. Most patrols were uneventful, and the policemen enjoyed a quality of life they had never known in Ireland—spare time and relatively peaceful encounters with a public that seemed to have respect for their authority.

After a little over three months in Palestine, Tudor felt comfortable enough to write, in a long personal letter to Churchill, that he was finally feeling "quite fit" and that "this place is like a rest cure after Ireland."[15] He also offered Churchill strategic advice on how to deal with Arab tribes. One formidable tribal leader, Ibn Saud, founder of what is now Saudi Arabia, had joined forces with followers of a violent Wahabi branch of Islam, and they posed a threat to the whole region, Transjordan in particular. One way to box them in, Tudor felt, would be to move British forces closer, maybe even over the Jordanian frontier, into territory Ibn Saud had claimed. The letter was well informed and exhibited a level of self-confidence that often comes from proximity to power, an asset that was, in Tudor's case, entirely a product of his warm relationship with Winston Churchill.

Churchill had designed a bureaucratic structure to support a low-cost mechanism for delivering a high level of political stability in the region. It was a hybrid system, the product of a creative mind and an emphatic personality. Anytime Tudor encountered roadblocks in what he soon would find to be a baffling tangle of administrative obligations, he counted on Churchill for support. As Churchill's chosen leader to keep the complicated system running smoothly, his job would be, if not easy, at least secure and manageable. It seemed unthinkable that the weakest factor in the Winston Churchill security equation would be Winston Churchill.

30.

ON OCTOBER 16, 1922, Churchill suddenly felt ill. The pain was soon unbearable. The diagnosis was appendicitis. Two days later, he awoke after the operation to the news that, while he was unconscious, an independent conservative had beaten a Lloyd George coalition candidate in a by-election.[16] His doctors told Churchill to ignore the news and settle down. A few hours later they found him, once again unconscious, with five newspapers strewn across his bed.

Even in his post-operative haze, Churchill could grasp the political significance of the by-election that he'd missed. The Lloyd George government, a coalition of Liberals and Conservatives, had been staggering along since 1916. Conservative allies were becoming restless, tired of sharing power with the Liberals. The day that Churchill physically collapsed, the Lloyd George coalition fell apart.

The two events were unrelated, except perhaps symbolically. Evidence of his friend's mortality should have sparked a moment of reflection by the new security commander in Palestine. Within days there would be a new government and, significantly for General Tudor, a new secretary for the colonies. In a month Winston Churchill would lose his House of Commons seat in a general election and become a political nonentity for the first time in twenty-two years. As he would later write, "In the twinkling of an eye, I found myself without an office, without a seat, without a party, and without an appendix."[17]

And soon his formula for law and order and security in Palestine started to unravel. Even with an influential and supportive ally in the government, the job of running the hybrid mechanism Churchill had invented would have daunted an administrator of deep experience and skill. In the shifty world of colonial politics, Tudor found himself with neither asset.

From Tudor's point of view, the security arrangement in Palestine was effective where it mattered—on the ground. His officers were competent and disciplined. Fatalities were few and reprisals were unheard of. Tudor's main challenges, in his first year on the job, invariably involved personnel, contracts, pensions and promotions. But he would frequently ignore the normal bureaucratic channels and protocols created to handle such mundane matters. He preferred to deal with military officers of equal status—most often, the chief of the air staff and "father of the RAF," Hugh Trenchard—even on civil policing matters that should have gone to either the high commissioner in Jerusalem or the Colonial Office mandarins in London.

In one revealing exchange with Trenchard, early in 1923, General Tudor urged him "not to risk weakening or impairing the really fine force you have in the British Gendarmerie." That Trenchard had no responsibility for the gendarmerie was either lost on Tudor or he considered it irrelevant.

Trenchard usually tried to be helpful. But Tudor's inappropriately addressed requests and comments frequently annoyed other military officers and antagonized civil servants by ignoring their authority. At first, Tudor's indifference to the ways of bureaucracy was put down to inexperience. A more generous interpretation might have recognized the contradictions inherent in his job—two mutually exclusive roles, military commander and civilian police chief. But whispers about General Tudor's competence as an administrator soon grew into hostile murmurs and, within months, titillating gossip.

Shortly after his arrival, McNeill noted in his diary that General Tudor had "an unfortunate way of never praising anything, spends his time crabbing everything and everybody, rather tiresome." McNeill found him peevish and abrupt ("very short in the temper, irritable"), but in the early days of their relationship, he attributed Tudor's moods to physical discomfort caused by the old injury to his foot. In October, McNeill even recorded that he was "getting on much better with Tudor now. His foot is better. So is his limp."[18] But over time, McNeill's generosity toward his commander's performance and personality evaporated, and the commentary in his daily diary entries became explicitly antagonistic.

There was more substantial criticism higher up the pecking order. Senior officials in both the air force and the Colonial Office complained about General Tudor's inability or unwillingness to follow bureaucratic protocols. In February 1922, with Churchill still in power, a senior military adviser in the Colonial Office acknowledged the contradictions in General Tudor's job. He judged that Tudor's knowledge of Arabic, his police experience in Ireland and his military record made him "peculiarly fitted" for the job he'd been handed. He believed that Tudor could probably have handled one or the other role—either general officer commanding or director of public security—but not both jobs simultaneously. Both roles added up to "more responsibilities than one man could conveniently assume."

With Churchill at the apex of the complicated system he had personally designed, it had worked. But with Churchill gone, the structural arrangement generated animosities in both camps—military officers annoyed by problems more appropriately directed toward the colonial service, colonial officials feeling snubbed by what they saw as disrespect from an overbearing army officer. Before the year 1922 was over, a senior official in the Colonial Office in London declared that Tudor was "entirely ignorant" when it came to running the various police establishments.[19] But given what would soon be general knowledge about pressures in his private life, it was impressive that General Tudor was able to focus on his work at all.

31.

FROM THE TIME they were first married, Eva Tudor had spent long intervals living with her husband on foreign postings. Ireland was an exception, but she had planned to join him in Palestine once he was settled there. She might have gone with him in June, but her father had recently died and she had to stay behind.

While there seems to have been little communication between them after she and Elizabeth waved farewell in Victoria Station in June, the letter she received some time in December landed with a crash. He was asking her to divorce him.

She clearly had no warning of Tudor's plan to end the marriage and she had no intention of co-operating. In the dry reporting of a later court action, "she cabled declining to do so," announcing instead that she was coming out to see him.

He cabled back. His words were harsh: *just don't*. The marriage, at least as far as he was concerned, was over. There was nothing to discuss.

If the drama in his personal life was causing him emotional distress, Tudor managed not to show it. To most of his associates he had always seemed remote, but that was normal for an officer of high military rank. Family circumstances were, as was conventional at the time, sheltered behind social conventions that assured important people a scrim of privacy.

Tudor's visits to Jerusalem while he was based in Bir Salem, and his contacts with the civil government, including the high commissioner, were rare. His relationship with McNeill, the commander of the British Gendarmerie, was not warm but it was collegial, correct. McNeill and his wife, Lillian, would occasionally invite Tudor to dinner at their home at Sarafand, near Ramla. On Christmas Day 1922, the two senior officers made courtesy visits together to the gendarmeries, where "Tudor made a suitable speech at each mess." The general was good at that sort of thing. He could be distant, impatient, aloof among people he didn't know well, but he was able to project a likeable personality when it was appropriate, especially among the lower ranks.

He generally avoided personal disclosure, but on January 2, 1923, Tudor quietly informed Colonel McNeill that he had just had news from London—that he had been knighted in the King's New Year's list of honours. It was a rare moment of intimacy and McNeill seemed touched. "He deserves it," he recorded warmly in his diary.

When Elizabeth Tudor found out in January that she and her mother were going out to see her dad in Palestine, she might have thought the trip was a birthday gift. She turned eighteen that month. Or maybe it was to celebrate her father's becoming a Knight Commander of the Order of the Bath (KCB)—henceforth to be known as Major General Sir H. H. Tudor. Her mother was now Lady Eva Tudor.

Elizabeth's memory of the journey, recorded many years later, gives no evidence that she was aware at the time that there were serious problems in her parents' marriage. She appeared to read nothing into the fact that when they arrived at Kantara, Egypt, border officials found their travel documents to be "inadequate" and prevented them from continuing. It is unclear why they were stopped—possibly because her father, a powerful man in Palestine, wanted to avoid a showdown with his wife. But when he realized that Elizabeth was with her, he'd have certainly backed down and cleared the way for them to continue on their journey. Whatever the explanation, they were on their way again before Elizabeth had time to wonder why they had been stopped in the first place.

Tudor had promised to referee a boxing competition in Bir Salem on February 8 but was nowhere to be found that afternoon when the bout was set to start. At noon the next day, he was at the railway station when Lady Tudor and Elizabeth arrived by train, after crossing the Sinai Desert from Kantara. Years later, Elizabeth would continue to believe that her father was "very surprised but very pleased" to see them.[20]

She wrote that her father noticed she had brought her golf clubs and "deputed one of his staff, a very nice subaltern called Frank," to look after her, as he knew Frank played golf. He may have also regarded the young officer as a convenient distraction for Elizabeth while he parried awkward questions from his wife.

January had been cold and wet, and there was a heavy rainstorm the first night they were at Bir Salem. But on the next day, February 10, the sun shone, and the weather remained clear and dry for the six days of their visit. "Frank asked me to play next morning, and we set off in his car and played a round of nine holes," Elizabeth wrote in her memoir of the trip. She and Frank soon discovered another common interest besides golf. They were both fascinated by insects— butterflies (Elizabeth) and beetles (Frank). The two spent a lot of time together, touring the historic sites in and around Jerusalem, playing golf and hunting bugs. Elizabeth's account, in fact, is entirely focused on smart young Frank.

Then, on February 15, she and her mother were back at the railway station with their bags. Angus McNeill, arriving at the station to meet other visitors, was surprised to see them there, obviously on their way back home. It had been a brief visit, he wrote, "a very expensive trip and rather mysterious." The mystery, naturally, inspired gossip in the small expatriate community.

Waiting for the train that day, Elizabeth noted with disappointment that Frank was not among the officers from her father's staff who had come to say farewell. The scene, however, would not end without a sentimental resolution.

Soon we could hear the train some distance away and then we saw someone galloping at speed towards us. I saw it was Frank. He dashed up, leaped off [his horse] and threw the reins to a driver, rushing up to me saluting the senior officers on the way.

"Thank heavens I'm on time. I spent nearly all night making this!" and he thrust a small packet into my hand. "Hide it now and open it when you are alone," he whispered.[21]

Then they were on their way, the beginning of a long and soon, for Elizabeth, unhappy journey back to England: back to Kantara by rail, then another train to Port Said, where they boarded a ship for the last and longest segment of their journey home. Soon after leaving Port Said, she opened the package Frank had surreptitiously handed to her. Inside she found a beetle. It was "a beautiful beetle, perfectly stuffed," and she would treasure it for years, long after Frank, whose surname she never recorded, had become a wistful memory.

The fine weather ended as they crossed the Mediterranean and the ship thrashed in high winds. Nearing Gibraltar, her mother broke the news: the visit to Palestine had been the start of a campaign to save her marriage, but she had failed. Lady Tudor and the general were separating.

General Tudor seemed to be more relaxed in the weeks following the "surprise" visit from his wife and daughter. In March, he and Angus McNeill were part of an expedition to Jordan, with a side trip to the ancient Nabataean capital, Petra, where they spent three days as guests of the emir (and later king) of Jordan, Abdullah, an important British ally in the region.

Tudor and Abdullah were friends. They played chess, shared an interest in horses, and occasionally exchanged memories of the Great War, in which they were allies against the Ottomans. The emir also presented Tudor with gifts, including an Arab mare and binoculars he claimed to have taken from a Turkish military officer after a decisive battle in the war.

Colonel McNeill would write poetically of the Petra visit, during which he and General Tudor, along with several other members of the British party, shared a tent. From a high ridge overlooking Petra, he described "sunset light on red sandstone rocks" and "pink cliffs all carved with temple facades," and a "wild and vast" wadi running from the south end of the Dead Sea almost to the Gulf of Aqaba, "shimmering in the mirage." It was a high point in the relationship between Tudor and McNeill, and one of the few pleasant memories either would recall from the time they spent together.

Soon after their return to their respective military bases in Bir Salem and Ludd (today Lod, Israel), it became apparent that major changes were being planned for security in Palestine and for the British Gendarmerie in particular. A new British government and a new colonial secretary, the Duke of Devonshire, had begun the process of redesigning Churchill's unwieldy scheme for cutting costs while bolstering security. Though revealed vaguely and bit by bit over time, the new plan was a drastic one; central to it was a determination to gut the British Gendarmerie.

McNeill would become increasingly embittered by what he saw as Tudor's indifference or, at worst, collaboration in the new government's degradation of the British paramilitary force. Behind the scenes, however, Tudor tried to find savings other than by emasculating his creation. In one new configuration, he hoped to *increase* the size of the gendarmerie.

In a note to Hugh Trenchard in mid-January, Tudor suggested replacing two Indian army battalions with four new companies of "white" policemen. The Indian troops didn't "pull their weight," he said. But he was proud of the British Gendarmerie and enthused by the prospect of saving money while expanding it. Trenchard had no responsibility for policemen, but he agreed to test the idea in London and reported back that there was general approval for eliminating the

Indian battalions. But he also reported an unwelcome question: Why couldn't Tudor cut the Indians without adding another three hundred costly British bodies to the gendarmerie?

The haggling went on for months, with Tudor facing resistance at every turn. He wasn't good at politics, and he added to his difficulties by sidelining a strong potential ally, a military man with the same intense commitment to their British paramilitaries—the gendarmerie commander, Colonel Angus J. McNeill.

32.

TUDOR RETURNED TO England on leave late in April and soon discovered that ending a marriage wasn't the simple matter that he had presumably imagined when he made his declaration in December. Divorce in 1923 was legally complicated, invariably messy and usually scandalous.

In London, he moved into the Army and Navy Club, a social fortress on the corner of Pall Mall and St. James's Square, where senior military officers enjoyed their privacy and, when desired, the company of men of equivalent distinction. It was an old establishment, founded in the 1830s as a place where army officers could relax without civilian interference and, especially, the distracting presence of women. "Ladies," according to the rulebook, were allowed "to be shown over the club by a member between 3 and 5 p.m." The club was known affectionately as "the Rag," for a memorable complaint by a rakish former member about a meal, which he compared to food served at a London dive called "Rag and Famish."

An early patron, the Duke of Wellington, insisted that the club expand its membership to include naval officers. Membership had, from time to time, also enabled temporary "hospitality to distinguished strangers," one of whom was Napoleon III, a frequent guest while he was living in exile in London.[22] Tudor had been a member since 1900.

Lady Tudor soon discovered he was living there and on June 4, 1923, wrote to him. The letter was warm, conciliatory. "My Dear Hughie," it began. "It is time this absurd estrangement ended." He sent the letter back unread, with instructions that future communication should be through his lawyers. She wrote again. One week later, on June 11, he responded:

> Dear Eva. In reply to your registered letter I want you to clearly understand that I am not going ever to return to you under any circumstances. Nor will I consent to see you or receive you, either here or in Palestine. I am leaving England shortly.

The cold, injured tone implied he had a grievance, but the reason for his abrupt decision to leave the marriage remains a mystery to this day.

Was his decision caused by some traumatic stress from Ireland? Was there a secret chapter in his life in Palestine? A rumour that surfaced and persisted for a while in the family was that "a friend" had written to Lady Eva to report that, in Palestine, her husband was involved in an affair with the wife of another military officer. Neither the letter nor the rumour was ever substantiated.

The breakup was traumatic, especially for Eva Tudor, the military spouse who had diligently raised their children and managed family affairs for years on end while her soldier-husband served their King (and Queen) and country in far-off places. But for General Tudor, who had precipitated the marriage crisis, the timing of the split could not have been worse for his reputation, his credibility and, ultimately, his career. On top of that, he never did get his divorce from Lady Eva.

July 1923 was a crucial period in what was an evolving British role in the Middle East. On the ground in Palestine, the Churchill formula appeared to be successful. The new British Gendarmerie was, by all accounts, impressive. Where there were disturbances, the Black and Tans managed to prevail without killing people. In March 1923, Herbert Samuel, the high commissioner, had praised them for an ability to "dispose of an unruly crowd at the cost of a few bruises when a company of [troops] would probably find themselves obliged to fire." Samuel agreed with Tudor that the force deserved to be supported and expanded by the new colonial administration.[23]

As if to prove Sir Herbert's point, Colonel McNeill reported an encounter on March 14 with a potentially hostile crowd near the Damascus Gate in Jerusalem. After police had unsuccessfully attempted to disperse the mob, an officer in charge "called in the BG [British Gendarmerie] who quickly did the trick, breaking a few heads in the process." Similar scenes in Palestine and other places where the British army had been involved had ended up in rioting and bloodshed.

Officially, however, the new government in London didn't acknowledge the success of the gendarmerie in Palestine. The serious resentment and confusion in the bureaucratic backrooms deflected any positive evaluation of achievements by Tudor and McNeill.

On July 2, Tudor was still in London and scheduled for an important meeting with senior officials in the Colonial Office. The high commissioner was to attend, as was the head of the Middle East Department, Sir John Shuckburgh. Angus McNeill was also present. The agenda for the late afternoon meeting was the budgetary problems anticipated in the coming year.

Half an hour before the meeting started, McNeill later noted, "the War Office sprung a bomb by offering a British cavalry regiment for Palestine."[24] Presumably, the thinking was that bringing such a regiment, funded by the War Office, into the Palestine security equation would reduce financial pressures on the Colonial Office. A new cavalry regiment would inevitably lead to the elimination of one of the two mounted squadrons of gendarmes. For as long as the War Office proposal was on the table, planning by the Colonial Office for the future of the British Gendarmerie had to be suspended.

Meanwhile, a more intriguing story was unfolding in a nearby London courtroom. Lady Tudor had abandoned hope of reconciling and, earlier that same day, had appeared before a judge demanding "restitution of her conjugal rights," among which would be entitlement to financial support from her husband.

The Tudor family's dysfunction was reported by the newspapers in London and Dublin on July 3. The story was discreetly understated but guaranteed to attract the attention of a wide and influential readership, including the top brass at the Colonial Office and a disapproving, prudish high commissioner. As his son would one day describe him, Herbert Samuel was "puritanical in the extreme." He would have cringed while his tea went cold that morning, as he read the article headlined "TUDOR V. TUDOR" in his copy of the *Times*. The story in the *Irish Times* that day was more forthcoming, under an explicit headline: "Restitution Decree Granted to Lady Tudor. Fruitless Visit to Palestine."

Human foibles were to be expected. Human nature was given to corruption. But one should never permit one's peccadillos to be on display in public places.

The court had reacted swiftly to Lady Tudor's application. The judge "pronounced a decree of restitution of conjugal rights, with costs, the decree to be obeyed within fourteen days of service."[25] Two days later, General Tudor left the country, heading back to Palestine.

The newspaper coverage confirmed what Colonel McNeill had suspected for some time—his GOC was going through personal difficulties that were interfering with his work. McNeill had spent two futile weeks in London trying and failing to meet one-on-one with General Tudor. Finally, he wrote him "a long letter on many points," noting sourly in his diary that Tudor was "very much otherwise employed endeavouring to get rid of his wife."[26]

On June 26, McNeill and Colonel Richard Meinertzhagen, a senior military adviser in the Colonial Office, had met for lunch with Churchill. The former colonial secretary, now a private citizen, was anxious to reassure the officers that they shouldn't fret about the future of the British Gendarmerie, that he "could not dream of coming out of Palestine." Churchill's optimism would have been at least in part a product of high spirits, given that he had just published the first of the five volumes of his memoir, *The World Crisis*. The early reviews were positive. The *New Statesman* described it as a book that was "remarkably egotistical but which is honest and which will certainly long survive him."[27]

Tudor, it seems, had avoided his old friend while he was in London but received a cheerful and reassuring letter from him when he was back in Bir Salem. Churchill wrote: "I'm sorry we didn't meet before you left . . . I am very glad to know you are pleased with your work in Palestine, I am sure there is no one who could do it half as well as you."[28]

Churchill disclosed, sort of by the way, that the Duke of Devonshire, the new secretary for the colonies, had asked him for input about the future of the gendarmerie, and Churchill said he had explained "why it would be a great mistake to substitute a British Cavalry Regiment for an addition to the gendarmerie." Churchill assured Tudor he would have no difficulty arguing that diminishing the gendarmerie in any way would be a big mistake. "Pray write me and let me know how things are going on and how you feel about them."

Churchill's input had obviously had no influence on the plans of the new government, nor had Tudor's distracted presence in London.

"Thank God," McNeill wrote on July 5, when he heard that Tudor had returned to Palestine. "I can't get him to do anything."

McNeill had lunch a few days later with Sir Herbert, the high commissioner, at the Reform Club, just along Pall Mall from Tudor's Army and Navy Club; obviously the Tudor "situation" arose in their conversation. McNeill reported later in his diary: "I gather [Sir Herbert] doesn't think much of Tudor and is amazed at this domestic upheaval."

For McNeill, who was a dedicated family man and devoted husband, General Tudor's messy marital situation on top of his own exclusion from discussions about the future of the gendarmerie would soon turn a distant working relationship into a personal and professional estrangement.

33.

LONDON WAS SWELTERING in a heat wave in July, which added to the gendarmerie commander's irritability and anxiety. With Tudor gone, Colonel McNeill found himself hanging about in the stuffy offices of the colonial and war departments, waiting for decisions that would offer clues about his future and the future of his men.

On July 23 he spent what he described as a "humiliating" afternoon going over budget estimates he and Tudor had prepared. To his amazement, "young whippersnappers" in the Colonial Office had defaced their paperwork with rude inquiries and sarcastic marginalia. One of the whippersnappers was Gerard Clauson, thirty-one, a graduate of Eton and Oxford, a linguist and a rising star in the British civil service. According to internal documents from the period, he was already a ferocious critic of the gendarmerie and its senior officers, and his sniping at Tudor and McNeill had only begun.

McNeill's private response to "the d— ignorance" of the bureau-crats on July 23 was a timeless expression of frustration from someone working in the trenches of reality over "bean-counter" quibbles about money. In the privacy of his diary, McNeill allowed, "It's no use get-ting ratty with them, much as one despises them. Otherwise, one would never get anything through in future. But how I would like to have them as subalterns under me. Ye Gods!!!"

On July 25, he sat in the gallery of the House of Commons for five and a half hours listening to a tedious debate about Colonial Office budgetary estimates. There was a lot of discussion about Kenya and other colonial responsibilities, "but not one word about Palestine!" The uncertainty was ominous; the War Office proposal to send a cavalry regiment to Palestine was becoming a greater like-lihood as each day passed. From Palestine, General Tudor was sig-nalling "despondency." His clout in London and in Palestine was rapidly diminishing.

For McNeill, the last straw fluttered down on August 10, when he received a cable from a military officer in Palestine ordering him to evacuate his army bungalow in Sarafand in case it would be required to accommodate officers from the proposed new cavalry regiment. Normally, McNeill would have protested to his boss—General Tudor. But he blamed Tudor, at least in part, for his predicament. He shared his fury with his diary: "It is damnable . . . I can't understand Tudor—why doesn't he say 'I'm d—d if I am going to turn out old and perma-nent residents for newcomers.'"

He turned for help to Richard Meinertzhagen, who tried to reas-sure him that he and the other gendarmerie officers would never be "turned out in the streets." Even with that assurance, McNeill slipped into a darker mood every time he thought about General Tudor. "I gather from what gunner [artillery] friends of his say at the Rag that he is known to have become rather peculiar."

On September 6, when McNeill was back in Palestine, General Tudor finally "blurted out" in the middle of a general conversation that he had recommended scrapping a mounted gendarmerie squadron to further reduce expenses. For McNeill, the disclosure amounted to betrayal. It now seemed clear that all along, behind his back, General Tudor had been part of the restructuring that would compromise the gendarmerie McNeill was trying to protect. And there was a larger political reality, perhaps not yet apparent to McNeill. Tudor's days in Palestine were numbered.

General Tudor was a Churchill man, a distinction that had been a source of power and deference in Ireland and in his early days in Palestine. Being apolitical, perhaps he didn't realize how much of his authority flowed from Winston Churchill's imposing presence and political prestige. Now that both Churchill and Lloyd George were out of power, the association that was once a priceless asset had become a heavy liability. A new political team in London was already busily evaluating Churchill's complicated schemes for cutting the cost of Britain's foreign obligations, and Palestine was high on the list of their priorities for major alterations.

Tudor's job wasn't necessarily vulnerable just because he was a Churchill man. His unwieldy responsibility for both civil and military security services in Palestine could easily and logically be simplified by splitting it and sharing it with someone else. His larger problem was that he had acquired influential enemies in Palestine and that the enmity was, to a large degree, personal.

McNeill now detested him. The high commissioner was repelled by Tudor's domestic situation. But perhaps more fatal was the silent animosity that had been growing in the Colonial Office bureaucracy. Now that Tudor had become politically disabled, the bureaucratic opposition was about to become overt and vocal.

The fallout from a minor incident in April 1923 would perhaps have the greatest impact on his future—a car accident just outside Jerusalem. Gendarmerie officers were in a military vehicle when a wheel dropped off and the car rolled over on the roadside.[29] Injuries were minor, but the accident would lead to an official inquiry that lasted all summer and into the autumn, and eventually it involved General Tudor, the high commissioner and the colonial secretary, the Duke of Devonshire, and, ominously, the hostile Colonial Office "whippersnapper" Gerard Clauson.

According to established rules and practice, government officials were not allowed to use government vehicles for private purposes. The men of the gendarmerie, with the approval of their commanders, didn't consider themselves to be government officials. They believed that they had a special status as paramilitary policemen and made it their practice to rent military vehicles for personal excursions in the countryside. The accident exposed the practice and created bureaucratic outrage.

By August 6 the high commissioner was involved. He agreed that the private use of government vehicles by the gendarmes was against the rules and had to be discontinued. General Tudor disagreed with Samuel and two days later weighed in aggressively on the side of his policemen:

> I consider it most desirable that officers and men of the
> British Gendarmerie should be encouraged to make
> themselves acquainted with the country in which they are
> serving, and their presence on the roads must act as a
> deterrent to the bands of highwaymen who frequent them.
>
> I am also of the opinion that to deny the means of
> allowing members of the force to get a change away from
> their stations—many of which are monotonous and far
> removed from civilization—is not conducive to improving
> the morale of the men.[30]

On September 7, Gerard Clauson offered his opinion: the sooner
the members of the British Gendarmerie realized that "they are government employees like everybody else, the better." They should never
be allowed to use government equipment for their personal amusement, he insisted in a detailed memo setting out his objections.

It would come as a shock for Clauson, a week later, when his boss,
the Duke of Devonshire, agreed with Tudor. An exception would be
made for the British gendarmes. Clauson blew a gasket. He sat down
that day, September 13, and wrote a blistering critique of Tudor and
his attitudes toward rules and regulations.[31]

General Tudor is constantly adopting an attitude of
independence with regard to the Palestine government . . .
treat[ing] the Palestine government and the Secretary of State
for the Colonies' orders with disrespect whenever it suits him
to do so.
     This is not my personal view only . . . I have heard that the
Air Ministry have just as many difficulties with him as we have.

He wrote that he had discussed the General with colleagues and

it was their firm conviction that it was a matter of fixed policy
on General Tudor's part not to obey orders except when it
suited him to.
     This is demoralizing, not only to General Tudor himself but
to his subordinates also, who are encouraged by his attitude to
adopt an equally independent attitude themselves. Col. McNeill
is a case in point.

To Clauson, the car accident revealed that General Tudor was undermining the authority of the bureaucracy and "if we don't put our own

views quite clearly we shall be letting down the Palestine government and weakening our own case still further."

Tudor won the day in his appeal to the Duke of Devonshire. But his successful advocacy for the right of his policemen to rent military vehicles and tour the countryside, for what Clauson and his colleagues considered frivolous reasons, would turn out to be a consolation prize.

34.

ON SEPTEMBER 21, 1923, General Tudor sent a long letter to his old friend Winston Churchill. He wrote that he had done his best to achieve one of Churchill's top priorities, cutting costs, but he had perhaps been too successful.[32]

He'd made drastic cuts to the security operation in Palestine, but tensions in the region were rising as Arab political aspirations collided with the expectations of a rapidly expanding Jewish population. His policemen had recently uncovered a plot to assassinate Sir Herbert Samuel, who "was not personally unpopular before." There would have to be "extra precautions for his safety," and increased security would be expensive. "Otherwise, I do not think the country will become anything like Ireland," he wrote. "They are a different people, and it is unlikely that the Arab, if handled firmly, will ever do much more than agitate and talk."

Still, Tudor shared that his summer had not been without its challenges. "The Arab" was learning tactics that had worked in the IRA campaign against the RIC and the British army. Roadside ambushes were becoming more common. Several British officers, veterans of Ireland, had recently been killed in Palestine. If he could have seen the future, he might have also warned his friend that Jewish settlers out to defend and, eventually, expand their new homeland would come to adopt the IRA's guerrilla strategies, and that their leaders would embrace Michael Collins as a model for conducting a successful armed insurgency.

In his letter, Tudor seems to understand that his job is on the line—at least his role as military GOC. But it is obvious that he isn't ready to leave the Middle East. Where could he go? Was there anywhere on the planet where he might feel safe, after Ireland? He was physically and culturally comfortable in Palestine, and he had the presumed loyalty of the hundreds of RIC veterans who had volunteered to serve there with him. Clearly, Tudor saw Palestine as a potential long-term refuge.

But having made "drastic" reductions in the British military garrison in Palestine, the question of his position was "bound to be raised," he wrote. "It would naturally seem that I must now abolish myself." On the other hand, he felt that it would be "advisable to have a military officer of highish rank here to deal with Trans-Jordan and carry sufficient weight on military matters with the High Commissioner." It clearly did not occur to Tudor that, by this point, he was in the high commissioner's black books.

Tudor's tone reflects a weary resignation.

I have done my best . . . but for you I should probably have been
on half pay long ago for a considerable time instead of having
three or more extremely interesting years.
    I don't know what prospects there now are of further
employment. There are plenty of men for every vacancy.

He mused that it might be time to leave his military life behind. Perhaps his expertise with horses would offer a way into a new career. "I almost think I should like to manage a stud farm . . ."

———

By the end of 1923, Tudor knew that his job as GOC in Palestine was soon to disappear and that the police were to be reorganized. The British Gendarmerie would become part of a new, amalgamated force. Late in autumn he was still clinging to hope that he would get a chance to run it. But his desire to keep even a part of his job in Palestine was futile. By November 20, the Duke of Devonshire had made up his mind—Tudor had to go.

Devonshire advised the Air Ministry that he wanted to give the general "as long notice as possible," and asked that they convey his "high appreciation of the manner in which he has performed the duties of his appointment and . . . regret that the change in the circumstances of Palestine should now make it necessary to bring that appointment to an end."[33]

A memorandum the next day, November 21, from the duke to the high commissioner, is more explicit.

> As from the 1st of April, 1924, the rank of the Air Officer
> commanding in Palestine will be reduced to that of Air
> Commodore. Simultaneously, it is proposed that the
> arrangement by which one single officer holds the two posts
> of Air Officer commanding and Inspector General of Police
> and Prisons should be terminated.[34]

Herbert Samuel made no attempt to save Tudor's job, but in mid-December the high commissioner made a strong case that Tudor should be replaced by another military officer. London wasn't buying it. Top advisers in the Colonial Office were scathing in their opposition.

Gerard Clauson's appraisal of General Tudor's time in Palestine was blunt: regardless of his military talents, Tudor had been the wrong man in the wrong job, and had wrongly been given too much power.

The department has suffered very severely in the last two years
from the fact that it has been under a professional soldier without
any ordinary police experience (and only about two years
extraordinary experience in Ireland).

It would be, I think, disastrous to perpetuate the system.[35]

The Duke of Devonshire agreed, writing to Samuel that "military
experience was not only not essential but might even be regarded as a
handicap . . . in a post of which it is our policy to emphasize the civilian
character." General Tudor would be replaced by a career policeman.[36]

There were subtle signs that Tudor saw it coming. Ordinarily a
stickler for discipline, he began to occasionally show up late for meetings. In one case, he kept a funeral waiting in Ramleh Cemetery for
five minutes, "cortege, mourners and many others all formed up."
Five minutes would normally not be considered egregious. But the
funeral was for a British air force officer killed accidentally the day
before in a highway accident in Amman and, given the circumstances,
the lapse was noted by Colonel McNeill with sour disapproval.

On September 13, General Tudor was an hour late for a meeting in
Jerusalem with senior colonial officials. On February 19, 1924, he kept
the mayor of Ramleh waiting forty minutes for an important scheduled conference.

Once decided, the termination proceeded with impeccable civility.
There were expressions of appreciation. The Duke of Devonshire and
Herbert Samuel were regretful that "the circumstances of Palestine
should now make it necessary" to get rid of him. There was a rare note
of sincerity in a farewell message from the commander of the air
force, Hugh Trenchard, who thanked General Tudor for "making our
task here as easy as possible in running a new responsibility."

On March 21, General Tudor inspected units of his British
Gendarmerie for the last time. According to Angus McNeill, the

gendarmerie commander, he "made a favourable speech" after which they "gave him three cheers." Nine days later, McNeill was at the Ramleh Aerodrome, where on June 22, 1922, he had greeted General Tudor as they started what would become an awkward, often stormy personal relationship.

"So that's that," McNeill wrote in his diary later that day. "I never wish again to serve under such a man. He has been no asset to us either officially or socially since he dropped out of the clouds at the same spot 20 months ago."[37]

Tudor now faced a future darkened by uncertainty. He had just suffered a drastic loss of income, yet he still carried the unavoidable financial burdens of supporting a wife and four dependants. His civilian job prospects were possibly best in England, but because of his leadership of the Black and Tans, for the rest of his life England would be a place to visit cautiously, never again a place that he could call his home.

He was no longer young, but not yet old. He had turned fifty-three on his birthday, March 14. Seventeen days later, for the first time in his adult life, he was unemployed.

Winston Churchill had in no small way authored his predicament. But Churchill, in April 1924, was no longer in a political position to help him out of it.

35.

AFTER LEAVING PALESTINE, Tudor disappeared into the sanctuary of the private club that had served as his retreat for many years—the Army and Navy Club, the Rag, a place to meet and reminisce with old soldiers and now a place where he could live in safety, at least for the moment. As a member of long standing, he had many friends there, one of whom, a Royal Navy captain, had been a member for almost as long as he had been. Tudor joined in 1900; Captain Victor Campbell became a member in 1902.

Campbell had an impressive British pedigree from a noble Scottish family, and he had a heroic First World War record from service in the Dardanelles campaign and the North Atlantic. He was more famous, however, for having been a senior officer on Robert Falcon Scott's expedition to Antarctica in 1911, a doomed attempt to claim the empty continent for the British Empire. Campbell had managed to survive what turned into a disaster for Scott in the winter of 1912–13.[38]

Like Scott, Campbell, leading a separate Antarctic exploration under Scott's direction, became stranded in the frozen wilderness. Battered by the wind, tortured by the dropping temperatures, it soon became apparent that Campbell and his companions would be spending an Antarctic winter there. His six-member team carved out an ice cave that became their home for seven months, during which they survived on penguin meat and seal blubber. In one miraculous discovery when they were almost out of food, they found a nutritional bonanza of thirty undigested fish in the stomach of a seal they had killed.

Once liberated from the ice cave in September, they had a 230-mile trek ahead of them before they reconnected with other members of the expedition. They would learn that Scott and four members of his team had actually reached the South Pole, only to discover that a Norwegian group had been there thirty-four days earlier. Scott and his group died on the return journey—a fate that Campbell had avoided by physical endurance and ingenuity.

Campbell and Tudor were, it seems, kindred spirits. In 1924 both were living at the Rag. It was probably through Campbell that Tudor first considered an unlikely island as the potential sanctuary that would become his lifelong home.

Campbell had property in Newfoundland, a place that Tudor had never visited but knew about from his experience as a divisional commander in the Great War. Alongside the Scottish units in his infantry division, he remembered commanding a battalion of extraordinary fighting Newfoundlanders. Beyond that, Tudor would have known nothing about Newfoundland, only that it was an isolated place, a forbidding rock in the middle of the North Atlantic with a ferocious climate. Campbell described a more bucolic prospect.

He owned land near Stephenville Crossing, in the district of St. George, on Newfoundland's west coast. The area had fertile soil, rivers teeming with trout and salmon, a forest full of wildlife. Campbell had just built a home there, at a place called Harry's Brook. His dream was to establish a small colony of like-minded souls, British military men with experience and adventures to share in the twilight of their interesting lives. Tudor became one of a half-dozen former officers who bought into Campbell's vision of a lifestyle that was private and secure, in the company of comrades and survivors. He purchased three acres of land close to Victor Campbell's farm and started planning to build a home there.

There was one catch. Much of Tudor's army pension was committed, by court order, to his wife and children—about six hundred pounds a year. He would need a job if he was to be able to live the way Campbell was imagining. But in 1924, jobs were hard to come by, even for a major general with a KCB.

Churchill was also unemployed. But he was busy, writing and all the while insisting that he had "not given a thought to politics." However, the instincts of an old politician were still vibrant. The

Conservative prime minister, Stanley Baldwin, called a national election for early December 1923, and Churchill was unable to resist. He ran for a Liberal seat. He lost.

Baldwin was unable to form a viable government and was soon replaced by a coalition of Liberals and Labour members of parliament. Churchill ran again in a by-election in March 1924, this time as an independent. He lost again.

There was another general election October 29, 1924. It had been twenty years since Churchill had called himself a Tory, but he ran as a "Constitutionalist" with Conservative support and won in a decisive Tory sweep. Given the size of the Baldwin majority, Churchill expected that the new government would be "composed only of impeccable Conservatives." No one was more surprised than he was when Baldwin offered him one of the most important jobs in his new government— chancellor of the exchequer. Overnight, Winston Churchill was once again one of the most influential politicians in Britain.

The fallout from the years that Tudor had spent dutifully tackling hard assignments from his influential friend had left him personally and professionally stranded at the age of fifty-three. It would have been reasonable for him to expect that Churchill, now that he was back in power, might feel obliged help a faithful friend to find a job that was perhaps less interesting but surely safer than his previous employment. And perhaps he did. But whatever Tudor's expectations were, it would soon become apparent that the next transition in his life would be secured by his military reputation and connections among Great War survivors in Newfoundland and England.

By late November 1925 he was on another railway station platform, this time bound for Liverpool and onward, to North America, once again to say goodbye to England. Lady Tudor wasn't there for this departure.

36.

November 18, 1925, Liverpool Station, London

FOR ELIZABETH TUDOR, one consolation on the day of her father's departure to a distant, unimaginable country was that Newfoundland would probably be safer for him than any other potential refuge in the world. She had not forgotten the day he'd left for Palestine, in June 1922, or what had happened to Sir Henry Wilson shortly afterwards. By now she understood that Palestine had been more than a career move. Her father had needed distance from his experience in Ireland. Now twenty, she also understood more about the circumstances of Sir Henry's murder, how he was doomed as much by his extremist political opinions as by his rank or anything he'd done to incite the men who killed him. Her father was nothing like Sir Henry, but as a polarizing figure in the Irish war, he was no less imperilled.

Hugh Tudor didn't talk about it. He didn't have to talk about it. She had figured it out from the occasional publicity, the scraps of information, that his job in Ireland had been controversial and that, for many years, his life would be in danger. And yet she was reluctant to believe that he was running away from the Irish or from his family. There would be gossip that he was running away to *protect* his family. Gossip that he was running away from family responsibilities. Gossip—never right, never wrong, never fair.

The father she knew was not a man to run away from anything. Elizabeth preferred, instead, to think that he was moving to Newfoundland for business reasons. After all, he had an investment there. In fish. As he had told her, he had taken a substantial portion of his pension entitlement in cash and invested it in a business opportunity on the advice of "a military friend."

Now it was November 1925, appropriately gloomy. This time the departure was from Liverpool Station. And there was only Elizabeth on the platform to say goodbye as he set off for Newfoundland, wherever that was. Was it Canada? America? Newfoundland was neither. Just Newfoundland. A former colony, Britain's oldest colony, now, in 1925, a dominion of the British Commonwealth, like Ireland.

Elizabeth and her father had a lot in common. Like her father, she too had grown distant from her mother. It probably started with Lady Eva's unilateral instructions after their failed visit to Palestine that Elizabeth must never again have anything to do with her father. It was an order she never honoured.[39]

Lady Eva had once intercepted a letter Tudor had written to his eldest daughter and had torn it up in front of her. Elizabeth was almost an adult then and resented being treated like a child. After that her father routed his letters to her through a friend.

She confided to him as they said their farewells at Liverpool Street Station that she was desperate to get away from home. She wanted a career. She wanted to begin her life, to become a self-supporting, independent woman.

Tudor promised he would make her independence possible. As soon as she was legally an adult, on her birthday, which was just a little under two months away, he would pay for a secretarial course and a place to live until she got a job. He was confident in her potential to build her own life, to create her own family. He understood her need for independence and personal security. They had that much in common.

They hugged each other, then said goodbye. And then he was gone.

Part VI

AMID THE NORTHERN MISTS

"I made two attempts to see you in Newfoundland . . .
in your retreat amid the northern mists."

CHURCHILL TO TUDOR, AUGUST 26, 1942

37.

IT HAD PROBABLY occurred to Tudor more than once in the long night of thrashing and tumbling on the North Atlantic, waiting for the winds to die and the sea to settle, that the complex circumstances that were bringing him to Newfoundland were neither of his making nor under his control. General Tudor was familiar with foreign destinations and uncertain prospects far away from home: India. Egypt. France. Belgium. Ireland. Palestine. But before this moment, there had been a logical consistency to the unfolding of his life. He had chosen, while still a schoolboy, to become a soldier when in 1888 he enrolled in the Royal Military Academy at Woolwich. Everything after that decision made sense in retrospect. The soldier's business is maintaining peace by threat of force or waging wars and winning them by force of arms. The future Tudor now faced was, as the place was once described on maps, *terra incognita*.

And the prospect of an open-ended stay in this grim seaport clinging to these rocky hills was daunting—living in a settlement with centuries of history but little evidence of human creativity except for the overbearing churches high above the town. The situation had a bright side, though, as he would remind himself in the days ahead: he could expect no existential drama here. Newfoundland in 1925 was economically and politically unstable, but peace was not an issue in St. John's.

Life had been a thrilling blur since that Christmas Eve in France in 1914, when he had first fired his big field guns in the war that would consume his next four years. And now that momentum had ended unpredictably in this uncertain moment, at the ragged end of a North Atlantic storm, in the middle of—nowhere. While he must have been apprehensive, he was, above all, tired. Boredom, given the past five years, might just turn out to be restorative.

Though it had started well enough with his knighthood, 1923 had been a hellish year for Tudor. There had been the awkward visit from his wife and daughter in February. Then there was the court case and publicity in July. He was certain that it was the cause of much of the later sniping by fellow officers and bureaucrats, ultimately leading to unemployment, exile. There was a streak of priggishness in the upper classes. He knew this from experience.

Lloyd George, Asquith, General Macready. All people he knew very well. All two-faced hypocrites when it came to matters matrimonial. Asquith didn't even try to hide his infatuation with Venetia Stanley, who was his daughter's age. Everyone who mattered knew that part of the cordiality between Prime Minister Lloyd George and General Macready came from the fact that both were sleeping with their secretaries.[1] But Tudor had committed an offence that was worse than adultery. He had exposed his private life to public curiosity. Bad form, in the social circles he inhabited.

He had carelessly let Lady Tudor go to court. That was inexcusable. The judge, like everyone else, had decided that Tudor was the villain in the sordid little drama. This came as a shock. Ireland had been a well-intentioned if dubious career move. Palestine, looking back, was a bad but unavoidable decision after Ireland. The marital scandal was a miscalculation that should have been avoidable through frank communication.

Tudor's future now was an open question. His whole life had been devoted to military or quasi-military jobs. That the last two jobs had saddled him with deadly enemies was a reality he would have to keep in mind. Perhaps Newfoundland was where at last he might feel safe, now that his soldiering days were over. It was time for a whole new line of work. In business. Though he knew nothing about any kind of business, his political and military credentials and connections, and his knighthood, should make this professional deficiency irrelevant in a distant, more forgiving place.

The business Tudor had settled on was selling codfish, caught, salted and exported from this rock in the middle of the Atlantic Ocean, 2,300 miles away from London. Newfoundland, war had taught him, was a breeding ground for the people he admired most in the world—fighting men. Surely they would reciprocate his admiration.

As a cover story, the Newfoundland salt fish trade was a shrewd choice. General Tudor needed work in a safe place. Newfoundland, thanks to its geographical isolation, was safe. Never mind that the general didn't know a codfish from a halibut, the support of credible and well-established merchants in London and St. John's would satisfy the doubtful. He would have plenty of assistance from people who, after generations of engagement, intimately knew the fishery and the salt fish markets of the world. More important than that, they knew the general.

They knew him from the Great War. They knew him from the military brotherhood that wars create. They didn't care about his time in Ireland or in Palestine. Like Churchill, they could be counted on to be loyal. And so it came to pass—Newfoundland became a refuge and, whether he had an inkling of it in 1925 or not, his life.

Tudor was an Englishman, from Devon. But, like the many Englishmen from Devon who came before him, he discovered a spiritual connection with Newfoundland—an enduring bond formed in bloodshed and survival in the final weeks of the greatest war of his career.

38.

September 29, 1918

THE DISASTER OF Cambrai, late in 1917, was already fading in the memories of the people who had planned it and the soldiers who had paid the price for the failures of their leadership. Tudor had helped plan the British strategy for Cambrai but his division hadn't been involved in the fighting. The Newfoundlanders had been in the thick of it, while still part of the 29th Division.

As of September 13, 1918, they were together in the 9th Scottish, where Tudor, now a major general, was commander.

The 9th Scottish Division was composed of three infantry brigades, the 26th, 27th and 28th. A battalion from the Newfoundland Regiment, along with battalions from the Royal Scots Fusiliers and the 9th Scottish Rifles, made up the 28th Brigade. Their brigade commander was Brigadier General J. L. Jack, known among the troops as "Mad Jack" for what seemed to be his suicidal disregard for danger.

Captain Sydney Frost, a Newfoundland company commander, described General Jack as "a daring and able leader except for an occasional lapse bordering on insane heroics." In fighting on September 29, Newfoundlanders won fourteen major citations for their own insane heroics—including three awards of the Military Cross, one of which went to Captain Frost. Official reports barely capture the horror and the heroism that won the medals and the war.[2]

[Pte. James O'Quinn, South Branch, Newfoundland] voluntarily went forward one hundred yards in advance of his company . . . suddenly came upon three enemy snipers whom he bayonetted . . .

[Pte. Newman Gough] when his platoon was held up by an

enemy machine-gun . . . crawled one hundred yards in front, killed the machine-gun crew, thus enabling his platoon to advance . . .

[Pte. Albert Lee] advanced straight toward the enemy post firing his Lewis gun from shoulder and hip, [and] gained superiority of fire, which enabled his platoon to come forward and capture the machine-gun and crew . . .

October 2, 1918

The Newfoundlanders, alongside a Scottish battalion from Tudor's 26th Brigade, were pinned down by a strong German defence in the Belgian town of Ledeghem. German snipers and machine-gun crews sent the Scottish soldiers and the Newfoundlanders scrambling for cover near a railway station.

The generals, Jack and Tudor, were a quarter-mile behind the front line. In his postwar memoir, General Jack recalled crouching alongside General Tudor in the shelter of an embankment with shells exploding all around them. "Feeling sure that the barrage is the prelude to a hostile attack, I keep watch and am presently horrified to see considerable numbers of men from another [British] brigade drifting back from the front over the open ground; we suppose the Germans will be on their heels at any moment."[3]

But there were no Germans, just the retreating British soldiers. General Jack couldn't believe his eyes—British soldiers, Scotsmen, on the run from nothing he could see. "Springing across the road and running forward, pistol in hand I threaten to shoot the first man who passes me. The rascals halt. Tudor and I 'fall the men in' in the open . . . the General [Tudor], monocle in eye and cool as a cucumber, orders 'slope arms, quick march,' and himself leads the parties back in extended formation to their posts."

General Jack then hurried off to find his Newfoundlanders, uncertain what he'd encounter when he caught up to them. Had they been slaughtered? Were they, too, in a panic, retreating from the enemy? But he found them exactly where they were supposed to be. "Colonel Mathias [Newfoundland battalion commander] and his adjutant, both the acme of composure, are leaning against a hut beside the advanced lines of their Newfoundlanders, who lie behind a shale bank . . . bayonets fixed, waiting for the Germans and as unconcerned as their officers."[4]

Within weeks of his arrival in St. John's, Tudor had settled into the social routines of his new home. If he was worried about the probability that he was high on an Irish list of enemies worthy of assassination, he didn't show it. From the day he stepped ashore in Newfoundland, he was in the company of friends. English accents and English titles were no handicap in St. John's. Even among the Fenian diaspora in Newfoundland, the general's involvement in the Irish War of Independence was little more than an exciting sidebar.

Tudor presented an unfailing air of confidence when on the go in Newfoundland, but the instincts of a fugitive were never entirely dormant. He often carried his revolver, a .455 calibre Wilkinson Webley popular among British army officers. For backup, he had a second gun, a weapon so small he could conceal it in a closed fist. In case he ran into a minor conflict, he usually had brass knuckles in the pocket of his overcoat.

General Tudor went straight to work the day after his arrival. He had a lot to learn about the salt fish trade. By November 28, he had made his presence known on Water Street, the business centre of St. John's. Edgar Templeman, a St. John's–based son of the merchant-politician Philip Templeman, reported to the company's main business operation in Bonavista that "Major General Sir Hugh Tudor . . . has been in here twice . . . just calling on the trade."[5]

Tudor represented a company that the Templemans knew well—Holmwood and Holmwood, an old British trading firm with whom Philip Templeman had been doing business for decades. Tudor's assignment was to open an office on Water Street for Holmwood.

The Templeman business was struggling financially. Philip Templeman owed a lot of money to the Holmwoods. Whether the Templemans knew it or not, one of Tudor's main responsibilities was to monitor their company's affairs to protect the interests of the English trader and ex-soldier who had hired him, Percy Holmwood.

Percy Holmwood, still young, had been permanently damaged by the war. Philip Templeman had never quite recovered from the loss of a son in the carnage at the Somme, July 1, 1916. Donald Templeman, a soldier in the Newfoundland Regiment, was twenty when he fell at Beaumont-Hamel, one of 233 Newfoundlanders who died that day in battle.

General Tudor's mission was to protect the financial interests of the ailing Percy Holmwood, even if it meant putting a grieving Philip Templeman out of business and taking over his remaining assets. Business, Tudor would soon discover, was another form of war. No blood, no bullets, but no mercy for the weak. Survival of the fittest.

October 14, 1918; 5:35 a.m.

An impenetrable mist from the soggy soil met a drifting pall of smoke from a twenty-minute artillery barrage, turning the rising dawn back into nightfall. And then, friend and foe alike were baffled by a midnight darkness at the break of day. For every high-explosive shell that struck that morning, there were two others exclusively for making smoke.

Before the blinding mist and smoke obscured the battlefield, B Company of the Newfoundland battalion had swiftly silenced three concrete pillboxes that had been blocking the advance of their division. But the return of darkness disoriented everyone. As Captain

Sydney Frost would later write, "the Battalion was automatically split into little groups of two or three who could keep in touch with one another only by shouting."

In the darkness, the Newfoundlanders and Scots of the 28th Brigade were stumbling and running into one another, but they soon noticed that the deadly German machine guns had all but fallen silent. Frost later wrote, "An officer and his runner actually fell over a machine gun manned by a couple of Boche, one offering a bag of sugar cubes as a ransom for his life."[6] As the soldiers straggled through the fog, "the accumulation of captives was becoming an embarrassment as a party of two or three Newfoundlanders would find itself saddled with an enemy group three or four times as large."

The confusion and delays caused by the fog and smoke lasted until noon. Then the real fighting started. The Newfoundlanders made easy targets as they struggled, carrying sixty-pound backpacks and assorted tools and weapons, over open ground. They were nearing the summit of a ridge—perilously beyond the range of their own big guns—when enemy artillery and machine guns opened up on them again. As Frost saw the situation, "Something had to be done quickly . . . before our battalion would be annihilated."[7]

He consulted his second-in-command, Lieutenant Stanley Newman, who had led the successful early-morning B Company attack against the concrete bunkers blocking their advance. Newman recommended a repeat of the morning strategy, a few men moving forward in quick, evasive sprints to outflank the German stronghold—where four artillery pieces were protected by four machine guns—now about six hundred yards away.

By then, seventeen-year-old Private Tommy Ricketts was a seasoned combat veteran. He and a section commander, Matthew Brazil, a former iron miner at Bell Island, were the only two unscathed survivors from another Newfoundland platoon that had been practically wiped out. When Newman asked for volunteers to try to outflank the enemy position, Ricketts and Brazil stepped forward.

Sprinting ten yards at a time, weaving and ducking through a plowed field, firing from the hip, Ricketts and Brazil were still nearly three hundred yards from the enemy when Ricketts ran out of ammunition for his thirty-three-pound Lewis light machine gun. Somewhere along the way they had lost two of the spare containers they'd packed with extra ammunition.

The enemy took advantage of the stalled attack and summoned teams of men and horses to move their field guns to a safer place, while pinning down the two attackers with sustained machine-gun fire. Ricketts looked back over the rough ground he had just covered, realizing his missing ammunition was somewhere in the muddy field. He started running back the way he'd come, bullets whizzing all around him. After about a hundred yards, by some miracle, he found what he was looking for.

Feeling either fatalistic or invincible, Ricketts grabbed the heavy ammunition packs, crouched low and sprinted back to where he had dropped the Lewis gun. He quickly reloaded and, with the machine gun balanced on his hip, resumed firing as he and Brazil charged toward the enemy position. The German gun crew fled toward a farmhouse. Ricketts chased them all the way inside, where he captured eight of them.

In the larger picture of that day, the Newfoundland battalion had advanced three miles, taking five hundred prisoners, seven field guns and ninety-four machine guns. The cost was high. More than a hundred Newfoundlanders had been wounded; forty-nine of the battalion's fighting men were dead or dying. The glory would come later—nineteen decorations, including a Military Cross for Stanley Newman and, for Matthew Brazil, a Distinguished Conduct Medal, second only in prestige to the Victoria Cross.

It is unlikely that General Tudor would have been immediately aware of the particulars of the Newfoundland battalion's exploits on that busy day. He was in charge of more than fifteen thousand soldiers—nine battalions in three infantry brigades. His focus was on the "big picture," success and failure from the perspective of the generals and field marshals, parliaments and heads of state, a vastly different experience of war than that of, as he wrote at the beginning, "an army of civilians stirred up by the propaganda of hate."

It was in the less hectic days that followed that Tudor would notice and reward the Newfoundlanders. In later years, when he lived among them, he would reap his own subtle but significant rewards for his association with their deeds.

The River Lys was a major objective on the way toward what would be a decisive crossing of the River Scheldt, one of the last strategic barriers before the Rhine and the German frontier. German defenders fought hard in what had become a desperate rearguard effort to slow down the enemy, stopping three separate attempts to cross the river. They drove back two British divisions, the 29th and the 36th. Tudor's 27th Brigade had also tried and failed.

Then it was up to his 28th Brigade—the Royal Scots Fusiliers, the Scottish Rifles and the Newfoundlanders. Engineers laid pontoons and rafts across the river. The heavy German guns promptly blew many of them to splinters, but finally the soldiers got across and began marching through the open Belgian countryside. As Captain Frost recounted, "The civilians would pour out of farms and villages as we passed them by, offering us coffee and welcoming us as deliverers from bondage."

Half an hour after the Newfoundland battalion had passed Deerlyck (now Deerlijk), a small Belgian town that had survived the war relatively unscathed, the Germans turned their fury and their guns on the civilians there, shelling the terrified inhabitants with high explosives and poison gas. The townspeople, who'd assumed they were safe, had just offered gratitude and hospitality to the Newfoundlanders. A hundred of them died in the bombardment. Captain Frost's cryptic comment: "No more prisoners were taken that day."[8]

Tudor's 9th Division was advancing steadily toward the Scheldt and, they were now confident, headed all the way to Germany. Temporarily stalled near the Steenbeek River, Belgium, during this last push, they were surprised when a former commander from their old unit, the 88th Brigade in the 29th Division, galloped past. The officer, Brigadier General Bernard Freyberg, suddenly stopped his horse, wheeled around and shouted, "Who are you?"

"Newfoundlanders," someone hollered back.

"Thank God," General Freyberg shouted. "My left flank is safe."[9]

But these soldiers had by now endured a solid month of combat. In his diary entry on October 24, General Tudor wrote: "Our men are very tired and it is asking too much to expect them to be able to attack for much longer."

Just days later, "within a rifle shot of the Scheldt," Tudor realized that to cross the river would now require a murderous assault. He decided that his troops had done enough. As Captain Frost would later write, "General Tudor . . . gave orders in the following words . . . 'Absolute murder, boys, do not attempt it, consolidate and defend the ground already taken.'"

"Thank God," Captain Frost wrote, "we had learned from bitter experience that the way to win the war was not to rush recklessly and madly into the mouth of guns and pay a life for every yard of ground, but to use brains and tact, shrewdness and skill."

The shooting war was all but over for the Newfoundlanders. The armistice that would end what was being hopefully described as "the war to end all wars" was only weeks away. Tudor's diary, as October 1918 ended, was typically dry:

> From September 28 we had advanced, fighting all the way 'til the 27th of October, a distance of about thirty miles from Ypres to the R[iver] Scheldt.
>
> The infantry Scots and Newfoundlanders had attacked with remarkable dash and bravery right up to the end; their casualties had been considerable but light if judged by the gains in ground and prisoners taken.

Tudor won high praise for the stubborn resilience of his fighters. Even before the exploits of mid-October, his corps commander, General C. W. Jacobs, had effused that during action in the first days of that decisive month the successes of the 9th Scottish Division "will be considered by history to have eclipsed all their previous performances."

In his diary, later in October, Tudor noted wryly: "On October 3 the corps commander had sent the division a Special Order saying how well the division had fought. And it is now the 24th of October!"

And he let the Newfoundlanders know how highly he regarded them. On December 4, 1918, it would be foot soldiers from Tudor's 28th Brigade—the Royal Scots Fusiliers, the Scottish Rifles and the Newfoundlanders—who would lead a victorious army of occupation across the Rhine into Germany, behind the massed pipe bands of the two Scottish battalions.

As General Tudor watched, he might have imagined that this moment would mark the beginning of a shift from the turmoil and uncertainty of war toward the welcome tedium of peace. He was almost wistful as he records a final, lasting image in his war diary:

"As the battalions crossed, the massed pipes of the two Scottish Battalions played 'The Blue Bonnets are Over the Border.' The Pipe Major of the 9th Scottish Rifles presented me with his pipe banner."

The final push to victory had been costly: one of every three soldiers in his infantry battalions killed or wounded. Tudor had no idea that the first shots in his next war, the bloody Irish conflict that would define his life and legacy, were just weeks away.

On December 23, 1918, the Newfoundlanders were still in Germany as part of the occupation forces on the Rhine. They were relaxed, rehearsing the rituals and ceremonial parades that are part of the rewards of military victories and looking forward to going home. That afternoon, they received sudden orders to report to the parade ground and "form three sides of a hollow square" and wait there for further information.

Once they were assembled, Tommy Ricketts was as surprised as anyone and probably more shocked than most to hear the formal proclamation read by his commanding officer, Major (later, Lieutenant Colonel) Adolph Bernard. For his actions on October 14, when he had charged through a fusillade of enemy fire, machine gun blazing, to capture an enemy artillery position, Tommy Ricketts received the highest military decoration in the British Empire.

The announcement was brief: "His Majesty the King has graciously awarded the Victoria Cross to Number 3102, Private Thomas Ricketts."

As Captain Frost reported later, Ricketts, still four months away from his eighteenth birthday, stepped forward and "with his usual military bearing, marched to where the Commanding Officer was standing, saluted and stood at attention." His regimental commanders shook his hand, "whereupon Ricketts turned about and marched back to his place in the ranks."

Private Ricketts might have known that, after such an honour, his life would never be the same. What was less predictable was how the moment would inform the destiny of his divisional commander.

When General Tudor arrived in St. John's at the end of 1925, the most famous of the Great War veterans in Newfoundland was not yet twenty-five. Tommy Ricketts would have been indifferent to the general's arrival. The army and the war were nightmares that he was struggling to forget as he tried to establish a life and a career far from the social epicentre of the city. While the general made his rounds among the merchants, Ricketts was in school, at long last acquiring a formal education. Eventually, he would become a pharmacist with a business of his own, a drugstore, on Water Street.

For years Ricketts tolerated fame, but as he grew older, he became reclusive, even hostile, shunning attempts to treat him as a celebrity. In 1929, on December 10, he attended a regimental dinner at a restaurant in St. John's to celebrate the tenth anniversary of his Victoria Cross. General Tudor was also there that night. For Tudor, it was also, by then, a rare public appearance. He proposed the toast to the guest of honour, who responded shyly, hardly mentioning the war. Ricketts spoke mostly about the aftermath, the hoopla and the ceremonies.

Tudor, like Ricketts, avoided casual conversation about his battles, but that night he went into detail about the heroism of the Newfoundlanders and how they had fought, paying tribute to the spectacular performance of Tommy Ricketts and his comrades on October 14, 1918.

Approaching middle age, Ricketts became withdrawn and, for the remainder of his life, avoided public gatherings. During a visit to St. John's in 1951 by then Princess Elizabeth, he declined an invitation to attend a royal reception. It has become part of local Ricketts lore that he agreed to meet the princess only when she stopped her motorcade on Water Street and waited outside his drugstore until he reluctantly emerged.

Perhaps, like many people who survive catastrophes, Tommy Ricketts felt survivor's guilt, or worse, survivor's shame. Perhaps he felt unworthy of being singled out when so many others who risked as much as he did received lesser recognition or no accolades at all. St. John's military historian Frank Gogos wrote, in 2013:

> Ricketts believed his action was just one of many made during the war for which countless others received no recognition. Fate would drop the Victoria Cross on him and he bore that burden like a true soldier. He was respected by many of his comrades, as he made no outlandish displays or pushed his Victoria Cross to curry favours.
>
> In fact, once he stepped away from the limelight it was rare to see him at remembrance parades or anywhere else besides a dark corner in his pharmacy. His medals lay in a desk drawer for many years undisturbed.[10]

Memories of glory would be forever overshadowed by a sorrowful reality. Nearly 1,300 young Newfoundlanders had died in action; nearly 2,300 survivors came home damaged, physically and psychologically.

39.

HAVING INTRODUCED HIMSELF to the St. John's "trade" in November and December 1925, for a time the general turned to the creation of what now seems to have been a necessary but carefully controlled social profile in the city. On January 1, 1926, he was among the throngs of locals at the annual New Year levees hosted by the Catholic and

Anglican archbishops. Later that month, according to the local press, he helped to establish a chess club in the city.

Tudor soon became a member of the Newfoundland Board of Trade, an association that was essentially controlled by half a dozen of the most influential merchant families in the city. He would, in time, become a member of the exclusive Bally Haly Golf and Country Club. In late January 1926, he attended a founding meeting of a local Boy Scouts group and promised to speak at a future gathering of scouts about the valour of the Newfoundlanders who had served with him in the recent war in Europe—a promise that he kept just one week later.

He didn't need to touch base officially with the Great War Veterans' Association, many of whose members he would have known from the crucial final months of 1918, when together they sealed their reputations as fighting men. The veterans who mattered most to General Tudor would have been well represented in the elite business, political and social circles he was already infiltrating in St. John's.

In the early days of 1926, it seemed that Tudor had left an eventful life behind him and was now contemplating a few years of peace and quiet, relaxing among other old warriors in Captain Victor Campbell's community at Harry's Brook, while handling manageable business obligations in St. John's and making occasional discreet visits back to England. What he could not have possibly foreseen was that two unexpected funerals in mid-1926 would force him to become an active player in a place and in a business that until then had been a convenient cover story: the Newfoundland fishery.

There were signs that should have worried Tudor if he had really gone to Newfoundland to participate in the business of exporting dried salt codfish to the world. Newfoundland exporters were being trounced in the marketplace when, given their geographic position and long experience as a fishing nation, they should easily have been dominant.

But the exporters and merchants on Water Street were too busy competing with each other to mount a coordinated campaign to confront aggressive European brokers.

Since more than 300 million Roman Catholics around the world were still obliged to avoid eating meat on Fridays and assorted other holy days, which invariably meant eating fish, the busy men on Water Street were confident that there was no good reason to change the way they had been doing business for centuries. They always seemed to muddle through their crises. That the majority of Newfoundlanders were poor, vulnerable to hunger and disease, isolated and exploited was a reality the well-to-do could easily ignore.

Conservative by nature, General Tudor would have accepted the fable during his early months in St. John's that a sensible political administration was managing the country's business. The government of Newfoundland was basically run from Water Street. The arc of Newfoundland prosperity followed the interests of politicians, the unpredictable migrations of codfish and the whims of foreign bankers. In 1926, as a future historian would wryly note, the government of Newfoundland, was "another merchant junta."[11]

But the entire economy was based on borrowing. Anyone dependent on the fishery, from the top to the bottom of the economic pyramid—the fishermen in hundreds of small outport communities scattered along nearly eleven thousand miles of coastline—was a hostage to the price of fish, but also at the mercy of interest and currency exchange rates. The vulnerability inherent in dependence on a single industry would soon lead to an economic and political crisis that a newcomer with no background in business and a visceral disdain for politics might not have anticipated.

In June 1926, Philip Templeman seemed to have been in robust health when he stood up to deliver what would be remembered as an upbeat speech in the Newfoundland legislature. It would also be remembered as the last words he uttered in public. The next day, June 2, as General Tudor closed the deal to buy his piece of paradise next door to Captain Campbell at Harry's Brook, he received the shocking news that Templeman had died. He was sixty-six years old. There were whispers that his death was suicide.[12]

Templeman had been a major presence in the salt fish trade and, as a member of the legislative council, an influential politician. In Bonavista, his hometown, two thousand people turned out for his funeral. Templeman's death sent his company into terminal decline, creating major headaches for people to whom he owed money, creditors such as Percy Holmwood and Holmwood's representative in Newfoundland, General Tudor.

Then, on June 29, Percy Holmwood, who had never fully recovered from war-related illnesses, died in England. He was thirty-nine. Whatever the reasons motivating his move to Newfoundland, Tudor now had a real job there, whether he wanted one or not.

40.

FOR THE NEXT eight years, while his military friends were fishing trout and salmon and hobby-farming on the distant west coast of the island, spending long summer evenings regaling one another with adventure stories, Tudor lived in St. John's, a struggling merchant, never fully understanding fish or foreign markets. Already caught off balance by the sudden death of Philip Templeman, with the loss of Percy Holmwood, both companies were now adrift.

Templeman's life story embodied the volatility and peril of any business connected to the sea, one moment serene and rich with possibilities, the next a vast and potentially catastrophic mess. From all outside appearances, Templeman had been, like the fishery itself, robust and healthy. But, also like the fishery, appearances were frequently deceptive.

In the salt fish trade, prosperity was frequently ephemeral and always transient. Optics often made the difference between failure and success, so it was important for the credibility of everyone in his class that Templeman was always seen to prosper. When his affairs were finally untangled by lawyers and accountants after he was gone, Templeman's company was technically bankrupt.[13]

The two deaths, just a month apart, cast a shadow over Tudor's future. The Templeman connection with Percy Holmwood would have assured him that, come what may, the business would probably have rolled along as always, propelled by a momentum established during centuries of history. Fish caught mostly by poor people and processed, stored, shipped and sold mostly by rich people; bills paid, books balanced despite inevitable financial challenges.

Tudor now had to roll up his sleeves and get to work at a job that, until then, had probably been little more than an elaborate disguise. Any chance of success meant he had to leave the comforts of St. John's and get to know the distant outports. By August 20, 1926, he was on the North Atlantic once again, this time sailing northward along the rugged northeast coast of the island.

Tudor's destination was a remote fishing community on Notre Dame Bay, but he made a strategic stop along the way. No one in the export business knew the fishery, its weaknesses and strengths, better than Sir William Coaker, prominent in politics and business, a man who had been knighted, like Tudor, in 1923. Tudor spent the evening with Sir William, and it is easy to imagine what they talked about. Fish and marketing. Coaker would have had useful advice for making influential contacts on Water Street.

———

Another contact high on the list of potentially important allies was George Hawes—an influential London trader who had strong ties with both Newfoundland exporters and European buyers of salt codfish. Hawes became critically important as Tudor struggled to learn the basics in his new career.

Hawes and Tudor had an impressive military connection. His son, Cecil Hawes, like General Tudor, had served in the Great War as an artillery officer on the Western Front. Equally significant, Cecil Hawes was married to the daughter of George M. Barr, a prominent St. John's fish exporter who had been born and raised in Liverpool but had been living in Newfoundland for decades.

George Barr's son, James Barr, had served with the Newfoundland Regiment while it was under the command of Major General Tudor. Passenger manifests for ships travelling between St. John's and Liverpool in later years would show James Barr and General Tudor on the same ship at the same time when both James and the general had become active in the salt fish trade.

George Barr and his British in-law, George Hawes, obviously impressed upon the general that, as in war, survival in the fish business meant playing hardball. There would be no room for sentiment. And it would soon become apparent that, with George Barr's help, the general and his allies were determined to take down and then take over the struggling remnants of Philip Templeman's failing business.

The competition was paying close attention. One major Bonavista trader reported in September that "George Barr bought Edgar Templeman's fish . . . for Hawes & Company and [Edgar] did not get the prices." By October the struggling Templemans' correspondence showed them wondering "was Tudor and Barr in league," manipulating prices to the disadvantage of their company? "One can never tell. It looks somewhat suspicious." Tudor and Barr were putting pressure on the Templemans by offering fish prices that were "ridiculously low."[14]

There was little the Templemans could do about the situation as the general moved aggressively to control the future of their business. Beginning in 1927, he became a frequent visitor to the Templeman operations in Bonavista and nearby Catalina. His visits were clearly part of a takeover strategy that became overt by the middle of that year, when he incorporated a new company called Philip Templeman Ltd., a Holmwood entity created to exploit the established Templeman identity while pillaging its assets.

In October that year, the St. John's press made it official: "The Bonavista business of the late Hon. Philip Templeman has been taken over as a going concern by Philip Templeman Ltd. with Major General Sir Hugh Tudor as the company's representative in Newfoundland."[15] The Templeman business would live on, but only in a name.

For businesses everywhere, 1929 was a catastrophic year. By mid-November a worldwide economic crash was under way. In late November, a tsunami, following an offshore earthquake, ravaged part of Newfoundland's south coast. In 1930, Newfoundlanders would be shocked by a sudden decline in codfish stocks, a phenomenon probably exacerbated by the tsunami. The decline lasted for several years.

During the slump, the corporate identities of both Percy Holmwood and Philip Templeman would slowly disappear from Newfoundland. Soon the struggling dominion was dependent on the self-interested generosity of bankers for its economic survival. There would be civil strife in St. John's, the sacking of the dominion legislature by a mob, even an attempt to capture, maybe harm, the Newfoundland prime minister.

Within a decade of Tudor's arrival in St. John's, political activity would cease, democratic institutions suspended indefinitely. Newfoundlanders would be rescued from bankruptcy in 1934 by the Mother

Country, for which they had invested lives and gone into suffocating debt in the bloody years of 1914–18. In return, they were required to surrender their political autonomy; for fifteen years, 1934 to 1949, public life in Newfoundland would be strictly administrative, a bureaucratic process managed by "commissioners" appointed by the British government.

But General Tudor was able to become a spectator on the sidelines of the turmoil. By 1934, he had stepped away from the salt fish business in which he had, because of unanticipated circumstances, become entrapped. If he had invested his own money in the fishery, as he had told his daughter, it's possible he recovered at least part of it through a share transfer when Templeman's remaining assets passed to a company the general controlled in 1929. Like many aspects of his life in Newfoundland, the details of his withdrawal from the business world and his personal finances are obscured by the privacy he cultivated there.

By the mid-1930s, Tudor was living in a small but elegant apartment on the top floor of George Barr's mansion, where he would remain in relative security for more than a decade. Barr's house was but a brief stroll from the residence of the British governor of Newfoundland, in whose stables, according to local gossip, General Tudor, an avid rider and polo player in his younger days, kept a horse.

It was a neat arrangement all around. The common experience of the First World War, connections with the British army and (by war's end) the *Royal* Newfoundland Regiment, had created bonds of trust to last a lifetime. And the salt fish trade gave everyone a comfortable lifestyle—until it no longer did.

Tudor's social circle in the city was eventually limited to a few business associates like George Barr and his family, and the extended family of his lawyer, Fred Emerson, whom the general had met soon after his arrival in 1925. Tudor abandoned his plan to live at Harry's

Brook and, in 1932, he sold his property there to another military acquaintance, a Scottish baronet named Sir John Hume Campbell, a relative of Captain Victor Campbell.

General Tudor might not have been troubled by Newfoundland's slide into democratic limbo after 1934. He might even have felt more comfortable under a government of unelected bureaucrats selected by the British political establishment than being subject to the whims of mercurial politicians from the Newfoundland elite. But British members of the new regime seemed unimpressed, if not disdainful, of his military reputation, which was obviously tarnished by his time in Ireland. And General Tudor might have been surprised, if not offended, when they created a police force for the island without consulting him.

One of the senior officers in the new police force was a Newfoundlander who had served under Tudor in the Auxiliary Division of the RIC in 1920–21. But Raymond Fraser, who had held an administrative job with the Auxiliaries in Dublin, clearly kept a tactful distance from his former RIC commander in St. John's.

Sir John Hope Simpson, the British commissioner who hired Fraser to be second-in-command of the new police force, the Newfoundland Rangers, noted (somewhat imprecisely) in a letter home that while Fraser had once served with "the Black and Tans . . . I expect that he is sorry for that episode as we all are . . . except General Tudor who was in command." He continued, "[General Tudor] by the way lives in NFL but we never see him."[16]

41.

FREDERICK ATTENBOROUGH, a schoolmaster and musician from Burton-on-Trent, Staffordshire, was obviously having second thoughts about his decision to start his first trip to North America in St. John's,

Newfoundland. The place was a mess. On a street that he later discovered to be the city's "chief shopping thoroughfare," he feared that he had strayed into a slum. He decided to redeem the experience by finding someone local who was worthy of a visit. He had the name of someone mentioned in a conversation back home in England before he had started out: George M. Barr.[17]

Attenborough dropped by the address he had for an office on Water Street, but Mr. Barr hadn't yet arrived for work. It was a Saturday morning in August 1935, but he was expected to be there by noon. To kill time, Attenborough "stepped out again into the unlovely street" and was disconcerted by the number of people he met who were "carrying big fishes."

But when he finally connected with Barr, Attenborough's impression of St. John's immediately brightened. He found Barr to be intelligent and hospitable, a trait Attenborough would soon discover to be fairly common among city residents, notwithstanding the distressing squalor in their streets.

Barr had been born and raised in Liverpool. He'd come to St. John's as a young man, saw opportunities in the fish business and soon cornered the lobster trade, which had been largely ignored by Newfoundlanders. Barr was keen for Mr. Attenborough to see a few "pretty spots" around the city. He promised he would either take the visitor around himself or ask a friend—a retired British army general, Sir Hugh Tudor—to be the tour guide.

Tudor's name didn't seem to ring a bell with the schoolmaster, but "a British general" clearly piqued his interest. George Barr assured him that the general had "nothing at all" to do, and he was sure that Tudor would be "pleased to show [him] what there is to see."

Tudor was now nearly sixty-five, his days of fretting over fish and foreign markets behind him. The two companies with which he'd been intimately involved would soon be history. Philip Templeman

Ltd., the Holmwood company that he had helped to create, was already in receivership.

Barr invited the English tourist to come to his home on Circular Road, St. John's, later that afternoon. It was in a neighbourhood that also improved Attenborough's impression of the city—leafy streets and large, elegant houses, many of them the homes of merchants in the salt fish trade. Attenborough was accompanied by two female acquaintances he had met on board the ship that brought him to St. John's. Shortly after the guests' arrival, Barr excused himself to finish up some office work. But he insisted they were all to stay for dinner and, in the meantime, the general would make them feel at home.

After half an hour of small talk, Tudor, courteous but obviously restless, suggested that he bring around his car and take them to his club—the Bally Haly. There he left them in the clubhouse with buttered toast and tea while he set off to play a round of golf.

The schoolmaster, who clearly fancied himself a literary diarist, offered detailed commentary on any sight or subject that interested him. The lovely golf course; the Avalon Peninsula, which reminded him of Devon, England; flakes of codfish drying in sunny coves. Yet he seems to have found nothing worth remembering or writing down about the substance, if any, of his conversations with General Tudor, over a visit that lasted through a chatty afternoon and evening and a follow-up get-together days later.

The Empire. The Western Front. His experience in Ireland. Why he was in Newfoundland. Clearly, Tudor didn't share enough about his life to stimulate the curiosity of an interested traveller from "home." This discretion may have been the key to his survival. He could be friendly, but he was generally aloof in unfamiliar company. Or he became pedantic sometimes, as if to shift a conversation that threatened to stray into personal disclosure.

Newfoundlanders who encountered him would remember with amusement the little arguments he launched about the cricket origins of baseball or the abuse of English grammar by the English. In fact, Attenborough found only one of their conversations worth commenting on—that the general had "a bee in his bonnet" about certain silly English speech mannerisms and planned to write a letter to the *Times* about some of the more ridiculous examples. It was as if all his personal experience in the mainstream of history—in India, South Africa, Belgium, Ireland, even Newfoundland—was off limits.

The literary landscape, even then, was littered with the diaries and memoirs of Tudor's military peers in the Great War and Dublin Castle. Less noteworthy generals and colonels; the politicians he had known, especially Churchill and Lloyd George; countless soldiers, and even RIC policemen, sharing memories of peril in the trenches, in the Irish countryside, in poetry and prose—all had been driven by a need to shape a future understanding of their life-and-death decisions and experiences, to find meaning in the catastrophes that they'd survived, significance in how they had lived their lives. Regardless of their motives, innumerable participants in events in which Tudor had played a part left raw material for future storytellers. Whether from a lack of literary skill, caution or indifference to posterity, he didn't even try.

As the years went by, he would occasionally deliver an opinion on world affairs to the one friend who had remained at the centre of the events that defined the times they had lived through. In a 1936 letter to Churchill, Tudor argued that Britain and France should form an immediate alliance with Hitler's Germany to stop what they both saw as an even greater threat—the Soviet Union and Communism. In his reply, Churchill, out of power again but always influential, did not agree or disagree but noted that Tudor's opinion was widely held among British Conservatives at the time.

Perhaps Tudor really wanted to be ignored by history. It was of sufficient satisfaction to his ego that Churchill valued his opinions and shared his insights and, above all, was grateful for his service. The general seemed to understand that he would become notorious in Irish history and that he should therefore strive to be, at most, a footnote in the records of "outrage and reprisal" in which he had played a central role, an accidental villain in the epic Irish drama.

For the most part, in Newfoundland, where he was unavoidably conspicuous, Tudor kept silent. That silence sparked enduring curiosity, creative speculation and, as time went by, the entertaining substitute for knowledge—mythology.

42.

FOR THIRTEEN YEARS Tudor stayed in touch with England. From 1926 to 1938, he returned, almost every year, for visits that usually lasted at least two months. He would live at the Rag, his club on Pall Mall in London, where he'd reconnect with old military comrades.

It was a familiar pattern for British expatriates in Newfoundland. George Barr was back and forth to Great Britain almost every year on business. Captain Victor Campbell and members of his little colony would escape back home during the worst months of the North Atlantic winter. Tudor made his final visit in 1938, the last year for a long while when the only perils on an Atlantic crossing came from Mother Nature.

He might have risked a trip in 1939, even though war clouds were ominous, but England came to him—a royal visit in June, during which he was selected for a private moment with King George VI. According to local lore, the King left Sir Hugh speechless when he loudly asked if he was "the man who commanded in Ireland." The

King also inspected a party of veterans of the Royal Newfoundland Regiment on that visit and "shook hands warmly with and spoke to Sergeant T. Ricketts, V.C."[18]

In 1941, Tudor suffered what was probably a heart attack. For him it was a double blow—it reduced his mobility and it deprived him of a last opportunity to reconnect in person with an old friend. Winston Churchill was then prime minister and the Second World War was going badly for Britain and her allies. In mid-August that year, Churchill spent several days on a battleship, HMS *Prince of Wales*, anchored in Placentia Bay, on the south coast of Newfoundland, holding secret talks with the president of the United States, Franklin Roosevelt.[19]

Churchill needed help from the Americans if his country was to survive. He was worried about the future of democracy, even if he and his allies could find a way to win the war. But he made time to socialize. He dispatched a coded message to the governor of Newfoundland: come to lunch on board the *Prince of Wales* and please bring General Tudor with you. He offered to send a float plane to collect his guests.

The governor accepted. But Tudor had to turn him down. Carla Emerson Furlong, a daughter of his friend and former lawyer, Fred Emerson, remembers that the general was devastated. Her sister, Anne Holt, confirmed in a brief memoir years later that he had been too ill to travel. Along with the repercussions of the heart attack, Tudor was suffering from arthritis. His old foot injury was causing problems with mobility. His eyesight was failing because of cataracts. For a while, at least, he was unable to read. He bought a typewriter and tried to learn how to type, but he never fully mastered the machine.

In a sympathetic letter a few years later, in January 1946, Churchill tried to comfort him, advising that an operation for cataracts was "simple and not severe." But by 1946, transatlantic travel seemed to have become too much of an ordeal for a man in his seventy-fifth year. Tudor became more reclusive, and as he faded from public view, unanswered questions about his past gradually spawned legends.

A persistent myth about the general is that he fled to Newfoundland in secrecy to evade his Irish enemies; settled in a remote outport, Bonavista, where he would feel safe in a large community of Protestants and Orangemen; lived there for three years and then finally felt secure enough to move to St. John's, where he worked and lived for many years with another English transplant, George M. Barr, who provided him with an income and secure accommodations. Like most mythology, it's a tangle of truth, fantasy and gossip.

Tudor, according to the local legends, was isolated from society; estranged from members of the family he had abandoned back in England; divorced by his wife; ignored by his embittered children, who even shunned his funeral; hunted by the IRA; despised by many in the local Irish population. Even what was true was exaggerated.

He was not divorced. Whether he liked it or not, he remained legally married until Lady Tudor died in 1958. His life in Newfoundland was mostly of his own design and lived mostly in St. John's. He had a military pension—maybe reduced by bad investments or maybe not. He had influential, loyal friends in Newfoundland, mostly merchants, lawyers and military veterans. He was a frequent visitor at the governor's residence.

In 1945, Tudor was still living in an apartment on the third floor of George Barr's house. In a census document that year, he reported total earnings of $1,100 for the previous twelve months. He had been retired for at least ten years by then.

He maintained contact with his only son, Henry "Harry" Tudor, for many years a banker in Hong Kong, and Elizabeth, his eldest daughter. Her son, John Davenport, recalls meeting his grandfather in England when he was six or seven years old, likely during the general's last visit to his homeland.

John's older brother, David Davenport, worked for Canada Life, a Canadian insurance company, and stopped to visit his grandfather in St. John's in 1954 while on his way to Toronto.[20]

Tudor had boasted about his grandson a year earlier, in 1953, when David was selected for the Oxford University rowing team for the annual race against rival Cambridge. He had obviously been following the rowing achievements of both grandsons, David and John, through his contacts with their mother. John and David rowed for Oxford while students there, and, like their grandfather and their mother, also become formidable competitors at bridge.

Tudor's son, Harry, had visited his father in St. John's twice, once in 1932 and again in 1947. Harry Tudor had served in the RAF in North Africa during the Second World War and spoke warmly about his father when he met a Newfoundlander there, Joseph O'Driscoll, who knew Tudor socially in St. John's and had served with him in the First World War.

On his last visit to St. John's, in October 1947, Harry brought his wife, Sonia Sawrey-Cookson. They stayed for about a week. Harry was unwell at the time, suffering from malaria, and soon retired to a small farm in the English countryside. By 1947, General Tudor had the full-time care and companionship of a nurse named Monica McCarthy. They probably met while he was recuperating from the heart attack in 1941; Monica's sister, Mary, worked for George Barr as a secretary. Monica would be at his side for twenty-four years, until his final illness in 1965.

Like much of General Tudor's private life, his relationship with Monica McCarthy remains a subject of speculation never confirmed or specifically denied. If the general had been looking for a mistress or a spouse, Monica was an unlikely choice. Four decades younger than Tudor, she was part of a large Irish Catholic family in St. John's. She is fondly remembered by relatives as a woman of dignity, integrity and fierce independence.

Monica McCarthy smoked cigarettes and drank in moderation. She wore slacks in public. She seemed indifferent to social curiosity. She was kind to the youngsters in her family; her nieces and nephews adored her and visited frequently. They remember the general as an "old man in a bed." She was the vivacious Aunt Monnie.

One nephew, Paul Woodford, a university professor in London, Ontario, recalls boyhood visits to his aunt's apartment and being asked by the old general, whose eyesight was failing, if he would read aloud to him. Professor Woodford remembers Tudor's choice most clearly: *Alice in Wonderland.*

Aunt Monnie made no effort to explain why she was living with a man to whom she wasn't married. He was old and she was the same age as his son. So what? She was a nurse, a professional caregiver. Full stop. Any more than that, no one—not even her closest family—deserved to know, and she swiftly shut down anyone who pried.

Her mother remained convinced that Monnie was "a lot more than a nurse" to the general and never concealed her disapproval. Her father, according to the family, disowned her. Her closest surviving friend, Carla Emerson Furlong, insisted for many years, long after both Monnie and the general were gone, that their relationship, while close, was essentially platonic.

Carla Emerson, born in 1922, three years before the general arrived in Newfoundland, was part of his social circle for decades. When he wasn't lawyering, Carla's father Fred was a musician and a linguist. Carla inherited her father's love of music and became a professional harpist. She taught the instrument to students until the end of 2021, when she was almost a hundred years old. Even after she retired, she remained a committed learner of Irish Gaelic.

Fred Emerson, because of his language skills, was honorary consul in St. John's for several small nations, and his home was a social mecca for international visitors. Carla remembers frequent visits from the general in her childhood. He was a regular for dinner on Sundays and special days like Christmas.

Carla's sister, Anne Holt, recalled that Winston Churchill intended to visit the general in St. John's and had accepted an invitation to stay at the Emersons while he was in the city, but he never made the trip. Another war got in the way.

Her uncle, Edward Emerson, another lawyer, friend and occasional business adviser to the general, later became a commissioner in the island's unelected government, and after that, chief justice of the Supreme Court of Newfoundland.

As they both grew older, Carla became a faithful friend of Tudor, and by the end of his life, she and Monica McCarthy were trusted substitutes for a distant family.

When the climb to the third floor at George Barr's home on Circular Road became too much for Tudor, he and Monica moved together to other houses in the neighbourhood. They later moved to a new apartment complex, located in an area with a name that would have resonated strongly—Churchill Square. And there they stayed for the remainder of his life.

It might be true that she was just his nurse. But one long-hidden detail about their life together offers a clue that perhaps the relationship ran deeper. At some point before he died, the general asked Monica if she would marry him. She confided to her friend Carla that he was serious. The proposal, as Carla Emerson Furlong insisted many years afterwards, was not at all romantic. It was, she felt, nothing more than practical estate planning.

Romantic or not, Monica declined. "Now could you just picture *me* as Lady Tudor?" she scoffed as she revealed the proposal to her friend.

The most intriguing of the Tudor mysteries in Newfoundland involves a failed attempt to kill him. As is the case with most mythology, it sounds plausible but there is little evidence to prove it.

Tudor wouldn't have been hard to find. His move to Newfoundland had been reported in the British press and, from day one, he was conspicuous around St. John's.

In the early days, he was probably high on a list of enemies marked for vengeance by republican survivors of the Irish war. Even if there was no official list, Tudor believed he would always be a target for a spontaneous attack or a random act of retribution, as had been the fate of Sir Henry Wilson on the doorstep of his home in London in 1922. There were many angry men with guns and grudges and hatreds burning in their hearts.

For a potential assassin, it wouldn't have been difficult to get to Newfoundland. Passenger liners from Liverpool, Halifax and Boston arrived weekly. There were Irish citizens in Newfoundland, many of them priests who, unlike most Irish Newfoundlanders, had strong nationalist sympathies and bitter memories of the Black and Tans. They could have helped in a murder plot.

According to the most frequently repeated version of the story, two Irish gunmen arrived in St. John's in the early 1950s and easily discovered where Tudor was living. One of the hitmen, both of whom were obviously Catholics, was said to have realized that, when the deed was done, he would be burdened by a mortal sin. He had a flash of fear about the future state of his immortal soul. It wasn't likely that he'd have time for the sacrament of penance if he was on the run, so he decided to seek pre-emptive absolution. He confessed to an Irish priest, who, regardless of his politics, felt obliged to break the sacred seal of the confessional and passed the information on to the Catholic archbishop in St. John's—who passed it on to the authorities.

In a less elaborate version, three men with Irish accents showed up on a priest's doorstep one night inquiring where they might find "Hughie Tudor." The priest notified the police, who picked them up and arranged for a speedy unofficial deportation. The weakness of that story is that there would have been no need for the Irishmen to have asked around for "Hughie." Tudor's name and address were in the St. John's telephone directory for many years, and certainly in the 1950s.

All the versions of the assassination story suffer from the same flaw—the target was easy to locate and an easy mark for any competent assassin. But Carla Emerson Furlong, the last survivor among the people in St. John's who were personally close to the general, firmly believed it. She didn't hear about it from the general himself, though, and if the attempt had actually happened in the early 1950s, she was living in England at the time. But she knew that the IRA had murdered others in his Dublin circle, and to her it was entirely credible that he was in danger of assassination for as long as he was alive.

She had heard that the IRA was still hunting him long after he had come to Newfoundland, and from too many impeccable sources for it to be untrue. They would have had him, she believes, but for the fact that the archbishop found out "and sent them packing."

Besides the lack of first-hand confirmation, the compelling yarn has other obvious weaknesses. The general was nearly eighty at the time of the alleged conspiracy. Most of his old adversaries from the Irish war were already dead or too busy with their lives and/or Irish political intrigues to embrace the risks, not to mention the expense, of committing murder in another country. And while it was simple to get to St. John's as a tourist, leaving as a fugitive would have been more challenging. The likelihood of getting caught was high.

The larger question would have been, why bother? The passions that might still have been inflamed in 1925 would surely have dissipated by the 1950s. And yet the Tudor assassination plot is common currency in the history of Newfoundland, especially among clergy in St. John's.

Larry Dohey of St. John's, a devout Roman Catholic who was once, in his younger days, a candidate for the priesthood, heard the story in the 1970s from an older priest named Thomas Moakler. In conversations not long before he died in 2019, Dohey, who became a highly respected historian and archivist, was unprepared to say that he believed the story but was equally reluctant to dismiss it.

John Fitzgerald, a St. John's historian, has made an exhaustive search of diocesan records for clues that could add credibility to the story. His search turned up one vague reference to a parish priest with Irish ties who was mildly reprimanded for his pro-republican pronouncements, but no evidence of any threat to Tudor. Asked if he believes the story, Fitzgerald shrugs. Like almost everyone who is familiar with it, absence of corroborating proof is insufficient to support a firm denial.

The Irish author Tim Pat Coogan visited St. John's and included the assassination plot in a study of the Irish diaspora he published in 1999. While his account offers little new by way of proof, Coogan's renown as a chronicler of the Irish independence struggle became a kind of imprimatur for those who find the plot to kill the general too delicious not to swallow.

A retired judge in Newfoundland, Gerald Barnable, has made an extensive study of Tudor's time there and has heard many versions of the failed assassination story. Like any honest lawyer, he has an open mind about it. "The very frequent repetition improves plausibility," he believes. "No one wants to give up this good story. The IRA wouldn't deny it, showing as it does determination and long reach. What's the harm? All ends well. No one is killed. What makes it unlikely? By 1950 you could kill Hugh Tudor with a rolled-up newspaper."

Also, he argues, by 1950 "the IRA was not a force to be able to send men overseas." The old warriors had more important things to occupy their time than tracking an old man in a distant, stormy place and raising the ire of yet another government—Newfoundland had become a province of Canada in 1949. From the IRA's point of view, decades of exile on a foggy rock in the middle of the North Atlantic might have been punishment enough for anyone. Also, most of the old gunmen were by then busy being statesmen.

Ireland had long since ditched the hated oath of allegiance to the British Crown. She was a republic, free of entanglements with the English. The social problems and economic challenges of real independence were sufficient to keep her leaders focused on the here and now and the home front for as far ahead as they could see. The hatred lingering in the hearts of the aging hard men of the 1920s was mostly directed at former comrades, a blinding hangover from the civil war that followed independence.

Whether true or fanciful, General Tudor would almost certainly have known about a plot to kill him. If the events were true, he would have been officially informed. If the plot was nothing more than rumour, he would have heard the gossip. If Carla Emerson Furlong had known about it and believed it, he surely would have known as well. He might indeed have asked himself the question raised by Judge Barnable: Why deny it?

What's the harm in a dramatic story that ends well for the victim and, when all is said and done, even for the unsuccessful murderers? They presumably got back to Ireland with their immortal souls still pure. For the general, the plot would have embellished the persona of a man who saw himself as a survivor, indifferent to danger, indestructible. It would send a message to his enemies—don't even think about it. To his family in England, the story verified one of the excuses he gave when leaving them behind—that he had to go in order to secure their safety.

The peril that Tudor faced in 1925 was reconfirmed in the 1950s, if only as a myth. And all myths originate somewhere in the depths of truth. For those determined to believe the story, including many of Tudor's friends, there was a tantalizing hint of confirmation in April 1953, when he successfully applied to the Newfoundland Constabulary for a permit to own the handgun he had possessed and carried with him since his early soldier days—the Webley .455 revolver. In the space for explaining "purpose for which firearm required," he wrote "self defence." He was eighty-two years old, obviously still wary, maybe even sleeping, as he had once suggested to his estranged wife Eva, with a loaded gun underneath his pillow.

43.

ON THE DAY he turned ninety-two, March 14, 1963, General Tudor granted an interview to a reporter in St. John's. The journalist knew she had a scoop, exclusive access to an old man with a controversial history that she tactfully ignored. Her admiring profile reviewed a lifetime of importance, referring to powerful friends (Churchill) and grand achievements as an artilleryman in the First World War.[21]

His battlefield innovations (smoke cover for infantry assaults) "saved hundreds of thousands of lives," she wrote. Having fought in "two major wars" (South Africa and the Western Front), he was content, in the twilight of his life, to spend his free time reading "whodunits" and scrupulously avoiding military history, especially, it seems, a significant chapter of his own. In the interview—in all likelihood, the only formal media interview he'd ever granted—Tudor avoided any mention of his most personally consequential war, the Irish War of Independence.

Perhaps because it was his birthday, a day of celebration, the journalist made no mention of the general's experience as a belligerent policeman in Ireland or in Palestine, the two assignments that had sent him into exile. By 1963 the Black and Tans had vanished from the news agenda, at least in Newfoundland, but it is doubtful that the reporter was unaware of the Irish chapter in his life, given that his name was permanently linked to the darkest part of one of Ireland's darkest stories.

That the most consequential four years in his life were omitted from his story suggests a prior undertaking by the writer to avoid a topic that the subject didn't want to talk about. This fact alone would indicate that, at ninety-two, the general was still deeply sensitive about the two years he'd spent in Ireland and what he'd had to do there to fulfill the expectations—and the agenda—of his government and the close friend who was then the British minister for war.

In May 1960, Tudor had complained in a letter to Churchill about a book published the year before, *The Black and Tans* by the British journalist Richard Bennett, which he said was "full of inaccuracies" and nothing but "a bare-faced stunt to cash in on the title." For the first time since he'd left Ireland, he felt obliged to write his own account of his two years there, he told his friend. Churchill replied, in light of Richard Bennett's book:

> It would be a very good thing . . . for you to write an article about Ireland.
>
> If you would make me a first proof, I sh'd certainly like to see it.

Tudor was keen to start—and promised to send a "readable" copy "for editing as soon as it is written."[22]

Churchill, however, had second thoughts, and just weeks later walked back his encouragement: "I shall be much interested to read what you write about Irish affairs, but I do not think that I could undertake to edit it as you ask. I have now quite ceased my literary activities."[23]

Tudor understood. But he seemed sufficiently provoked by Bennett's "stunt" to create his own record of his time in Ireland.

It would perhaps be wiser to rest on my one [literary] effort—
the First War—but though I am about four years older than you,
I think I will have a stab at it; I can always tear it up.
Those two years were the most exciting, and perhaps the most
dangerous of my life; so my memory of them is still fairly vivid.[24]

Maybe, on reflection, the memories were a bit too vivid, even after nearly forty years, or maybe Tudor was daunted by a sudden consciousness of passing time. It had taken three years to assemble his written record of the four years he had spent on the Western Front, and he'd had detailed diaries to work with. Or perhaps he realized that, nearing ninety years of age, he'd be wasting the little bit of life he had left on a futile struggle to remember and make sense of the tumultuous two years he had spent in Ireland.

There would be no more discussion of a memoir about Ireland. Perhaps he had realistic doubts that he could ever finish one. Or perhaps he did begin and eventually decided to "tear it up."

General Tudor was, in many ways, an angry man by then. He had spent decades far from home and family. Because of his physical decline, he could no longer even visit England. The glory of the 9th Scottish Division seemed to have been cancelled by the infamy of the Black and Tans, his grand achievements hijacked by one brief, controversial episode.

Growing old and angry laid bare seams of disappointment that, as often is the case late in a long life, expressed themselves in bitterness that easily mutated into bigotry. The casual racism that had informed many old imperial opinions was obvious even in June 1958, when he wrote to Churchill praising volume four of Churchill's *History of the English-Speaking Peoples*.

Tudor was especially taken with his friend's account of white migration to Australia and New Zealand and speculated that, these days, "they would both, especially Australia, like to have millions more of British stock and overcrowded England could well spare them." The most thrilling part of the book, for him, was Churchill's treatment of the American Civil War. General Tudor supported the Confederacy. "The Southern army was composed of pure British stock; they were superior to the Northern Army in generalship, fighting ability and in everything except numbers and arms and equipment."[25]

His approval of the American rebels might well have been an essentially professional evaluation of military competence, tactics and the gallantry of soldiers, indifferent to the underlying politics and social issues. But in an earlier letter, from September 1958, Tudor displayed a race-related animus that caused his friend the politician to offer a gentle reprimand. Tudor had decried the British social schemes that he felt would foster immigration from former colonies.

This "Welfare State" racket has got Britain in a real mess. I have just read an article in The Times which points out that 500m people in the Commonwealth have now the right to invade Britain to obtain a higher standard of living. How can any country stand the financial strain?

Other nationalities arrive. Americans, Egyptians and even Russians come for free medical treatment.

The "No Colour Bar" slogan is just tripe and is against nature. Try selling it to the Australians!

There is naturally a strong feeling in England against our becoming a half-caste race, which finds expression in the present racial rioting that is causing anxiety. I hope steps will be taken to stop the inflow of coloured people.[26]

Churchill's reply is cautious, perhaps aware that their correspondence might one day be of interest to a more socially enlightened generation: "I entirely agree with you about the free importation of colonials. I think there should be no distinction on colour grounds, but that no one of either colour should enter Britain if he is undesirable or for whom there is no room."[27]

It is unlikely that General Tudor's eventual reluctance to write about Ireland—and Churchill's unwillingness to be associated with what it might reveal about them both—was evidence of a guilty conscience. It is more likely that Tudor was unwilling to expose the outrage that he still felt about the Irish people and the land he had stumbled into, and what he'd learned about himself while fighting a guerrilla war— that he, himself, had a capacity for hatred that transcended military rules and discipline.

There is a revealing anecdote about an incident when he was closer to the end of his life, nearly blind and confined to a hospital bed in the living room of his apartment at Churchill Square. After more than half a century, the Irish War of Independence could still arouse his fighting spirit.

Tom Coleman, one of Monica McCarthy's nephews, was a frequent visitor at the apartment. He was a veteran of the Second World War. He had conflicted feelings about the general's time in Ireland but, like most Newfoundlanders, had genuine respect for Tudor's service on the Western Front. Coleman was known in the family to be a talented singer, and on one Sunday visit, Monica asked him to entertain her and the general with a song—an Irish song, she suggested innocently. She loved that sad Irish ballad about an Irish martyr, Kevin Barry.

Perhaps she didn't realize that Kevin Barry was an eighteen-year-old Dublin medical student hanged on November 1, 1920, for his involvement in a shootout in which three British soldiers had died. Or that one of the most influential voices calling for Barry's execution had been General Tudor's. Tom Coleman would later tell his son, Michael, what happened when he started singing. "The song was short-lived as Tudor came up out of his bed, rested on his elbows and admonished [me] saying, 'Don't dare sing about that little bastard in my presence.'"

Carla Emerson Furlong recalls the ringing of her telephone just after 1 a.m. on September 25, 1965. Messages arriving after midnight rarely bring good news. It was Monica McCarthy on the line. "The baby is gone," she said quietly.

Tudor was four years older than Winston Churchill. He had outlived him by eight months and one day.

Churchill's death, at ninety on January 24, had followed years of slow decline. In his final public appearances, he was in a wheelchair. When he'd finally retired from politics in 1955, he wrote a letter to the US president, General Dwight Eisenhower, confessing to a feeling of "relief and denudation." Shortly afterwards he elaborated in a letter to General Tudor that "the worst thing about [retirement] is that when you let all these responsibilities drop, you feel your power falls with the things it held."

Churchill had a foretaste of the feeling in 1945, when he was defeated in the first election after his heroic political performance during the Second World War. He wrote to Tudor at the time: "I found it odd being turned out of power just at the moment when I imagined I would be able to reap where I had sown, and perhaps bring some lasting settlement in this troubled world." He found it "none too easy to change over so quickly from a life of intense activity and responsibility to one of leisure in which there is nothing to be looked for but anticlimax."

General Tudor could easily have identified. By 1945, his life had been in a state of "anticlimax" for more than twenty years.

Churchill's last words, before the stroke that silenced him forever, were spoken to his son-in-law Christopher Soames, fifteen days before he died: "I'm so bored with it all."[28]

The sentiment would have resonated strongly with his friend in Newfoundland. General Tudor spent most of his last year unable to get out of bed and nearly blind. He passed his final days in the Veterans' Pavilion at the St. John's General Hospital.

We can only imagine his reaction to the telegram announcing Churchill's death and inviting him to the state funeral one week later. A brief conversation with faithful Monnie and a sad instruction to decline the invitation. An avalanche of memories.

Churchill lay in state in Westminster Hall for three days as 320,000 mourners filed past his casket, a river of humanity flowing past a monument, as one biographer described the scene.[29] An estimated 350 million people watched Churchill's funeral on television. In the United States alone, the broadcast was said to have drawn more viewers than the funeral of John F. Kennedy fourteen months earlier.

General Tudor lay in state in Oke's Funeral Home, St. John's, dressed in his military uniform in an open casket. Hours would pass before anyone came.

Carla Emerson Furlong was first to arrive. Fifty-seven years later, she still remembered a long, silent vigil beside his casket waiting for the visitation to begin. It was an eerie scene, as she recalled it, her ninety-four-year-old friend in an open casket, a dead infant, also lying in an open casket, in another corner of the visitation room.

Gradually they trickled in, the small group of citizens who knew Tudor from his time in Newfoundland and a somewhat larger group of former officers and soldiers of the Royal Newfoundland Regiment, men for whom the only chapter of his life that mattered to them had been written in the final days of the war they won together.

His family in England, when notified about his death, had replied that no one would be able to attend the funeral.

Both Churchill and Tudor rode to their respective funerals on gun carriages. Churchill was hauled through the streets by 104 Royal Navy sailors. Tudor was escorted by a small contingent of aging army veterans.

Churchill biographer Andrew Roberts writes:

It took four majors of the Queens Royal Irish Hussars . . . to carry all Churchill's orders and decorations behind the gun carriage.

As the cortege passed the Cenotaph at Whitehall, one hundred flags carried by men and women of the wartime resistance movements of France, Denmark, Norway and Holland were raised in a final salute.

After the coffin had passed, a group of Danish Underground Fighters laid a wreath of lilies at the Cenotaph. When asked for their names by a journalist, one answered before slipping back into the crowd, "We were unknown at war; it must be the same now."

As Carla Emerson Furlong recalled the Tudor funeral, "there were only about six Protestants there . . . the rest were all Catholics." She knew them all. It is unlikely that the Catholics, mostly all of Irish descent, had any connection with the freedom fighters from his early life, or if they did, that any of them mourned.

There were choirs for Churchill at St. Paul's Cathedral. They sang "Battle Hymn of the Republic" to acknowledge Churchill's American heritage (through his mother). They sang "Fight the Good Fight with All Thy Might." And of course, as Churchill's coffin left the cathedral, they sang "O God, Our Help in Ages Past."

For Tudor, a bugler broke an awkward silence at his graveside when he played the Last Post, and after a regimental firing party gave a last salute, the bugler played Reveille. It was probably the only music that any soldier would have asked for. In a graveside photograph, there are eight mourners and a clergyman.

What was on Sir Hugh Tudor's mind in the final moment of an eventful life? What was on Sir Winston's mind? It is futile to wonder. In our final moment, we are all alone with everyone.

Tudor's grave is now difficult to find. It is marked by a small, nondescript stone with an incorrect inscription, "Major General Sir Hugh H. Tudor, KCB, CB, CMG." While he was known throughout his life as Hugh, it was his second name; his first was Henry.

The location of his grave is frequently identified by an ironic reference to the nearby walls of a penitentiary. It is most easily located by directions to a more famous grave less than twenty feet away, marked by a large, black, elaborately inscribed headstone that identifies the final resting place of Tommy Ricketts—the Newfoundlander who, while his battalion was serving under Tudor, won the highest military honour in the British Commonwealth, the Victoria Cross, at the age of seventeen. Along with the medal for his heroic actions on October 14, 1918, Private Ricketts had been promoted to the rank of sergeant.

Sergeant Thomas Ricketts, VC, another reserved, unhappy man throughout most of his postwar life, died at the age of sixty-six, just seventeen months after his divisional commander, Major General Sir H. H. Tudor, who had lived to be nearly ninety-five.

EPILOGUE

"What a wonderful thing it is, looking back,
to see all that we have survived."

CHURCHILL TO TUDOR, JANUARY 18, 1946

ON TUDOR'S LAST known visit to England, in 1938, he probably assumed that the perils of the early 1920s were now behind him and that his homeland would be a safe place for him to live. He was sixty-seven then. Perhaps he even considered a fresh start or writing a memoir, even delivering lectures about his wars. By then, another war in Europe was inevitable. He might have had a role to play in shaping public attitudes and opinions, using insights he had acquired in the First World War.

His time in Ireland would also have equipped him with expertise in guerrilla warfare. IRA tactics and organization were being copied widely in China, Palestine and Bengal, and would one day inspire the leaders of new rebellions in the former colonies in Africa, in the Balkans, Cuba, South America, Southeast Asia—even covert foreign operations by the British government.

By 1938, one of his contemporaries in Ireland, Major General Sir Colin Gubbins, was using what he had learned as an army intelligence officer spying on the IRA in 1920–21 to help create a new covert section in the British intelligence establishment, the Strategic Operations Executive (SOE). Gubbins had learned to respect and, eventually, to admire Michael Collins, and in Ireland he had "learned how much mayhem could be caused by a disciplined and shadowy army of operatives fighting on their own territory and employing hit-and-run tactics."[1] The SOE would go on to use IRA tactics for sabotage and terror against German occupation forces in Norway, Yugoslavia and France during the Second World War.

General Tudor, however, clearly had no interest in exploiting his experience in Ireland for any purpose. And he lacked the vanity that moved contemporaries like General Macready, Ormonde Winter and the Auxiliary commander, Frank Crozier, to write mediocre, self-dramatizing memoirs. And unlike Mark Sturgis, Tom Jones and Henry Wilson, he'd kept no Irish diaries.

During the visit in 1938, Tudor was in touch with Churchill, who, at the time, was busy fighting the Tory appeasement policy in Europe. The government of Neville Chamberlain was, on the one hand, allowing Hitler to expand his territory and his power while, on the other, neglecting Britain's defensive capabilities as war with Germany became inevitable.

Churchill wrote to Tudor on May 26, 1938, while the general was still in London, confessing: "We are in an awful mess and it is the Tory party, above all others, who have failed in their duty to the country. I have been so hunted lately that I have hardly had time to turn around."

He did have time for lunch, though, and he invited Tudor to his home on June 2, shortly before Tudor was to return to Newfoundland. Churchill had to make a speech in Birmingham that night, but he would "so much like to have a talk."

The subject would undoubtedly have been the coming war and

Britain's perilous unreadiness and, perhaps, some reminiscences about their time in Ireland, though it was a subject and a chapter in their lives that neither seemed enthused about revisiting. It was the last time they would speak together face to face.

Maybe, when he agreed to go to Dublin in 1920, Tudor knew, from a soldier's point of view, what his government was up to, what he was getting into. He was probably aware in a soldierly way of the political stakes. But throughout his life, he was explicitly averse to political engagement. Always just the soldier.

He joined the Irish struggle because he knew and trusted Churchill and it was obvious that Churchill needed him. Churchill saw in him someone whose loyalty and discretion were crucial for executing the ruthless agenda that he and Lloyd George had devised to maintain the relevance of Britain's diminished empire for just a little longer. They succeeded, but at a huge cost to the Irish. A civil war, a century of recrimination and political strife, unfinished business and lingering resentments to this day.

General Tudor must have realized at some point near the end of 1920 that he was destined to go down in history as a villain in the Irish drama. With that fate in mind, he prudently decided to leave historians scant material to illustrate that villainy.

Tudor could have tried to rehabilitate a controversial reputation by writing of his own importance in the larger context of the Irish war. He could have leveraged his experience in Ireland, where he became a witness to the emergence of a defining phenomenon in political conflict for the rest of the twentieth century—guerrilla warfare. Like many of his contemporaries, he might have written his own account of history, his own carefully remembered version of the role he had played in the violent drama of his century.

He chose instead to bury himself in a place where he would be left alone, where he could pretend that time was standing still, where he could enjoy the comfort and security of respectable irrelevance while avoiding the consequences of a brief political significance.

ACKNOWLEDGEMENTS

BEING NEITHER SCHOLAR nor academic, I am indebted to both disciplines for what is essentially a work of historical journalism. Two eminent Canadian historians inflamed my curiosity about the life and personality of Major General Sir Hugh Tudor, who, for a brief part of his very long lifetime, played a pivotal role in the campaign for Irish self-determination by leading a ruthless struggle to prevent it.

In 2016, Peter Neary, of Western University in London, Ontario, and Melvin Baker, from Memorial University of Newfoundland, published an account of the August 1941 conference between Franklin Roosevelt and Winston Churchill, held on a ship anchored in a bay on the south coast of Newfoundland, surrounded by a flotilla of twenty-four British and American battleships. In a footnote, they refer to Churchill's "old army friend, Major General Henry Hugh Tudor," whom Churchill invited to lunch while he was there for what would be remembered as a historic moment in the Anglo-American alliance.

Tudor was living in Newfoundland and Churchill seemed keen to see him. The reunion didn't happen, but the gesture seemed to be evidence of a deep and continuing relationship that had started as friendship in India and fused into a lifelong bond in Ireland. I was intrigued by two questions: What was the nature of the bond; and why did Tudor, whose closest family and friends all lived in England, spend nearly half his life in Newfoundland? The answers are largely embedded in the history of the First World War and the Irish War of Independence.

The Irish War of Independence has been well documented by British and Irish historians, on whom I have relied extensively to understand a story that has been complicated by perceptions and interpretation throughout a hundred years of storytelling. The principal sources will be well known among scholars—Charles Townshend, Michael Hopkinson, Keith Jeffery, Ronan Fanning, Paul Bew, Eunan O'Halpin, Seán William Gannon and many others. Less familiar will be a young Bosnian-Canadian historian, Igor Knezevic, a specialist in European history and contemporary conflict, who provided vital assistance in processing vast amounts of scholarly research and arriving at some understanding of Ireland's place in the history of twentieth-century liberation warfare.

Two Canadian historians have provided crucial scholarship and insight: the late Peter Hart, of Newfoundland and Ireland, and David Leeson, of Laurentian University, whose deep research into the roles of the IRA and the Royal Irish Constabulary in the War of Independence provided a crucial factual account of a struggle that has often been distorted by political bias and dramatic fancy.

Seán William Gannon helped with extraordinary generosity in sharing his extensive research into the period in which members of the RIC and General Tudor served in Palestine in a policing enterprise devised and executed by Winston Churchill during late 1921 and 1922. Father J. Anthony Gaughan, a native of Listowel and author of a comprehensive biography of Constable Jeremiah Mee, kindly offered access to photographs and biographical detail from his work.

I'm grateful to Linda White and Paulette Noseworthy of the Queen

Elizabeth II Library at Memorial University and to Colleen Field of the Centre for Newfoundland Studies, at Memorial, for their guidance; David Bradley, head archivist at the Maritime History Archive, and Melvin Baker, retired archivist-historian at MUN, were invaluable guides as I struggled to understand Tudor's activity in the salt fish trade. Melvin Baker and Hon. Clyde Wells, a former premier of Newfoundland and Labrador, led me to and through Tudor's relationship with Captain Victor Campbell. The late Edward Roberts offered valuable insight into Tudor's involvement with the Royal Newfoundland Regiment. Peter Neary was a constant source of encouragement and historical context prior to his untimely death, after a brief illness, in March 2024.

I had the good fortune to locate and establish a friendship with the last two living people with memories of personal contact with General Tudor, who died in 1965. John Davenport, one of two grandchildren, was a boy when he first met the general, possibly in 1938, but shared vivid memories handed on by his mother, Tudor's daughter Elizabeth, with whom the general maintained contact for most of his life.

Carla Emerson Furlong, at this writing 102 years old, knew Tudor throughout most of the time he spent in St. John's and was part of a small group of Newfoundlanders who took care of him in his later years. Carla and Monica McCarthy, Tudor's nurse and life-companion for many years in St. John's, arranged his funeral and burial in the fall of 1965.

General Tudor never planned to be a person of historic significance or interest. Perhaps deliberately, he left few clues from which to draw insight into his personality, his emotions, or how he saw his life and times. To tell his story required several years of research and, in the end, became a manuscript that called for the objective judgment of people with the courage to evaluate it honestly in its nearly final stages.

Among them I am especially grateful to Igor Knezevic; Bob Culbert, a long-time friend and colleague in journalism; Joan Ritcey, for many years head of the Centre for Newfoundland Studies; Barbara Kennedy, former journalist and television producer, and a voracious reader; my agent, Shaun Bradley; and my wife, journalist-author-broadcaster Carol Off. They all read and offered shrewd advice on how to improve the telling of a very complicated tale.

As usual, my deepest gratitude must be reserved for my most important reader—my long-time publisher and editor, Anne Collins, whose unflinching tough love for a compelling and important story once again rescued a troubled manuscript from the infatuations of an overly enthusiastic author.

ENDNOTES

PROLOGUE

1 Jim Herlihy, *Royal Irish Constabulary Officers, 1816–1922*, courtesy Police Museum, Dublin Castle (museum@garda.ie).

PART I: A NEW FOUND LAND

1 *As Others See Us* (Herbert Jenkins, 1924), a series of contemporary profiles published anonymously by "A Woman of No Importance," later self-identified as Mrs. Stuart Menzies / Amy Charlotte Bewicke. Clearly an admirer of General Tudor, she wrote that he was "a very quiet man and unobtrusive, but of great courage and nerve . . . Every now and then he likes to test his nerves to see that they are not deserting him." (Mrs. Menzies is referred to in a memoir by a Tudor associate, Brigadier General F. P. Crozier, head of the RIC Auxiliary Division, as "the Black and Tan political propagandist.")

2 Ormonde de l'Épée Winter, *Winter's Tale: An Autobiography* (London: Richards Press, 1955).

3 "Pepys behind the Scenes," *Evening Telegram*, June 5, 1925.

4 Melvin Baker and Peter Neary, "'So Many People in the Wrong Place': Edward Hale's Account of His 1936 Visit to Newfoundland," *Newfoundland and Labrador Studies* 35, no. 1/2 (2020): 107.

5 Paul O'Neill, *The Oldest City: The Story of St. John's, Newfoundland* (Boulder Books, 2003), pp. 39–40, 42; Peter Neary, *Newfoundland in the North Atlantic World, 1929–49* (McGill-Queen's University Press, 1988), p. 4.

6 Sylvia Wigh, *St. John's Evening Telegram*, March 15, 1963.

7 Joy Cave, "A Gallant Gunner General" (unpublished manuscript, Imperial War Museum), p. 12; Tudor Boer War diary, Feb. 4, 1900, courtesy John Davenport (grandson). Ms. Cave was a schoolteacher from Shrewsbury, England, who developed a deep interest in the First World War and, later, in the Royal Newfoundland Regiment. She established a relationship with General Tudor's daughter, Elizabeth Davenport, while researching books about the war, including her incomplete biography of Mrs. Davenport's father.

8 *The Fog of War*, Tudor's First World War diary compilation (self-published, 1959), Queen Elizabeth II Library, Memorial University of Newfoundland.

9 *Fog of War*, Dec. 1914, p. 3. (The manuscript is in segments, year by year, month by month, each segment paginated separately.)

10 Frank Gogos, *Newfoundland's Reluctant War Hero*, prepared for the Provincial Historic Commemorations Program of Newfoundland and Labrador, 2013.

11 Sydney Frost, *A Blue Puttee at War: Memoir of Captain Sydney Frost, MC*, edited and annotated by Edward Roberts (St. John's, NL: Flanker Press, 2014), p. 22.

12 Frost, *Blue Puttee at War*, p. 47.

13 Frost, *Blue Puttee at War*, p. 408.

14 Gogos, *Newfoundland's Reluctant War Hero*, p. 7.

15 *Fog of War*, congratulatory letter, Nov. 20, 1917, from Brigadier General Geddes: "Your scheme worked in the most splendid manner. It was a most brilliant victory and the merest accident prevented us from reaping the fruits of it to the fullest extent." The November 1917 attack at Cambrai became what Tudor, in his diary, lamented as "a severe defeat," with more than 75,000 British casualties (10,000 dead). First greeted as a victory, Cambrai became a scandal when details of the battle finally emerged. Tudor's plan had been for the attack to happen in late August or September. "Had this been done, it would have rocked the whole German line, they would not have dared to send troops to Italy, nor would we have had to send four divisions there, and it is probable that there would have been no disaster at Caporetto," where Italy, an ally, lost 800,000 troops, causing the collapse of the Italian government in October 1917.

16   Frank Gogos, *The Royal Newfoundland Regiment in the Great War* (Flanker Press, 2015), p. 249.

17   Churchill held the rank of lieutenant colonel; as of January 31, 1916, Tudor had been promoted to brigadier general.

18   *Speaking for Themselves: The Personal Letters of Winston and Clementine Churchill*, ed. Mary Soames (Doubleday, 1998), pp. 171–72.

19   Andrew Dewar Gibb with Nigel Dewar Gibb, *With Winston Churchill at the Front* (Frontline Books, 2016), p. 89. Andrew Gibbs's war story was first published in 1924 under the pseudonym Captain X by Gowans and Gray Ltd.

20   Martin Gilbert, *Churchill: A Life*, (Pimlico Books, 2000), p. 348.

21   Nigel Gibb, p. 134, quoting Lieutenant Edmund Hakewill-Smith in Martin Gilbert, *Winston S. Churchill*, vol. III, *The Challenge of War, 1914–16*, p. 658.

22   *Speaking for Themselves*, letter to Clementine, Jan. 27, 1916, pp. 163–64.

23   *Fog of War*, February 1916, p. 3. On February 6, 1916, Churchill commented, in a letter to Clementine, that a former adviser had recently reported watching field trials in which "my 'caterpillar' [tank] . . . performed miracles." *War Memoirs of David Lloyd George*, vol. 1 (Odhams Press, 1938), p. 383 (there are two volumes but pagination is continuous with volume 2, starting at p. 1069). Lloyd George describes witnessing what was possibly the same demonstration and the "feeling of delighted amazement with which I saw for the first time the ungainly monster . . . plough through thick entanglements, wallow through deep mud and heave its huge bulk over parapets and across trenches." Just seven months later, in September 1916, tanks would be deployed for the first time, during the Battle of the Somme. And at the First Battle of Cambrai, in November 1917, 460 British Mark IV tanks led an infantry assault that would succeed but later stall because of an overwhelming counterattack by the German army.

24   Lloyd George, *War Memoirs*, vol. 2, p. 1736.

25   *Fog of War*, April 1918, p. 11: "On the 17th of April the Corps Commander came to me and told me he had a verbal message for me from Sir Douglas Haig [commander of the British Expeditionary Force on the Western Front]. The exact words of the message were 'Tell Tudor that but for him and the 9th Division the situation of Flanders would have been very much worse and we might have had to go back and flood the country.'"

PART II: IRELAND: FROM MUTINY TO MURDER

1   Sir Roger Casement was a prominent British diplomat before he joined the Sinn Féin movement. In 1916 he tried to recruit rebel fighters among Irish prisoners of war in Germany. (According to one of them, "he was booed out of the room.") He tried to smuggle a shipment of German rifles to the Irish Volunteers but was caught after landing on the Irish coast from a German submarine on April 21, 1916, three days before the start of the Easter Rising. It became clear that British intelligence officers were well aware of the insurrection plan, and when Casement pleaded to be allowed to contact its leaders to cancel it, he was refused. According to Foreign Office files, British officials felt that Ireland was "a festering sore" and it was "much better that it should come to a head." Christopher Andrew, *The Defence of the Realm: The Authorized History of MI5* (Penguin Canada, 2009), p. 88.

2   General Sir Nevil Macready, *Annals of an Active Life*, vol. 2 (Hutchinson, 1924), p. 425. Macready recommended another general to run the police, Edward Bulfin, who had roots in Dublin (p. 459), but Bulfin replied that "as a Catholic and an Irishman" he would find such a challenge "distasteful." Macready's attitude toward the job was apparent in an observation in his memoir, that time would possibly reveal that "a people characterized . . . by a lack of discipline, intolerance of restraint, and with no common standard of public morality, can only be governed and held in check under the protection of a strong military garrison" (p. 444). Keith Jeffery, ed., *An Irish Empire?* (Manchester University Press, 1966), p. 108; David Leeson, *The Black & Tans: British Police and Auxiliaries in the Irish War of Independence, 1920–21* (Oxford University Press, 2011), p. 32.

3   Cave, "Gallant Gunner General," p. 309.

4   Macready, note to Iain MacPherson on his appointment as Irish Secretary in 1919. Quoted by Ronan Fanning, *Fatal Path: British Government and Irish Revolution, 1910–1922* (Faber and Faber, 2013), Kindle, citing Strathcarron Papers, Bodleian Library, MS Eng., hist. c 490/70.

5   For a more detailed biography of Gerald Smyth and his brother, Major Osbert Smyth, see Jerry Murland, *Departed Warriors: The Story of a Family in War* (Matador, 2008), pp. 191–213.

6   *Fog of War*, April 1916, pp. 6–7.

7   Peter Hart, *The IRA and Its Enemies: Violence and Community in Cork, 1916–1923* (Oxford University Press, 1998), p. 141.

8   *Fog of War*, May 1918, p. 13.

9   *Fog of War*, April 1917, p. 11. Tudor refers to a meeting with "Col. Wickham," who had succeeded him as an artillery brigade commander in the 7th Division when Tudor moved to the 9th Scottish Division. It is unclear whether this is the same Col. Wickham who later joined him in Ireland.

10 *Fog of War*, March 1917, p. 6.

11 *Fog of War*, October 1917, p. 26.

12 John W. Wheeler, *John Anderson, Viscount Waverly* (Bennett, MacMillan, 1962), pp. 65–66.

13 Ernie O'Malley, *On Another Man's Wound* (Roberts Rinehart, 1999), p. 228; first published in 1936 as *Army without Banners*.

14 O'Malley, *On Another Man's Wound*, p. 298.

15 John Borgonovo and Gabriel Doherty, "Smoking Gun? British Government Policy and RIC Reprisals, Summer 1920," *History of Ireland* 17, no. 2 (2009): 36–39.

16 Charles Townshend, *The Republic: The Fight for Irish Independence* (Penguin, 2014), p. 155, notes that Prescott-Decie had revealed official government policy "with startling candour."

17 Keith Jeffery, *Field Marshal Sir Henry Wilson: A Political Soldier* (Oxford University Press, 2008), p. 265, quoting *The Riddell Diaries, 1908–1923*, ed. John M. McEwen, p. 314.

18 CAB 23/21, meeting June 7, 1920: "Re Cabinet 31 (20) Conclusion 2, 'The prime minister stated that on the previous evening he had had a talk with General Tudor who had recently been sent to Ireland. As a result, he had come to the conclusion that it would be advantageous to make some public statement to show that the government were strengthening the administration.'" The prime minister would indicate (in the proposed statement) "in general terms, that in order to combat the campaign of assassination, the government are taking steps for reorganizing the [Irish] executive, reinforcing the police, and increasing the military garrison and that it will probably be necessary for the government to ask parliament to strengthen the law." There was already pressure within the cabinet (meetings on May 31 and June 2, 1920) to strengthen the law by giving military

tribunals expanded powers to impose the death penalty for crimes normally handled by civil courts.

19 Townshend, *The Republic*, p. 8. "They [the Irish national police] shared their founder, Robert Peel [Home Secretary, later Prime Minister], with the English police, but whereas English constables were 'bobbies,' their Irish counterparts were 'peelers,' reflecting their less amiable image."

20 Leeson, *Black & Tans*, p. 9: twelve police killed in the first three months of 1920, twenty-eight killed between April and June, fifty-five killed between July and September. Eunan O'Halpin and Daithí Ó Corráin, *Dead of the Irish Revolution* (Yale University Press, 2020), cites seventy-three RIC deaths in October, November and December.

21 Bureau of Military History, witness statement (WS) #379, Cst. Jeremiah Mee. Two other Listowel constables, John McNamara and Michael Kelly, provided sworn statements describing the June 19 mutiny, as appendices to the *Interim Report of the American Commission on Conditions in Ireland*, pp. 131–35. The commission heard evidence about British tactics in the Irish War of Independence during formal hearings in the US in November and December 1920 and in January 1921.

22 Bureau of Military History, Mee witness statement.

23 Hamar Greenwood's Weekly Survey, December 27, reports that from January 1, 1919, to December 25, 1920, rebel "outrages" included the deaths of 177 policemen (fifteen of them in 1919). Between December 25 and December 31, seven more RIC officers died, for a total in calendar 1920 of 169.

24 Leeson, *Black & Tans*, 32, citing National Archives (TNA), UK, PRO CO 904, pp. 148–49.

25 Listowel Police Mutiny 1920, online exhibition, Kerry Writers' Museum, https://www.kerrywritersmuseum.com/online-exhibitions/listowel-police-mutiny; "Jeremiah Mee," Glenamaddy Boyounagh Heritage Project, http://www.glenamaddyheritage.com/heritage/history/Jeremiah-mee.

26 Murland, *Departed Warriors: The Story of a Family in War* (Matador, 2008), pp. 2–6.

27 Paul McCandless, *Smyths of the Bann*, Appendix C, https://www.sinton-family-trees.com/smythsofthebann/contents.php.

28 Murland, *Departed Warriors*, p. 208.

29 O'Halpin and Ó Corráin, *Dead of the Irish Revolution*, p. 125.

30 Bureau of Military History, WS #719, Maurice Forde, Peadar McCann, Thomas Daly, Sean Kenny, Michael Keogh, Joseph O'Shea and Timothy O'Sullivan, p. 5.

31 American Commission on Conditions in Ireland: Evidence, Susanna Walsh, pp. 633–53.

32 Constable Thomas Hughes joined the Society of African Missions in the summer of 1920, was eventually ordained a Roman Catholic priest, served many years as a missionary in Africa and ended his career as a bishop in Nigeria.

33 Lloyd George, *War Memoirs*, vol. 1, p. 416.

34 TNA CAB 27/108 (Doc. 4), Tudor letter to Churchill, June 27, 1920, responding to points raised with Churchill by two unnamed RIC sergeants who were offering suggestions for how to better fight the IRA. Tudor was happy to get the suggestions, though he felt the points raised by the sergeants were already well in hand. But he decided to respond in detail for Churchill's benefit because he wanted the minister to see "what progress we are making and what further progress we hope to make."

35 TNA CAB 27/108, Tudor to Churchill, June 27, 1920.

36 Leeson, *Black & Tans*, pp. 97–98.

37 Bureau of Military History, Mee witness statement.

38 *Hansard*, UK Parliament, July 14, 1920, vol. 131, cc. 2385–91.

39 Bureau of Military History, WS #746, Seán Culhane.

40 Tim Pat Coogan, *Michael Collins* (Roberts Rinehart, 1996), p. 124.

41 Bureau of Military History, WS #1656, Daniel Healy, pp. 9–11.

42 Bureau of Military History, Culhane witness statement, p. 5.

43 *The Last Days of Dublin Castle: The Mark Sturgis Diaries*, ed. Michael Hopkinson (Irish Academic Press, 1999), Thursday, July 15, 1920, p. 12.

44 O'Halpin and Ó Corraín, *Dead of the Irish Revolution*, pp. 149–50.

45 Bureau of Military History, Forde et al. witness statement.

46 TNA PRO CAB 24/109, July 23, 1920, Cabinet conference notes, Sir James McMahon, Irish Under Secretary, quoting Ireland's Primate, Cardinal Michael Logue, p. 18.

47 Murland, *Departed Warriors*, p. 211, says the funeral was July 20; other sources state the date of his funeral as July 21.

48 Murland, *Departed Warriors*, p. 211.

49 *Belfast Newsletter*, July 13, 1920.

50 Murland, *Departed Warriors*, pp. 210–11: "Gerald was brought back to Banbridge by special train from Dublin. Accompanying the coffin were his uncles . . . both Warren and Jim [Murland] were armed."

51 *Fog of War*, October 1918, p. 28.

52 Garda Museum, Dublin Castle.

53 O'Halpin and Ó Corráin, *Dead of the Irish Revolution*, p. 157.

54 Bureau of Military History, WS #389, Roger McCorley, p. 9; WS #746, Seán Culhane, p. 14.

55 *Last Days: Sturgis Diaries*, July 20, 1920, p. 13.

56 Thomas Jones, *Whitehall Diary*, vol. III, ed. Keith Middlemas (Oxford University Press, 1971), p. 53.

57 TNA CAB 24/109, CP 1693, pp. 446–48, Irish Government conference, July 23, 1920, "The Situation in Ireland."

58 "The Situation in Ireland" conference, pp. 448–51.

59 "The Situation in Ireland" conference, pp. 452, 462.

60 "The Situation in Ireland" conference, p. 460.

61 "The Situation in Ireland" conference, p. 462.

62 Jones, *Whitehall Diary*, July 23, 1920, p. 28.

63 TNA LG F/48/6/37, French to Lloyd George, July 27, 1920.

64 *Interim Report of the American Commission on Ireland*, Appendix E, p. 132, statement by John McNamara, ex Constable, RIC, sworn March 7, 1921, New Haven, Conn., USA.

PART III: RETALIATION

1 Murland, *Departed Warriors*, p. 211.

2 "Tragedy Follows a Foolish Joke," *Star*, Bedford, England, September 3, 1904.

3 *Last Days: Sturgis Diaries*, p. 32.

4 *British Intelligence in Ireland, 1920–21: The Final Reports*, ed. Peter Hart (Cork University Press, 2002), p. 7.

5 J. B. E. Hittle, *Michael Collins and the Anglo-Irish War: Britain's Counter-insurgency Failure* (Potomac, 2011), p. 134, quoting Lieutenant General Sir Thomas Hutton, who served with Winter in the Great War.

6 Bureau of Military History, WS #387, Patrick (Paddy) O'Daly, p. 24.

7 Bureau of Military History, O'Daly witness statement, p. 26.

8 Bureau of Military History, O'Daly witness statement, p. 28.

9   Hittle, *Michael Collins and the Anglo-Irish War*, p. 31.

10 Hart, *British Intelligence in Ireland*, p. 69.

11 O'Malley, *On Another Man's Wound*, pp. 188–89.

12 Bureau of Military History, WS #1739, Dan Breen, p. 22. "The only regret we had, following the ambush, was that there were only two policemen in it instead of the six we expected, because we felt that six dead policemen would have impressed the country more than a mere two."

13 Richard Bennett, *The Black and Tans* (Pen and Sword Books, 1959), p. 22.

14 O'Halpin and Ó Corraín, *Dead of the Irish Revolution*, p. 2.

15 Carl von Clausewitz, *On War* (Penguin Books, 1968), p. 123.

16 William Y. Darling, *So It Looks to Me*, memoir quoted in Cave, "Gallant Gunner General," p. 324.

17 Hart, *The I.R.A. and Its Enemies*, p. 82.

18 John Ainsworth, "The Black and Tans and Auxiliaries in Ireland, 1920–21: Their Origins, Roles and Legacy" (Centre for Social Change Research, 2001), quoting from Patrick Shea, *Voices and the Sound of Drums: An Irish Autobiography* (Blackstaff Press, 1981).

19 See O'Halpin and Ó Corraín, *Dead of the Irish Revolution*, p. 191.

20 Bureau of Military History, WS #845, Tom Malone, pp. 47–49.

21 The number 156 is from testimony to the American Commission on Conditions in Ireland in late 1920–early 1921. On December 1, 1920, the Irish attorney general, Sir Denis Henry, told the House of Commons (*Hansard*, vol. 135, cc. 1240–41) that "no officers of the police forces" had been kidnapped that year. Winston Churchill, however, stated that ten army officers and soldiers had been kidnapped, six of whom were unaccounted for. But as Leeson points out (*Black & Tans*, p. 148), many policemen were "captured" for their weapons or after barracks battles and allowed to walk away unscathed. IRA leaders considered it prudent policy to disarm and release their captives as encouragement to other policemen to avoid futile resistance that would also cause IRA casualties.

22 *American Commission on Conditions in Ireland*, Evidence, pp. 60–62, testimony by Rev. M. M. English, an Irish-born priest, who had been visiting from Montana when Patrick Lynch was murdered.

23 Bureau of Military History, WS #1454, Jim Leahy, pp. 25–26; O'Halpin and Ó Corraín, *Dead of the Irish Revolution*, p. 119.

24 Bureau of Military History, Leahy witness statement, p. 27.

25 Bureau of Military History, Leahy witness statement, pp. 28–37.

26 Henry Wilson Diaries, Imperial War Museum, HW/23, September 1920, p. 25; Keith Jeffery, *Field Marshal Sir Henry Wilson: A Political Soldier* (Oxford University Press, 2006), p. 266.

27 Bennett, *Black and Tans*, pp. 84–85; Bureau of Military History, Leahy witness statement, pp. 41–47.

28 Bureau of Military History, Leahy witness statement, pp. 46–47

29 Townshend, *The Republic*, pp. 193–96; American Commission on Conditions in Ireland, Evidence, Mrs. Muriel MacSwiney, pp. 265–302.

30 Martin Gilbert, *Winston S. Churchill*, vol. IV, *World in Torment, 1916–1922* (Hillsdale College Press, 2008), p. 458.

31 Gilbert, *World in Torment*, pp. 458–59.

32 American Commission on Conditions in Ireland, Evidence, Mrs. Agnes B. King, pp. 130–35.

33 American Commission on Conditions in Ireland, Evidence, John Joseph Cadden, pp. 410–15.

34 American Commission, Cadden evidence.

35 American Commission, Cadden evidence; Leeson, *Black & Tans*, pp. 45–46.

36 Leeson, *Black & Tans*, pp. 25–26, 196; Bennett, *Black and Tans*, pp. 93–94; Bureau of Military History, WS #1398, William Rock, pp. 11–13; O'Halpin and Ó Corraín, *Dead of the Irish Revolution*, p. 179.

37 Bureau of Military History, Rock witness statement, p. 12.

38 *Last Days: Sturgis Diaries*, p. 43.

39 *Last Days: Sturgis Diaries*, p. 43.

40 Bennett, *Black and Tans*, p. 95.

41 O'Halpin and Ó Corraín, *Dead of the Irish Revolution*, p. 182.

42 Murland, *Departed Warriors*, pp. 212–13, refers to entries in a family member's diary in 1920: "It becomes clear that Osbert was making his presence felt in Dublin by hunting down Gerald's killers . . . [and had] already dispatched one of them and was on the trail of the others." A former captain in the Dublin IRA Brigade, Joseph O'Connor, investigated the shooting and testified that "we were satisfied that they thought it was Liam Lynch, O/C, First southern Division." Bureau of Military History, WS #487, Joseph O'Connor, p. 40. Lynch was not involved in the murder of Gerald Smyth.

43 Paul Bew, *Churchill and Ireland* (Oxford University Press, 2016), Kobo, p. 247.

44 Gilbert, *World in Torment*, p. 460.

45 Gilbert, *World in Torment*, p. 460.

46 Leeson, *Black & Tans*, pp. 167–70, from TNA PRO CO 904/45.

47 Leeson, *Black & Tans*, 167–70, from TNA PRO CO 904/45.

48 Leeson, *Black & Tans*, 167–70, from TNA PRO CO 904/45.

49 Leeson, *Black & Tans*, 167–70, from TNA PRO CO 904/45.

50 TNA CO 23/22/53A, Cabinet conference, 10 Downing St., Oct. 1, 1920.

51 *Last Days: Sturgis Diaries*, p. 51.

52 Bew, *Churchill and Ireland*, p. 249.

53 Dan Breen, *My Fight for Irish Freedom* (Mercier Press, 2011), Kindle, p. 172.

54 Coogan, *Michael Collins*, pp. 151–152; Breen, *My Fight for Irish Freedom*, pp. 171–72; Winter, *Winter's Tale*, pp. 315–16; "Major George Osbert Sterling Smyth DSO, MC," British Intelligence in Ireland, https://bloodysunday.co.uk/castle-intelligence/smyth/smyth.html.

55 Breen, *My Fight for Irish Freedom*, p. 172.

56 *Report of the Labour Commission to Ireland* (1921), pp. 81–82.

57 Murland, *Departed Warriors*, 213.

58 "Major George Osbert Sterling Smyth"; Murland, *Departed Warriors*, p. 213.

59 Breen, *My Fight for Irish Freedom*, pp. 179–80.

60 David Nelligan, a policeman who worked undercover for the IRA, was talking to Roche on a street corner when the shooting started. In his version of events, Roche, from Tipperary, had been enlisted to identify a wounded volunteer who was believed to be Dan Breen. Roche confirmed he wasn't Breen: "I would know his bulldog face anywhere." Bureau of Military History, WS #380, David Nelligan, p. 10.

61 Bureau of Military History, WS #663, Joseph Dolan, IRA Intelligence Officer, pp. 2–3.

62 O'Halpin and Ó Corraín, *Dead of the Irish Revolution*, p. 198, suggests one reason for the police reprisal might have been a complaint that a brother of the victims forced a local school to close on the day of Seán Treacy's funeral.

63 Bew, *Churchill and Ireland*, pp. 257–58.

64 TNA PRO CO 23/22 49(A) (20), Irish Situation Committee meeting re Lord Mayor of Cork; Jones, *Whitehall Diary*, Aug. 25, 1920, pp. 36–37.

65 Bew, *Churchill and Ireland*, pp. 260–61.

66 Hittle, *Michael Collins and the Anglo-Irish War* (Potomac, 2011), Kindle, p. 226. Note: The reference to "a London hotel" is obviously incorrect, as Ho Chi Minh was living in Paris at the time.

67 Hart, *The I.R.A. and Its Enemies*, p. 85.

68 O'Halpin and Ó Corráin, *Dead of the Irish Revolution* (p. 178) reports that Harold Washington was born on October 24, 1904, based on records of the Commonwealth War Graves Commission. M. A. Doherty, in "Kevin Barry and the Anglo-Irish Propaganda War," *Irish Historical Studies* 32, no. 126 (Nov. 2000), also refers in a footnote (p. 229) to the Commonwealth War Graves Commission entry for Washington and that he was still fifteen years old when he died.

69 Members of the IRA raiding party reported that Kevin Barry had been issued an unfamiliar weapon, a .38 Mauser semi-automatic pistol known as a Parabellum. The leader noted that Barry was "not pleased" with the substitute for his preferred weapon, a Webley revolver; Bureau of Military History, WS #493, Seamus Kavanagh, team leader. There were several Parabellum pistols in the hands of other raiders. When captured, Barry was underneath a military truck and his pistol had jammed; medical testimony at the court martial confirmed there were three bullets, one from a Parabellum, in the body of one victim, Marshall Whitehead, twenty, but it was not clear which of the bullets caused his death; Bureau of Military History, WS #1154, Seán O'Neill. O'Neill was near Barry when the shooting started and doubted whether he could have had a clear shot at the victim. Barry refused to recognize the court, refused legal counsel, ignored the process and was reported to be indifferent, if not pleased, when sentenced to death.

70 *Last Days: Sturgis Diaries*, p. 63.

71 Donal O'Donovan, *Kevin Barry and His Time* (Glendale Press, 1989), pp. 167–68. Canon John Waters, who was with Kevin Barry for his final hours and at his death, told Barry's mother, "Your dear boy is waiting for you now beyond the reach of sorrow . . ."

72 *Last Days: Sturgis Diaries*, p. 62.

73 T. Ryle Dwyer, *The Squad* (Mercier Press, 2005), p. 157.

74 Dwyer, *The Squad*, p. 158. The author states that the victim, Houlihan, was a teenager. According to the authoritative compilation of war victims, O'Halpin and Ó Corráin, *Dead of the Irish Revolution*, he was thirty.

75 O'Halpin and Ó Corráin, *Dead of the Irish Revolution*, p. 208.

76 Dwyer, *The Squad*, pp. 159–61.

77 *Hansard*, Nov. 4, 1920, vol. 134, c. 550.

78 Bew, *Churchill and Ireland*, pp. 261–62.

79 TNA CO 904/188 #608, Macready to John Anderson, Nov. 3, 1920.

80 O'Halpin and Ó Corráin, *Dead of the Irish Revolution*, p. 213. Teresa O'Connell's death was "allegedly in consequence of 'a wager between two Black and Tans as to which of them could shoot the best.'"

81 See: "Discipline," circular, D.446, 1920, TNA PRO HO 184/125, prepared by Tudor, Nov. 9, 1920.

82 TNA CAB 24/114/85; Montagu memo to cabinet, Nov. 10, 1920.

83 Hart, *British Intelligence in Ireland*, p. 83; Townshend, *The Republic*, p. 204; *Last Days: Sturgis Diaries*, Nov. 16, 1920, p. 73; Nov. 18, p. 74.

84 *Last Days: Sturgis Diaries*, Nov. 21, 1920, pp. 76–78.

85 David Leeson, "Death in the Afternoon: The Croke Park Massacre," *Canadian Journal of History* 38, no. 1 (2003); Michael Foley, *The Bloodied Field: Croke Park, Sunday 21 November 1920* (O'Brien Press, 2015).

86 Ernest McCall, *Tudor's Toughs: A Study of the Auxiliary Division Royal Irish Constabulary, 1920–22* (Red Coat, 2010), chapter 7, loc. 947. It was widely known that "King and Hardy operated together in the intelligence gathering from IRA suspects in Dublin Castle in a room called by the IRA . . . 'The Knocking Shop.'"

87 Leeson, "Death in the Afternoon," pp. 4–5; Foley, *Bloodied Field*, pp. 356–87; TNA WO 35/88B.

88 Leeson, "Death in the Afternoon"; F. P. Crozier, *Impressions and Recollections* (T. Werner Laurie, 1930), pp. 256–57; T. P. Crozier, *Ireland Forever* (Jonathan Cape, 1932), Kindle pp. 80–81.

89 *Hansard*, Nov. 22 and Nov. 23, 1920, vol. 135, cc. 38–43, cc. 199–202.

90 Winter, *Winter's Tale*, pp. 322–23.

91 Coogan, *Michael Collins*, p. 161; Townshend, *The Republic*, p. 202; Leeson, *Black & Tans*, notes in the digital edition, "McKee and Clancy murdered in the Castle Bloody Sunday"; Mark Duncan, *Century Ireland*, an online historical newspaper, 2020; Anne Dolan, "Killing and Bloody Sunday, November 1920," *Historical Journal* 49, no. 3 (2006): 791; Paul O'Brien, *Havoc: The Auxiliaries in Ireland's War of Independence* (Collins, 2017), p. 205.

92 Patrick Kennedy, IRA Intelligence, Dublin (Bureau of Military History, WS #499), reported that one of his Dublin Castle spies was an Auxiliary officer named "Reynolds" who "gave us full details as to the perpetrators of the murder of Peadar Clancy, Dick McKee and Clune." The victims had been "kicked and beaten" in a failed attempt "to extract information from them," then shot to death. Paul O'Brien, in *Havoc*, identifies the spy as John Reynolds of the Auxiliaries F Company, based in Dublin Castle, who became a prolific source of information for the IRA throughout 1920 and 1921. Ernest McCall, in *Tudor's Toughs*, also identifies the spy as Cadet J. C. Reynolds, ADRIC # 584, who, "whilst suspicion was there," was still promoted to section leader on Christmas Day, 1920, and to third-class district inspector in another ADRIC company on June 18, 1920.

93 Duncan, *Century Ireland*, 2012–2023.

94 O'Halpin and Ó Corraín, *Dead of the Irish Revolution*, p. 233.

95 For details and perspectives on the Kilmichael ambush: Leeson, *Black & Tans*, pp. 152–53; Hart, *The I.R.A. and Its Enemies*, pp. 21–38; Tom Barry, *Guerilla Days in Ireland* (Irish Press, 1949), pp. 71–94.

96 Townshend, *The Republic*, p. 218.

97 TNA CAB 23-23/1920-12-29/ 79A, pp. 341–42.

98 Leeson, *Black & Tans*, p. 204; O'Halpin and Ó Corraín, *Dead of the Irish Revolution*, p. 255.

99 *Last Days: Sturgis Diaries*, p. 95.

100 Bureau of Military History, WS #615, Frank Thornton, The Squad, pp. 30–31.

PART IV: WHIRLWIND

1 Fanning, *Fatal Path*, p. 335.

2 *Report of the Labour Commission to Ireland*, pp. 53–54, 56.

3 TNA CO 904/150/3.

4 TNA CAB 23-23/1920-12-29/79A /340.

5 TNA CAB 23-23/1920-12-30/81(20), pp. 368–69 ("The head of the Royal Irish Constabulary [Tudor], whose view was supported by the Chief Secretary [Greenwood], had however been more sanguine and roughly estimated the date at which order would be sufficiently restored to enable election to be held at 2 months time.")

6 TNA CAB/24/119/4: There were 42 attacks on police and military; 11 policemen killed that week.

7 Bureau of Military History, WS #1068, Michael Brennan, p. 74.

8 Bureau of Military History, WS #680, Nicholas O'Dwyer; #970, John Ahern; and #1123, Cornelius Brosnan. In their statements, John Ahern and Cornelius Brosnan detail their personal involvement in killing O'Sullivan. Four other men, who presumably had nothing to do with the shooting, were charged, tried and sentenced to death but were spared following the July ceasefire.

9 Hart, *British Intelligence in Ireland*, p. 12.

10 Leeson, "The Murder of Patrick Howard," *Éire-Ireland* 47, nos. 3 & 4 (Fall/Winter 2012): 111–40.

11 O'Halpin and Ó Corráin, *Dead of the Irish Revolution*, p. 402 (see "Patrick Starr").

12 O'Halpin and Ó Corráin, *Dead of the Irish Revolution*, p. 307; Bureau of Military History, WS #1467, Patrick Higgins; #1444, John P. O'Connell; #1589, Diarmuid O'Leary.

13 O'Halpin and Ó Corráin, *Dead of the Irish Revolution*, p. 247; Jones, *Whitehall Diary*, Feb. 15, 1921, p. 53; Eamonn Thomas Gardiner, "An Examination of the Auxiliary Division, Royal Irish Constabulary, Exploring Possible Links between Conduct and Conflict Related Injury, Traumatic Experiences and Stress" (PhD thesis, University of Galway, 2017), pp. 367–68. A Fermoy court awarded the widow and children of Nicholas Prendergast compensation of 6,000 pounds later that year; *Yorkshire Post*, Oct. 31, 1921.

14 *Last Days: Sturgis Diaries*, p. 123.

15 O'Halpin and Ó Corráin, *Dead of the Irish Revolution*, p. 296.

16 Leeson, *Black & Tans*, pp. 185–86.

17 Bennett, *Black and Tans*, p. 172; https://theauxiliaries.com/INCIDENTS/trim-looting.

18 Crozier, *Ireland Forever* (reprint: Lewisham Press, 2020), p. 102.

19 TNA CO 904/188/649, Macready to John Anderson, Feb. 14, 1921.

20 *Speaking for Themselves*, letter, Clementine to Winston, Feb. 18, 1921, p. 232.

21 Coogan, *Michael Collins*, p. 173.

22 Sean O'Callaghan, *Execution* (Frederick Muller, 1974), p. 155.

23 O'Callaghan, *Execution*, p. 128.

24 Trials for two seriously wounded men were delayed. One, Denis Murphy, was sentenced to death but the sentence was commuted. Jim Barrett, forty, died before he could stand trial.

25 O'Callaghan, *Execution*, pp. 175–79.

26 O'Callaghan, *Execution*, p. 180.

27 O'Callaghan, *Execution*, p. 182. Frank Busteed is quoted by the author: "They must have had some suspicion that I was responsible for the death of Mrs. Lindsay. I haven't any doubt about that. That is why they killed my mother. It was revenge, all right."

28 O'Halpin and Ó Corraín, *Dead of the Irish Revolution*, p. 398; Bureau of Military History, WS #1695, Maurice Brew, Donoughmore Battalion, Co. Cork.

29 Bureau of Military History, WS #881, James Kilmartin, pp. 13–16.

30 *Last Days: Sturgis Diaries*, vol. IV, pp. 134–35.

31 *Hansard*, Feb. 15, 1921, vol. 138, cc. 36–52.

32 Jones, *Whitehall Diary*, Feb. 15, 1921, pp. 52–53.

33 TNA LG/F/19/3/4; Lloyd George to Greenwood, Feb. 25, 1921.

34 *Last Days: Sturgis Diaries*, March 6, 1921, p. 138. Sturgis comments sarcastically, "The Mountains were in labour and brought forth—Umfreville."

35 Bureau of Military History, WS #806, Máire Clancy; and #688, Cáit O'Callaghan; O'Halpin and Ó Corraín, *Dead of the Irish Revolution*, pp. 325, 326; Richard Bennett, "Portrait of a Killer," *New Statesman*, March 24, 1961.

36 In the *New Statesman* article, Bennett claims, after a belated investigation of the deaths, that the killers were Auxiliary policemen led by an officer named George Nathan. In his 1959 book *The Black and Tans*, Bennett had suggested (p. 180) "there was good reason to believe" that the Limerick politicians, Clancy and O'Callaghan, were murdered by the IRA—a theory floated at the time by the British government, but soon discredited.

37 Bureau of Military History, WS #1036, John Moloney, pp. 13–17. Moloney was one of the two survivors.

38 Bureau of Military History, WS #1194, Bernard Sweeney, pp. 13–16.

39 Sir Henry Wilson's opinion of General Tudor would only grow more caustic as time passed. On May 5, 1921, he would refer to Tudor, in a note to General

Macready, as "an idiotic child"; Imperial War Museum, HHW/2D/49, quoted by Gardiner, "An Examination of the Auxiliary Division."

40 TNA LG F/19/3/7, Greenwood to Lloyd George, April 3, 1921.

41 Barry, *Guerilla Days in Ireland*, pp. 201–17.

42 *Mao Tse-tung on Guerrilla Warfare*, trans. Samuel B. Griffith (Praeger, 1961), p. 54.

43 Martin Gilbert, *Continue to Pester, Nag and Bite: Churchill's War Leadership*, Barbara Frum Historical Lecture, University of Toronto (Vintage Canada, 2004).

44 Jones, *Whitehall Diary*, p. 53. Lord Midleton (William St. John Brodrick) was a prominent Irish landlord and Southern Ireland unionist.

45 TNA LG F/19/3/8, Hamar Greenwood to Lloyd George, April 6, 1921.

46 Jones, *Whitehall Diary*, pp. 55–63.

47 Jones, *Whitehall Diary*, pp. 63–70.

48 O'Brien, *Havoc*, pp. 219–27; Bureau of Military History, WS #689, Liam O'Doherty, pp. 16–18; O'Halpin and Ó Corraín, *Dead of the Irish Revolution*, p. 444.

49 Jones, *Whitehall Diary*, pp. 72–74.

50 O'Malley, *On Another Man's Wound*, pp. 369–74.

51 Paul von Littow-Vorbeck, *My Reminiscences of East Africa* (1920); Edwin P. Hoyt, *Guerilla: Colonel von Lettow-Vorbeck and Germany's East African Empire* (Macmillan, 1981). Michael Collins referred to von Littow-Vorbeck as an inspiration for his own campaign in Ireland.

52 Jones, *Whitehall Diary*, July 6, 1921, pp. 82–85.

53 Jones, *Whitehall Diary*, July 6, 1921, pp. 82–85.

54 Jones, *Whitehall Diary*, p. 89.

55 Bureau of Military History, Brennan witness statement, p. 116.

56 Copy of the original document courtesy John Davenport, grandson of General Tudor.

57 Jones, *Whitehall Diary*, vol. 1, letter to Bonar Law, April 24, 1921.

58 Townshend, *The Republic* (p. 332) refers to de Valera's absence from the London negotiations as "bizarre"; Hittle, *Michael Collins and the Anglo-Irish War* (p. 210) refers to de Valera's "decision not to participate" as an act that would still be viewed nearly a century later as "cowardly."

59 Jones, *Whitehall Diary*, p. 183.

60 Coogan, *Michael Collins*, p. 276. Collins's grim comment would be seen as a prophecy eight months later, after his death on August 22, 1922, during a gunfight with anti-treaty IRA gunmen in County Cork, not far from where he was born and raised.

61 Jones, *Whitehall Diary*, p. 183, comment by Keith Middlemas, editor.

62 Lloyd George to Tudor, December 16, 1922, courtesy John Davenport.

63 Florence O'Donoghue, *No Other Law* (Anvil, 1986), p. 177.

PART V: THE HOLY LAND

1 Elizabeth Tudor Davenport, "It Pays to Grumble," undated notes for an unfinished memoir, courtesy of John Davenport, her son.

2 John Davenport, various interviews, 2021–2024.

3 Hittle, in *Michael Collins and the Anglo-Irish War*, writes (p. 171) that "no fewer than five secret service officers working for [Ormonde] Winter became so despondent that they committed suicide." Ormonde Winter reports in his memoir *Winter's Tale* (p. 289) that shortly after his arrival in Dublin, a mess steward (waiter) who was a member of the RIC shot himself "in a fit of depression caused by his surroundings." Sturgis wrote in his diary (p. 180) on May 19, 1921, "Another poor devil has committed suicide in O's [Ormonde Winter's] office—this is the fifth—there seems a curse on the place."

4 Bureau of Military History, WS #1285, Eamon Broy, p. 8.

5 O'Halpin and Ó Corráin, *Dead of the Irish Revolution*, p. 383.

6 Keith Jeffery, in *Field Marshal Sir Henry Wilson* (chapter 14), concludes that Wilson's killers acted alone and without approval or direction from Dublin. Peter Hart reached the same conclusion: "There is no solid evidence to support a conspiracy theory linking Michael Collins or anyone else to the murder"; Irish Historical Studies, Hart Collection, Queen Elizabeth II Library, Memorial University of Newfoundland, 3.01.065/coll. 455. However, Michael Hopkinson argues in *Green against Green: The Irish Civil War* (St. Martin's Press, 1988) that "the testimony of many of those who were involved in the events surrounding the affair [Wilson's assassination] suggests strongly that Collins was directly implicated."

7 Churchill Papers, Cambridge, CHAR 17/15, Churchill to Creedy, Feb. 21,

1921: ". . . to form a force [for Palestine] very similar to the Royal Irish Constabulary . . ."

8 Memorandum of Edwin Montagu to British Cabinet, Aug. 23, 1917. For full text visit Jewish Virtual Library, https://www.jewishvirtuallibrary .org/montagu-memo-on-british-government-s-anti-semitism.

9 Seán William Gannon, *The Irish Imperial Service: Policing Palestine and Administering the Empire* (Palgrave Macmillan, 2019), p. 25. General Congreve to Sir Henry Wilson, Nov. 23, 1921: "We shall never have any peace in this country until [Zionism] is ended, nor self-respect either for it is a detestable and odious policy."

10 Congreve "circular to all troops," Oct. 29, 1921, Churchill College, Cambridge, Churchill Papers, CHAR/17/11, quoted by Gannon, *Irish Imperial Service*, p. 25.

11 Churchill telegram, Sept. 11, 1921 (CHAR 17/15/136).

12 Memorandum to Cabinet by Herbert Samuel, January 1915.

13 Samuel to Churchill (CHAR 17/11), December 11, 1921, from Gannon, *Irish Imperial Service*, p. 32.

14 Gannon, quoting Col. Richard Meinertzhagen, military adviser in the Colonial Office Middle East Department, "The Formation, Composition and Conduct of the British Section of the Palestine Gendarmerie, 1922–1926," *Historical Journal* 56, no. 4 (2013): 992.

15 Tudor to Churchill, Oct. 1, 1922, copy in Trenchard papers, RAF Museum, MFC 76/1/285.

16 Gilbert, *Churchill: A Life*, p. 453.

17 Gilbert, *Churchill: A Life*, p. 454.

18 McNeill Diaries, Oct. 18, 1922, Middle East Centre Archive, St. Antony's College, Oxford.

19 Gerard Clauson, Colonial Office Minute, 26/12/1922, CO 733/29/403-406.

20 Elizabeth Tudor Davenport memoir notes, courtesy of John Davenport.

21 Elizabeth Tudor Davenport memoir notes.

22 London Metropolitan Archives, LMA 4179/02/018.

23 Gannon, *Irish Imperial Service*, p. 163.

24 McNeill Diaries, July 2, 1923.

25 *Tudor v. Tudor*, TNA J77/1990/2359.

26 McNeill Diaries, June 15, 1923.

27 Gilbert, *Churchill: A Life*, p. 458.

28 Churchill letter to Tudor, Aug. 2, 1923, courtesy John Davenport.

29 TNA CO 733/48/195.

30 TNA CO 733/48/195.

31 TNA CO 733/48/188.

32 CHAR 2/126/43–44.

33 TNA CO 733/53, pp. 638–54.

34 TNA CO 733/53, p. 654.

35 TNA CO 733/62/413.

36 Duke of Devonshire to Herbert Samuel, Jan. 7, 1924.

37 McNeill Diaries, vol. 2, March 30, 1924.

38 "Newfoundland's Polar Men," *Newfoundland Quarterly* 90, no. 3 (1996). The article was originally a lecture by the Hon. Clyde Wells to the Newfoundland Historical Society.

39 Elizabeth Tudor Davenport memoir notes, courtesy of John Davenport.

40 293

PART VI: AMID THE NORTHERN MISTS

1 Fanning, *Fatal Path*, p. 335: "She [Stevenson] had a soft spot for Macready, whose private secretary enjoyed a sexual relationship with the general as she [Stevenson] did with the prime minister, and he [Macready] invariably wrote to her rather than directly to Lloyd George, whose aversion to reading correspondence was notorious."

2 Frost, *Blue Puttee at War*, pp. 337–40.

3 John Terraine, *General Jack's Diary: War on the Western Front, 1914–1918* (Cassell & Co., 1964), pp. 277–78; Frank Gogos, *The Royal Newfoundland Regiment at War: A Guide to the Battlefields and Memorials of France, Belgium, and Gallipoli* (Flanker Press, 2015), p. 286. Frank Gogos and General Jack avoid identifying the retreating soldiers, but General Tudor revealed in his war diaries that they were from the Scottish Seaforth Battalion, part of his 26th Infantry Brigade. Tudor's version was sympathetic compared to General Jack's disapproving comment that there was "no excuse whatsoever for these fellows quitting their posts." Tudor wrote: "The Seaforths were being heavily strafed and some of the young lads came back from the front line. They did not seem panicky. I heard one boy complaining 'I've lost my

hat.' We had no difficulty in getting them forward again. There was a good deal of shelling and machine gun fire."

4 Terraine, *General Jack's Diary*, p. 278.

5 Maritime History Archive (MHA), Memorial University of Newfoundland, Philip Templeman Ltd. fonds, Templeman Diaries, 1925.

6 Frost, *Blue Puttee at War*, pp. 349–51.

7 Frost, *Blue Puttee at War*, pp. 354–55; Gogos, *Royal Newfoundland Regiment at War*, pp. 294–96.

8 Frost's provocative comment, implying that surrendering German soldiers were shot, was removed by senior officials in the War Office and replaced in an official war history, *The Fighting Newfoundlander*, with a less revealing sentence: "The news of the brutal act [shelling the civilian villagers] enraged the Newfoundlanders." See Frost, *Blue Puttee at War*, p. 377.

9 Frost, *Blue Puttee at War*, p. 364.

10 Gogos, *Newfoundland's Reluctant War Hero*, p. 24.

11 S. J. R. Noel, *Politics in Newfoundland* (University of Toronto Press, 1971), p. 183.

12 Maritime History Archive, Memorial University, James Ryan Ltd. fonds, June 2, 1926, letter from John McCarthy, manager of Ryan Brothers Bonavista operations (competitors of Templeman), to Dan Ryan: "The news of Philip Templeman's sudden passing this morning was a great blow to Bonavista. As far as I know there was no particular—except that—ha, ha—he died suddenly."

13 *St. John's Evening Telegram*, Aug 10, 1926: "At a meeting of creditors . . . a trustee was appointed to investigate the condition of the business of the late Hon. Philip Templeman . . . A rough estimate places the liabilities at $500,000 and the assets at $350,000."

14 Levi Templeman to Edgar Templeman, letter dated Oct. 22, 1926. Templeman Diaries, Maritime History Archive, Memorial University of Newfoundland.

15 *St. John's Daily News*, October 25, 1927.

16 Peter Neary, ed., *White Tie and Decorations: Sir John and Lady Hope Simpson in Newfoundland, 1934–1936* (University of Toronto Press, 1997), p. 189.

17 Frederick Attenborough Fonds MF 389, Archives and Special Collections, Queen Elizabeth II Library, Memorial University of Newfoundland.

18 Melvin Baker and Peter Neary, "Governor Sir Humphrey Walwyn's Account of the 17 June 1939 Royal Visit to Newfoundland," *Newfoundland and Labrador Studies* 37, no. 1 (2022): 1719–26, p. 15.

19 Melvin Baker and Peter Neary, "Governor Sir Humphrey Walwyn's Account of His Meetings with Churchill and Roosevelt, Placentia Bay, Newfoundland, August 1941," *Newfoundland and Labrador Studies* 31, no. 1 (2016): 1719–72, n20.

20 Interviews, Carla Emerson Furlong and John Davenport, 2019–2024.

21 Sylvia Wigh, *St. John's Evening Telegram*, March 15, 1963, p. 3.

22 Tudor to Churchill, July 15, 1960; CHUR 2/536/85 (re writing about Ireland).

23 Churchill to Tudor, Aug. 9, 1960, CHUR 2/536/81.

24 Tudor to Churchill, Aug. 26, 1960, CHUR 2/536/79–80.

25 Tudor to Churchill, CHUR 2/536/93.

26 Tudor to Churchill, Sept. 14, 1958, CHUR/2/536/91.

27 Churchill to Tudor, Oct. 4, 1958, CHUR 2/536/90.

28 Andrew Roberts, *Churchill: Walking with Destiny* (Penguin, 2019), p. 961.

29 Roberts, *Churchill*, p. 962–64.

EPILOGUE

1 Hittle, *Michael Collins and the Anglo-Irish War*.

INDEX

LINDEN MACINTYRE is the bestselling author of many award-winning books, including *The Long Stretch, Causeway: A Passage from Innocence, The Bishop's Man, Why Men Lie, Punishment, The Only Café, The Winter Wives* and *The Wake*. A distinguished broadcast journalist, MacIntyre was born in St. Lawrence, Newfoundland, and grew up in Port Hastings, Cape Breton. He spent twenty-four years as the co-host of *The Fifth Estate* and has won ten Gemini awards for his work. MacIntyre lives in Toronto with his wife, broadcast journalist and author Carol Off. They spend their summers in a Cape Breton village by the sea.